Our Common Welfare

PRACTICING THE TWELVE TRADITIONS IN ALL OUR AFFAIRS

Our Common Welfare

PRACTICING THE TWELVE TRADITIONS IN ALL OUR AFFAIRS

Chronic Pain Anonymous Service Board

© 2021 by Chronic Pain Anonymous Service Board
All rights reserved

ISBN: 978-0-9856524-9-4

Library of Congress Control Number: 2020912001

Chronic Pain Anonymous Service Board
8924 E. Pinnacle Peak Road
Suite G5-628
Scottsdale, AZ 85255-3615
E-mail: *Literature@chronicpainanonymous.org*
Website: *http://www.chronicpainanonymous.org*

CPA Conference Approved

First Edition

As we apply the Twelve Traditions, we are protecting the fellowship, so it is there for us as well as for those who will need it in the future. The Traditions guide us to create a safe, effective, and loving environment, within which we can all grow and thrive.

Serenity Prayer

*God, grant me the serenity
to accept the things I cannot change,
the courage to change the things I can,
and the wisdom to know the difference.
Thy will, not mine, be done.*

Contents

Preface xi

Introduction xiii

Tradition One 1
Our common welfare should come first; personal recovery depends upon CPA unity.

Tradition Two 25
For our group purpose there is but one ultimate authority—a loving God as He may express Himself in our group conscience. Our leaders are but trusted servants; they do not govern.

Tradition Three 45
The only requirement for CPA membership is a desire to recover from the emotional and spiritual debilitation of chronic pain or chronic illness.

Tradition Four 65
Each group should be autonomous except in matters affecting other groups or CPA as a whole.

Tradition Five 83
Each group has but one primary purpose—to carry its message to people living with chronic pain and chronic illness.

Tradition Six 105
A CPA group ought never endorse, finance, or lend the CPA name to any outside enterprise, lest problems of money, property, and prestige divert us from our primary purpose.

Tradition Seven 121
Every CPA group ought to be fully self-supporting, declining outside contributions.

Tradition Eight 147
Chronic Pain Anonymous should remain forever non-professional, but our service centers may employ special workers.

Tradition Nine 165
CPA, as such, ought never be organized, but we may create service boards or committees directly responsible to those they serve.

Tradition Ten 187
Chronic Pain Anonymous has no opinion on outside issues; hence the CPA name ought never be drawn into public controversy.

Tradition Eleven 207
Our public relations policy is based on attraction rather than promotion; we need always maintain personal anonymity at the level of press, radio, television, film, and the Internet.

Tradition Twelve 229
Anonymity is the spiritual foundation of all our traditions, ever reminding us to place principles before personalities.

Conclusion 257

Glossary 259

Appendix A: The Twelve Steps of CPA 261

Appendix B: The Twelve Traditions of CPA 262

Appendix C: The Twelve Concepts of Service of CPA 264

Appendix D: Additional Resources 267

Index 268

Notes 290

Preface

Chronic Pain Anonymous (CPA) was co-founded in 2004 by Dale and Barry, in Baltimore, Maryland. After Barry left CPA, Dale continued to contribute to the fellowship until he died in May 2016. At first, CPA had only a few face-to-face meetings on the East Coast of the United States. The creation of a website in 2005 increased awareness of CPA, and soon new groups were started in several states across the U.S. As technology offered new ways to hold meetings, the fellowship grew to include telephone, online, and videoconference meetings. In time, people across the globe were able to attend meetings, often from their homes, and they began to discover the gifts of recovery from the emotional and spiritual debilitation of chronic pain and chronic illness.

As membership increased, a service structure was established to ensure the needs of the fellowship were met. In October 2007, an Advisory Committee (later named the General Service Board) was formed to support the fellowship and plan for future growth. Having personally experienced the miracles of spiritual transformation, the first CPA committee members were dedicated to nurturing the growth of a new Twelve Step program according to the successful Traditions and principles of other fellowships. As one of their first actions, the Advisory Committee instituted the role of Group Representative in September 2008 so that all recovery groups had a voice in stewarding CPA.

In January 2008, since CPA had no literature of its own, the Advisory Committee approved literature written by other fellowships and authors. However, it became clear it was time for CPA to write its own literature. In July 2008, members began work on a collection of recovery narratives written by members. CPA published its first book, *Stories of Hope: Living in Serenity with Chronic Pain and Chronic Illness*, in September 2012.

The idea for a book about the Twelve Steps of CPA was proposed in 2010, and a group was formed to begin planning the new book. This led to the publication of CPA's second book in September 2015: *Recipe for Recovery: A Guide to the Twelve Steps of Chronic Pain Anonymous*.

In 2012, CPA was incorporated in Arizona, and in December of that year the legal entity of the Chronic Pain Anonymous Service Board received non-profit status as a 501(c)(3) corporation in the United States. The General Service Board was renamed the Board of Trustees and was delegated to oversee the legal and financial responsibilities of the newly formed corporation.

As CPA grew and needed to build a strong foundation, based on the examples of other fellowships, the Board of Trustees published the Twelve Concepts of Service for CPA in November 2016. Implementing the guidance of the Twelve Concepts, CPA held the first World Service Conference on January 8, 2017, as a teleconference. At this time, a second service body, the General Service Council, was created, which later became the General Advisory Council. The Board of Trustees was entrusted with the legal and financial business of CPA, and the General Advisory Council oversaw the fellowship and their needs.

Now there was literature about two of the three CPA Legacies, the Steps and Concepts. It was time to write a book about the Twelve Traditions, describing the spiritual principles that guide the interactions of groups and CPA as a whole, and provide literature that would bind, guide, unify, and support the fellowship as a community of compassion, kindness, and love. The Board approved the idea of the book, and development began in 2018.

Through the dedication, efforts, and voices of many members, along with special workers including professional editing and graphic design, CPA now has a book that helps all of us understand the value of the Twelve Traditions in helping us live peacefully, joyfully, and comfortably within our fellowship and in all our affairs.

Chronic Pain Anonymous Service Board

Introduction

As we complete our journey through working the Twelve Steps of recovery, we arrive at Step Twelve, which tells us to "practice these principles in all our affairs." The spiritual principles this Step refers to are presented in the Twelve Traditions of Chronic Pain Anonymous (CPA) and offer a set of spiritual tools for working together in our program. The Traditions guide us in our groups, service bodies, and personal lives.

The members of CPA have written this book to help us better understand these Twelve Traditions so they can inform and support our relationships with others in the fellowship and with the people we interact with in our daily lives.

WHY DO WE NEED THE TRADITIONS? AREN'T THE STEPS ENOUGH?

The Traditions are to the group what the Steps are to the individual. The Traditions are as important as the Steps in our recovery program, yet they are often not well understood and often not "worked" as fully as we work the Steps.

The CPA Twelve Traditions were adapted from the Traditions of Alcoholics Anonymous (A.A.). The Traditions were created to address problems that A.A. encountered in their early years of growth, so they could survive as a fellowship. CPA, like every other Twelve Step group, has found we need these Traditions. They help prevent the problems that naturally arise when a diverse group of people comes together, and they help maintain continuity and unity. The Traditions ensure that our program is loving and effective and that it continues to thrive.

In a world that is always changing, our fellowship needs to be flexible, adaptable, and inclusive as we offer meetings on different technology platforms and across different cultures. The Traditions help us practice cooperation; they create safety, clarity, and unity for everyone, teaching us how to treat each other with kindness and respect, reminding us to "place principles before personalities."

For those of us who hold the Steps in the highest regard but have not given the Traditions much attention, the Traditions are the spirit of the Steps applied to our group life in recovery. They support us in being balanced within ourselves, with each other, and with everyone we encounter. The principles they outline lead to group harmony and sustain our fellowship. They are not rigid rules but rather guidelines we agree to adhere to. The Traditions guide and ensure our unity and help us stay focused on our primary purpose: to live our lives to the fullest by minimizing the effects of chronic pain and chronic illness in our lives and helping others to do the same. The spiritual unity they convey supports our common welfare so that nothing distracts from or interferes with carrying the message of freedom and serenity to be found in recovery.

Along with the Twelve Steps and Twelve Concepts, the spiritual principles in the Traditions keep our program strong. They suggest ways to carry out the business of our groups, the relationships between groups, and the mission of CPA as a whole. They give us guidelines for our service work and help us keep our fellowship non-commercial and non-professional. As we apply the Traditions, we are protecting the fellowship so that it is there for us as well as for those who will need it in the future. The Traditions guide us to create a safe, effective, and loving environment, within which we can all grow and thrive.

In our meetings, we seek to create an atmosphere of kindness, safety, and anonymity. The Traditions help us do this. Rather than applying rules and authoritarian governance, we follow the principles of unity and autonomy that have worked for those who came before us. We need recovery, and when we apply the Traditions, we can come together in our groups and in our service bodies so that recovery is available to everyone who wants it. We join together as equals and surrender to the loving authority of a Higher Power.

The Traditions are built on a foundation of spiritual principles. Just as we need the Steps, we also need the Traditions. As with the Steps, this requires daily practice in our recovery journey. The Traditions provide tools and direction for our successful recovery and for "practicing these principles in all our affairs." When we are doing a task such as building something or cooking a meal, having the right tools makes all the difference; it becomes easier to do what we've set out to do, and we are more capable and effective. This book was written to help us "work" the Traditions, to understand them for ourselves, and to apply them to our life in recovery and in all our affairs.

The material presented here can deepen and expand our understanding of the Traditions, whether we have been a part of CPA for a while or are new to the fellowship. We can explore them together in our groups and on our own as individuals. This book can be used to start conversations between sponsor and sponsee and as a guide for our group conscience.

We have found that the principles and tools offered in the Traditions are also helpful in our personal relationships. Illness and pain alter familiar roles in our family, work, and community. Our health condition can change how we relate to others and how they relate to us. It may take time and practice to learn new ways to connect, work, or live together. We can utilize the tools of the program and the Steps, Traditions, and Concepts to bring harmony and cooperation into all our relationships.

Just like the Twelve Steps, the Traditions provide sound principles for living, offering beneficial guidance when we incorporate them into our fellowship and our personal lives. Whether in our families, work, or communities, there are always ways in which we can practice the principles of the Traditions. As we do, we find that not only do we continue to grow spiritually and emotionally, but we discover ways of creating harmonious, satisfying relationships that were not available to us before. Because we cannot separate recovery from daily life, we focus on bringing the Traditions into "all our affairs," and as we apply the principles in all aspects of our lives, we change, and the quality of our lives improves. These principles help us enjoy a balanced and serene life, inside and outside of the fellowship. Using the guidance offered by the Traditions, we begin to have healthy and supportive relationships in all areas of our lives.

It's important to reiterate that the Traditions are not rules but a set of guidelines that work to support the integrity of our fellowship. The best way to learn them is through experience—in our groups and service bodies, and with one another—in making decisions, working through conflicts, and supporting solidarity.

HISTORY OF THE TRADITIONS

The Twelve Traditions began as part of the foreword of the first edition of the *Big Book of Alcoholics Anonymous* in 1939. In April 1946, due to the quick growth of A.A. and questions that arose surrounding publicity, religion, and finances, Bill Wilson (co-founder of A.A.) published the "Twelve Points to Assure Our Future" in the *A.A. Grapevine* monthly journal. He studied different governments and societies as part of his research. The Traditions were officially adopted at A.A.'s first International Convention in 1950. In 1953, A.A. published the book *Twelve Steps and Twelve Traditions*.

"OBEDIENCE TO THE UNENFORCEABLE"

The phrase "obedience to the unenforceable," which is used in other Twelve Step fellowships, is applicable to the CPA fellowship as well. The Traditions arose from the early experiences of A.A. members when they learned that unless individual egos are set aside and our thoughts are directed toward the preservation of the fellowship, the very group we need for our own recovery is at risk. Therefore, these Traditions can be considered to be tested and true. They are well-thought-out guidelines to preserve our all-important unity—indeed, our very existence.

No one has the authority to tell us what to do. However, if we fail to honor the Traditions, we risk conflict and disintegration, and then CPA may not be around for those who need it, now or in the future. We each make the choice to apply the Traditions as we understand them. We have seen that if we don't adhere to these spiritual principles, it is possible that our groups will no longer function effectively and may not continue to carry the message of recovery and hope.

Our recovery depends upon the strength of our groups. It can be quite common for groups with even the best intentions to break apart when conflicts arise. The Traditions have stood the test of time as extraordinarily effective guidelines for maintaining the integrity, purpose, and unity of any recovery fellowship. Most problems that arise in our groups can be resolved through thoughtfully applying the Traditions. We start by respectfully listening to each other as we share our experience, strength, and hope and ask our Higher Power for guidance.

WHAT WE WILL GAIN FROM STUDY OF THE TRADITIONS

When we arrive at our first CPA meeting, we are there for our own recovery and are usually not aware of the larger fellowship. We are suffering and want to feel better. In time, we look beyond ourselves and discover there is more than just our group and the Twelve Steps.

For each of us to thrive, we need CPA as a whole to be strong, flourish, and grow. The Traditions help us to be spiritually fit and provide solutions for our common welfare. For our groups to be effective in carrying the message of recovery, we need these suggested guides for harmony—as individuals, groups, and CPA as a whole—to successfully meet the challenges that could threaten our unity. In time, we begin to get involved in service as part of our recovery and understand how the larger fellowship supports our groups.

The Traditions show us how to embody the principles of the program as human beings, in all our affairs, to help us be resilient and thrive individually. We can then focus on our primary purpose: to share the message of hope in our meetings and in CPA as a whole.

GETTING STARTED

Each Tradition is divided into sections describing how the Tradition is applied in our groups (the recovery meetings we attend); in our service bodies (which provide support to our groups); and in all our affairs (our life outside of the fellowship).

A Tradition's chapter begins with a brief description of the Tradition, followed by a list of spiritual tools and the ways we can apply these tools based on the Tradition. The chapter concludes with an associated spiritual principle that denotes the essence of the Tradition.

We find that stories of how individuals understand and use the Traditions make the Traditions come alive and help them be more relatable to our lives. Each Tradition has a collection of personal essays written by members of CPA, describing how the Tradition is applied in our groups, in our service bodies, and in all our affairs.

Also at the end of each chapter are questions to ponder and explore. These can be used on your own, with your sponsor or sponsee, or with your group to "work" the Tradition and deepen understanding and capacity to apply it—in groups, in service work, and in daily life.

The book concludes with a glossary of some common terms. In the Appendix, you will find the Twelve Steps, the Twelve Traditions, the Twelve Concepts of Service, and suggested resources available on the CPA website.

The Traditions give us tools and guidance for learning how to apply CPA's spiritual principles to keep all our relationships healthy and sustainable. This book can be used for literature study in a meeting. It can be studied with a sponsor. It can give us guidance when our meeting is taking a group conscience. It can guide us in personal relationships, showing us how to apply the Traditions with family, friends, work colleagues, and health professionals.

Any group we belong to is strengthened by mutually agreeable values. The principles of the Traditions help guide us to understand and uphold those values. The basic values of CPA include honesty, kindness, fairness, integrity, and respect. We find them to be applicable in our relationships with family and friends, at work, or with our healthcare team. These values define how we interact with others, how we speak and behave, and how we resolve conflicts.

In CPA, our recovery is defined as the ability to live peacefully, joyfully, and comfortably, with ourselves and others. We don't think our way into a life we love—we act our way into it. If we want respect, we behave respectably. Our deeds and words are what matter, not our best intentions. We study this book to receive guidance for our program of recovery in CPA and in all our affairs. These Traditions, applied in all areas of our lives, guide each of us into a life of happiness and serenity.

Tradition One

Our common welfare should come first; personal recovery depends upon CPA unity.

> Our common welfare should come first;
> personal recovery depends upon CPA unity.

All of us depend on the unity of our fellowship because we rely on the group for our personal recovery. The optimal environment for our recovery is to be in a loving spiritual community that is safe and accepting. We take care of the individual members by taking care of the group and working together. The survival of CPA as a whole comes from the collective group unity, and the Traditions help guide our group harmony. Participating in fellowship allows us to practice letting go of self-obsession, being part of the common welfare, and safeguarding our individual opportunities for personal progress and growth.

SPIRITUAL TOOLS FOR PRACTICING TRADITION ONE

- Unity
- Shared responsibility
- Communication
- Equality
- Consistent message
- Surrender

APPLYING TRADITION ONE

I. In Our Groups

UNITY
The Traditions help us to maintain unity and focus, and Tradition One sets the foundation. When we focus on unity, we create and preserve our fellowship as a specific spiritual community. How do we do this?

Unity means that *We* comes before *Me*. The individual can't recover without the group, and the community will thrive if we each do our part. We support the group, which in turn nurtures the individual. This is put into practice with the group conscience: a well-informed group consensus that each individual can participate in. With mutually agreed-upon values and the primary purpose of CPA held as the first priority, each member is provided with the best chance of personal recovery. By creating a healthy community, we grow in our recovery.

Our shared purpose is an expression of our togetherness and our commitment to recovery. Each meeting has a structure that is consistent with this goal of unity. Although each meeting is different—having different formats, different meeting locations, and different topics—all groups are focused on the same common problems and work from the same spiritual principles. This makes our fellowship inclusive, with flexibility for members who are at different stages of recovery and attend meetings in many different ways. Newcomers can feel welcomed and experience the warm connections of our unity, trusting that it will be there the next time they return and in any CPA meeting they attend.

SHARED RESPONSIBILITY

A group's safety and inclusivity will suffer if someone is disruptive to the unity. This can show up in different ways: perhaps someone dominates the meeting, brings outside literature into the meeting, or treats a fellow member disrespectfully. The existence of a group can be threatened if we don't accept and apply the suggestions of the Traditions. Though they are not rules, we have learned from experience that groups are both loving and effective when we abide by them. We feel part of the whole and practice obedience to the unenforceable, each sharing in our responsibility to apply the Traditions.

We are all tasked with safeguarding the fellowship. This includes both newcomers and longtimers—all members are essential. When each member commits personally to the fellowship's unity, we create a caring and safe environment in our meetings.

We each are responsible for contributing to or distracting from the group harmony. This responsibility is seen in our shares during the meeting.

- We are thoughtful when we speak. This thoughtfulness includes talking within the allotted time or choosing to not share many details about our conditions.
- Dwelling on our problems does not help others if we do not also include a focus on the solution.
- We don't gossip or "take another member's inventory." (That is, we focus on our own recovery rather than what we think someone else ought to do.)
- We don't discuss politics or religion.
- Whining and complaining doesn't help others, nor does wallowing in our problems. There are times, however, when this is the best we can do and when what we need is a safe space to do so while trusting that no one will judge us.

In CPA, we say, "We share our mess with our sponsor and our message in a meeting." When we share, we don't generally share many details about medical conditions. We usually discuss our personal details one-on-one with our sponsor or a fellow member.

We share our struggles and also include how we are applying the program as we deal with our pain and chronic symptoms. Sometimes newcomers need time to adjust; they may need to unburden themselves and get relief. We want to provide them with acceptance and time—we are not in a hurry. We lovingly introduce them to the Traditions.

Each individual comes to know what is appropriate at a meeting. Someone who is disrupting the meeting may not realize this and may need to be gently reminded of the Traditions. This reminder is in support of the welfare and recovery for all. Generally, this is best done in private, but sometimes a gentle, direct reminder is needed. Only when someone is being blatantly disruptive would we interrupt them during a meeting. After the meeting, we can courteously remind them of the Traditions.

It is particularly important to help newcomers understand the Traditions. We want to orient them to the meeting format and our service structure so they can be comfortable in our meetings and begin to feel a part of our fellowship. We want to prevent others from embarrassment or feeling like they don't belong because they are unfamiliar with the Traditions that guide our meetings.

We choose to put our attention on all we share in common. By focusing on our common experiences, we keep our meetings healthy and strong. We are supportive as we work together, even when we have disagreements. We are not expected to like everyone; however, it is important to respect and listen to everyone and remember that everyone gets a voice. There is wisdom available in every share in a Twelve Step meeting.

Contributing to the safeguarding of our common welfare supports our personal progress. Everyone needs to participate and give what they can. As each of us pitches in to strengthen our unity, we start to feel like we belong.

COMMUNICATION
In support of our unity as a group of individuals, we must all have a voice. As members of the group, we choose to listen and choose to speak: listening with respect and sharing with honesty. Because each opinion is valuable, we have a responsibility to express our views. We share our truth and let others do the same.

In the meetings of CPA, we learn how to be present for each other. Some of us are learning how to listen respectfully or may be experiencing being heard for the first time. Our communication is direct and authentic. We pay attention to tone as well as our words and avoid being aggressive and hurtful. Some members may never have had a safe place to communicate before coming to CPA. Here, our communication is valued, and our skills grow.

We learn that we can disagree and that disagreement does not have to be done disrespectfully or in anger. We don't need to take differences personally. We are a diverse group, and there is value in getting all perspectives. Sometimes we are in the minority, sometimes in the majority. We don't always know the best solution for situations that may arise. When we have conflicts, we work through them with the guidance of a Higher Power and the

Traditions. It is important to let this Higher Power work through our group conscience, as presented in Tradition Two.

EQUALITY
Unity is important for all of us to succeed. In our groups, unity means that no person has special privileges; we are all equal. The newcomer is as valued as the member who has been around for a long time. Each of us is a piece of the whole and is needed in the group for the greatest possible experience of recovery.

In a Twelve Step meeting, no one is more important or has more power than anyone else. This is a foundational principle of Twelve Step recovery that makes it truly unique, attractive, and effective. It means that when we enter a CPA meeting, we detach from our egos and personal choices in support of the common welfare. We allow for different ways to work the program, to understand the principles, and to carry the message.

CONSISTENT MESSAGE
One expression of our unity is our Conference Approved Literature (CAL). Our literature is one means of accessing the experience, strength, and hope of the program. It is written by our members and new literature is approved by the membership at the World Service Conference. By having mutually created and agreed-upon literature, CPA ensures that its message of recovery is not diluted or distorted and that it remains clear and consistent.

If someone does bring outside material into our meeting, we can speak up and remind the group that outside literature may take the group off course and has the potential to interfere with our unity. CPA unity is not just important within our own meeting — it goes beyond the individual group and connects the entire fellowship. We want to protect the unity of CPA as a whole (Tradition Four) so that whenever and wherever anyone needs CPA, they can be sure it is carrying a consistent message they can count on.

SURRENDER
Prioritizing unity means that we surrender, just as we do in Step One. We recognize that we are part of something greater than ourselves, which matters to us. Just as we do in our personal program of recovery, in our groups we let go of our desire to control outcomes and accept the results of the group conscience. We learn to accept the group majority and trust that we are guided by a loving Power greater than ourselves.

We have found that our happiness and ease in life follow from our spiritual condition and our efforts to deepen and maintain it. In CPA, one solution to our problem of self-obsession is shifting our focus toward unity. As we each participate in creating unity with our fellow members, we accept that we don't always have to be right. We learn to surrender our personal preferences and desires to the common welfare.

II. In Our Service Bodies

In order to attend to the business of CPA, we need a functional environment. The Traditions help guide us as we work and serve on behalf of our fellowship. How can we use Tradition One to support us in service?

In our practice of unity, we recognize that no voice is greater than any other. This means that when we find ourselves in service positions or at business meetings, we listen to each other with open hearts and minds. We remember that we don't control people or outcomes—even when we have only the best intentions and are sure we know the best way forward. We participate; contribute our experience, strength, and hope; and make room for our Higher Power to guide us and provide answers.

We also mentor each other as we take on new service roles. Many positions have an apprentice, who will take over the role next. This apprentice is slowly introduced to the tasks and duties of the position; in this way, they have time to gain the knowledge and experience from the current service provider and will be confident and feel fully prepared when they take on the position. The apprentice is also available as a support to the person in the lead service role, thus maintaining continuity for the group. However, we keep in mind that each of us has different ways of performing tasks, and each member is a trusted servant and needs to do what they see as necessary and in their own way. We provide loving support and clear guidelines, and we trust in the abilities of our fellows.

Being accountable to others in our service work supports unity. If we can't complete a task, we ask for help. In CPA, many service roles are shared by two people so we can take care of ourselves and serve our fellowship. No one is expected to be perfect or show up for every single meeting; that is an unreasonable expectation in our fellowship. Unity is built right in to how we do service—we do it together. When we share commitments in this way, we can experience a deep feeling of belonging as we contribute to the whole, working alongside others with confidence and in unity.

III. In All Our Affairs

Tradition One can be applied to our relationships outside of CPA. To do this, one way our members have reworded Tradition One is: "*Our common welfare should come first; personal growth for each person depends upon unity.*"

In this section, we explore how we can contribute to unity in our home, our workplace, our community, and with the people involved in our healthcare. We can see through the same lens of unity we use in our meetings and work toward the common good. When we are unified, our relationships will thrive, and so will we.

A good question to ask is: *Is what I'm doing best for the "common welfare" of the relationship, or is too much attention being directed toward one person's personal desires?*

Some of us are dependent on others for our daily care and functioning. Some of us interact with others at a workplace. Some of us live with family; some of us live alone; some of us live in a care facility. Some of us are in the hospital from time to time. No matter our situation, we strive for harmonious cooperation with others for our spiritual recovery and overall well-being.

It helps to be clear about the common goal. This will look different in each situation. What is the common welfare in our home? At work? With our healthcare relationships?

In applying Tradition One in all our affairs, we remember that communication is vital to effective functioning and unity, as is equality. We all matter, and we all enhance the whole. We employ a willingness to listen to others and have an open mind. We share our feelings and thoughts so we can consciously engage in a free exchange of ideas.

When we are working toward a common goal with others, we need to find a balance between being dominating and being passive. We learn how to clearly express our needs, feelings, and boundaries, knowing that they matter, as do those of the group. We ask ourselves if we are speaking with an attitude of kindness and compassion. "Say what I mean, but don't say it mean," is one way our members remind themselves of this. We recognize the need to be flexible to ensure our needs are met along with those of the whole, and we don't try to control or manipulate. We are not more or less important than others just because we have an illness or live with pain. By practicing this Tradition, we become aware of when we are focusing too much on our needs and not on the common welfare, and then we find ways to balance our own needs and desires with the common good.

Because we've seen how Tradition One works in our groups, we've had practice and can apply its principles to life outside of the program. We learn to listen even when we don't agree. We don't need to take it personally when we have differing opinions with family members, coworkers, or healthcare professionals. We recognize that each person's opinion is valid and that another person's ideas and ways of doing things are just as legitimate as ours. We learn to appreciate what others have to give, even if it is not what we expected. By contributing to solutions and unity in this way, we reinforce our own welfare.

Our connection with our Higher Power, which we strengthen by working the Twelve Steps, can also be expressed in our relationships. We loosen our hold on how we think things should look and invite the guidance of our Higher Power. We do our part and let go of the results, detaching from others and outcomes, with love.

In our quest to have all our relationships benefit our well-being and be of value, we offer our support to the people in our daily lives. For instance, we make a point of thanking a store employee who helped load groceries into our car; this strengthens our connection with others and the common good. We take care of ourselves by being aware that our actions affect the common welfare. We don't gossip, we don't offer opinions when they are not requested, and we don't give advice. There may be a treatment that works for us, but we don't encourage others to try it or give them advice about their healthcare unless they ask us.

Just like in our meetings and personal recovery, we work to maintain relationships outside of the fellowship. In CPA, we are asked to practice humility and adaptability and to be teachable. We can practice these very things with everyone we encounter. It may be helpful to speak with our sponsor and explore any old patterns that appear to be keeping us from unity in all our affairs. In doing so, we may discover there are ways in which we are self-centered or engage in behaviors that disrupt the stability at home, at work, or in our healthcare relationships.

> **ASSOCIATED SPIRITUAL PRINCIPLE:** *Unity*
>
> The group requires unity; otherwise, it will not have consistency and direction, and members won't find recovery and progress in their program. We need others for our recovery, and they need us. For all of us to recover, we all share our voices and points of view as equals and surrender at times to the whole.

TRADITION ONE IN ACTION

Our common welfare should come first; personal recovery depends upon CPA unity.

VOICES OF OUR MEMBERS

When I was new in CPA, my sponsor said that I could share as much mess as I needed to in the meeting as long as I spent an equal amount of time sharing about how I was applying the Steps and the Principles, so I was also carrying the message of hope for myself and others. Later in my recovery, when I complained about a meeting, my sponsor asked me, "Are you only going to meetings for what you can get from them, or what you can bring to them?" This is where Tradition One is a great reminder about whether I am upholding unity or dividing it by bringing criticism. Am I bringing solutions or only my anger, frustration, and depression? Are my shares contributing to the love and safety of our CPA community?

We have no rules in CPA; however, we have agreed-upon etiquette that supports all of us. Although I am not challenged by perfumes and strong scents, I voted to ban them from our meeting when there was a group conscience about it, so I could support my fellow members. In that same spirit of inclusiveness, CPA video meeting etiquette includes asking all members to keep their cameras still or turned off if moving around because some members experience easily triggered motion sickness.

Tradition One asks me to think and behave with an all-inclusive attitude and to be mindful of what affects CPA as a whole and our ability to offer support and understanding to all members—instead of what just affects me. I am in CPA recovery not only from my obsessive, self-centered focus on my chronic pain and chronic illness but my self-centered focus, period. When I choose our common welfare over my own personal wants, I am practicing the principles of the program in all my affairs.

At our videoconference meeting, attendance is high, so we need two people to chair and a technical person to coordinate breakout rooms, none of which are assigned to anyone prior to the meeting. Yet at every meeting, people step forward to chair or handle the technical part. More people than needed always volunteer, and they are politely thanked. I really appreciate how everyone steps up to make sure all the positions are filled at every meeting.

It supports group unity when a group has a regularly scheduled business meeting. In our business meetings, eventually most decisions are unanimous because everyone is thinking about the group and how to make the meeting focused on our primary purpose and ensuring the newcomer feels welcome. Sometimes the group makes a decision that I don't agree with. I've learned it works well to try something new for a while, even if I really think it may not be a good idea. When we are not unanimous, we try out whatever we are considering until the next business meeting, be it a change in format or some issue of etiquette. Because we meet every month, when the next business meeting comes, we are fully informed by the trial period and can make a decision that best meets the group's needs.

At each business meeting, someone volunteers to chair the meeting, we each take turns speaking, and we listen to each other respectfully. Everyone has an opportunity to be heard. After the discussion, we often come to a unanimous decision. If we are still not unanimous, we table the issue or revise the trial. We trust Higher Power to reveal the best decision, in time.

I have found that the Traditions can be used to resolve most conflicts or dilemmas in meetings and fellowship. With a little thought, prayer, and feedback, we can take a troubling CPA relationship or conflict in a meeting and apply "principles before personalities."

For instance, sometimes people come to CPA with the practices of other programs, religious beliefs, or ideas about treatments. They are entering CPA with the stress of the emotional and mental suffering of longtime chronic pain and illness. I remind myself that they are stuck, like I was, unable to imagine doing anything differently. This is the cycle of defeat, despair, obsession, and fear that keeps us frantically doing the same things over and over, expecting different results. Trying to change by using the tools that worked in other programs, or by continuing with skills that one has used since childhood, is normal human behavior. I remind myself how important it was to experience compassion rather than judgment when I first came to meetings. However, if their behavior disrupts, divides, and creates conflict, Tradition One is very clear.

That doesn't mean I need to jump in and try to change someone's behavior, unless it is truly disrupting the meeting. If I challenge myself to stay within the purpose of CPA, I see that some folks need time to learn how to handle life more skillfully. Working the program in the face of chronic pain and illness takes time, practice, and a willingness to be teachable. Everyone needs as much compassion as I do, so I learned to send a special blessing to individuals who are struggling.

I need to trust my Higher Power and my friends to help me determine if I am projecting my own fears, judgments, and stories from the past, or if some corrective action needs to be suggested. Otherwise, my opinions and reactions are exactly that: my opinions and reactions. I can apply my new skills of compassion, acceptance, and kindheartedness to my own humanness. For me, this is Tradition One, in action.

In CPA, we say, "We share our mess with our sponsor and our message in a meeting." When I made that oh-so-hard first telephone call to a CPA member asking for help, she said, "Tell me your chronic pain and illness story." Her words left me dumbfounded and disarmed. Nobody had ever asked to hear anything about what it felt like to be me in a body that I believed betrayed me, let alone was willing to listen to the story of 30 years of health crises. But she knew what I would later learn: this story had been rattling around in my head, often leaking out in bits and pieces, looking like complaints, but nobody had actually reached in and invited me to say the words I'd swallowed for decades. And so I spoke and she listened and occasionally; she said, "I am sorry that you have suffered so terribly," which brought me to tears. I felt seen, heard, and engulfed in compassion. Not a fake "I'm sorry about that" as a half-listener checked her watch, nor a rush to blast me with the latest fix, sending me into rage or a shame spiral, but a witness who understood and held uninterrupted space until I was finished. I will never forget her generosity.

How does one repay that generosity and kindness? We pass it on, holding space for the new person. We realize that no matter how long we've been in other Twelve Step recovery, none of us had a solution or a message—only a mess—when we arrived in CPA. We try to be the kind of CPA member who meets a new member's mess with an open heart, inviting them—outside of the meeting—to finally fully say what they had been stuffing: anger, rage, frustration, physical pain and illness, despair and hopelessness.

I am grateful that we do not discuss the specifics of our individual illnesses, the medical community, or related subjects in meetings and instead, focus on our common solution, found through both the fellowship and working the CPA Twelve Steps. And I will be ever grateful for that member who took the time to invite this former sufferer in fellowship to "tell me more" in a one-on-one conversation.

I love the sharing of service we practice in CPA. I just had a lovely experience on a phone meeting in which the chairperson said, "What do you all think about someone who isn't usually the timekeeper being the timekeeper?" and "Would someone like to read the Preamble who has never read the Preamble?" She invited new people to participate. It was a large meeting, and she did something else I found lovely—and really effective. "Just a gentle reminder, if you have shared in another meeting today, please give someone else a chance to share since the meeting is so big." The more people who participate, the more inclusion, the more we all feel a natural tendency to take responsibility for our meeting. As someone new, I felt so included and was grateful for the invitation to step up.

In CPA, even as a newcomer, I can participate in the meeting and say yes, even if I am not sure I can do it. If I can't complete the task, I can ask for help, even in the midst of the service commitment. In CPA, we can always say, "I need help," and someone will step up.

This is the beautiful outcome of practicing unity that happens in CPA.

At my meeting, the format says we discourage crosstalk. Occasionally, someone introduces their share by saying, "I know this is crosstalk, but..." This is something we all may have done, but it is a problem when someone does it often and goes on at length. Someone at my meeting did this frequently, and I knew them well, so I called them and said, "It makes me feel uncomfortable when the guidelines for the group are being ignored, and I wonder if it makes the newcomers feel less safe." This person was grateful I helped them keep the meeting safe. I think there are times when things have to be dealt with at a group level and times when it's best to bring something up, one-on-one, as lovingly as possible. This is a gentle way to put our common welfare first.

I have found CPA to be a solution-focused fellowship. I feel my pain and illness are the things I have the most right to complain about. I have certainly spent a large percentage of my life complaining about my symptoms. And yet, when I come to meetings, I don't find complaining. I find others sharing about how they are dealing with the emotional aspect of their conditions. I hear how others are applying spiritual principles to their pain and illness. Luckily, I have made friendships in the program where I can vent privately about my day if I need to, and instead of pity, I receive understanding, respect, and connection. I have found that this allows me to stay solution-focused when sharing in meetings.

I will never forget the first time a committee chair stopped a heated discussion and asked us to join him in saying the Serenity Prayer. The immediate effect was palpable in the energy of the room. Unity was restored, and our focus was shifted back to our primary purpose and reliance on a Higher Power. When it came time to take the group conscience by vote, the chairperson again paused the meeting and suggested we say the Serenity Prayer. This intention allowed time for our own individual Higher Powers to guide our votes. In this way, unity and service and our primary purpose were being fulfilled. Not "I want to be right! I know I'm right!" Egos got put aside, simply through the use of that Serenity Prayer.

When I arrived in CPA, I was physically quite ill and couldn't reliably assume any service commitments, something that had never happened before. When I was considering doing service in CPA, questions ran through my mind: How could I possibly show up regularly on a given day to do anything when I had no idea what state I would awaken in? And then I asked myself, "What if it's easy?"

I regularly attend a meeting on videoconference where there is no standing chair, host, breakout room coordinator or leader for the breakout rooms. Attendees gather a few minutes early and whomever feels up to it jumps in and takes on one of those roles. I have been attending for more than a year and a half, and not once has a position not been filled. After my first time taking on one of the service roles, I found everyone so kind, generous in word and spirit, and helpful that I couldn't wait to try it again. In addition, I found myself leading one day only to discover I could not see well enough to finish the format. Without a moment's hesitation, another member jumped in.

I can't convey how much more a part of the meeting I feel when I can take on a simple task. Because my health is unpredictable, I do service on the days I can and appreciate meetings whose format allows that. I also attend drop-in meetings whenever I am able. CPA makes it easy to do service.

What kept me coming back to CPA was the love, kindness, and compassion that I witnessed. At my very first meeting, some folks were lying down, others wore their pajamas, most others were sitting in comfortable chairs, and one member fell asleep. Chronic pain and chronic illness are exhausting.

When the leader was partway through the meeting, she said it had been a hard day and brain fog was setting in. What happened next was remarkable to me. The leader simply asked if someone could help her and take the lead. Then a CPA member seamlessly, gently, and compassionately offered to step in and lead the rest of the meeting. Everyone knew that symptoms can rise up at any time.

My belief had been that I had to be perfect in everything I did or said. Have I ever asked for help? No. Have I ever put self-care first? No. Had I always muddled through my pain just so others would be pleased with me? Yes. Have I ever allowed myself to be comfortable in front of others? No, I was taught that wasn't proper. Have I always been afraid to lead a meeting and speak in front of others because I was afraid I would "mess up" in some way? Yes. These CPA members showed me that imperfection, being human, falling asleep, being comfortable, and asking for help were a normal part of life and part of our meetings. I no longer needed to be perfect! I finally had hope that my life would finally change for the better. And it has, in every way. With HP and my sponsor's patience and help, I led my first meeting—two months after my first meeting! I was imperfect, and I knew that was okay. My Higher Power and my CPA friends had my back. I once felt fear to offer to serve, and now I was able to give to others what they had given to me: Peace and hope for a better life.

For over a year, I had the privilege to apprentice a member in a service role she was going to fill, and it was an incredibly rewarding experience. We learned so much about ourselves and each other, and that's resulted in a priceless friendship.

Now, I am apprenticing in a CPA service position that intimidates me. I never would have dreamed of applying for a position like this in the business world, yet thanks to CPA's apprentice concept I feel safe and supported to say "yes" to a new role. My mentor has been so generous in sharing her knowledge and wisdom with me. She too has become a trusted friend. She has been gentle, encouraging, and patient and keeps reminding me of the importance of progressing slowly. Because of clear guidelines and her faith in me, my confidence grows with each task completed. We support each other, and my self-esteem grows as I assist her. I could not be doing this service role without her loving support. I love the saying "A shared load is a lighter load," but for me, "A shared load is a do-able load."

During a most difficult health challenge, I found myself unable to shower or warm a meal and barely had the ability to focus clearly enough to attend a virtual CPA meeting. I was actively working the Steps with my sponsor and worried that I could not give anything back—she told me that my service job was to *receive the care* given by my home health workers and all those who were helping me. I guffawed. Yeah, yeah, I thought. But she insisted that it is not a lower form of service. So I took it to heart and began treating the times my nurses come over as ones where I drop everything and deeply listen to them. I ask about their families and remember their children's names. I text each to say thank you or send a reminder of how much I appreciate them. As this continued, my husband and I noticed that each healthcare worker began to laugh more and spend more time at our home, not wanting to leave. They shared their hearts and challenges and I could tell they left differently, lighter than they arrived. Some began to tell me they loved me. These healthcare workers, angels all, have become beloveds, and for the first time in my life I actually believe that receiving with an open, grateful heart and acting from that consciousness is full-fledged service. It not only changed the experience of those who care for me, but it has changed me, too.

Before I began practicing Tradition One, I was a "scorekeeper." I obsessed about how much my husband was doing compared to how much I was doing. If he washed the cars, I had to do something of equal effort and value. Heaven forbid if the score cards came up unequal, as a resentment was sure to form in my mind.

Then I fell chronically ill. The whole basis of my marriage, that of equal partnership, fell apart. I kept coming up short on the score card. Shame and fear increased as my ability to function decreased. He would surely leave me because I could no longer contribute to our partnership.

My thinking shifted from the scorekeeping of separate individuals to viewing my marriage through the eyes of a unified entity. I discovered that my kind, supportive, and loving words were equally valuable to my partner as tasks, and I could choose this attitude regardless of my physical limitations. Our playful exchanges became way more important to the quality of our partnership than loads of laundry.

I now view my relationship as a team sport instead of a competition. My chronic pain and chronic illness take a back seat, when I place my focus on my family's common welfare instead of my own. Isolation and suffering decrease, and I become part of something greater than myself. Thanks to Tradition One, our marriage has never been better.

One of the main things I get from reading about Tradition One is selflessness and the importance of considering others. If I have a friendship that is valuable to me and that I want to last, I need to be willing to make some sacrifices for the benefit of that friendship. We don't always have to do what I want or eat where I want to eat or talk about my concerns. It is important that I consider the other person's needs and wants as well as mine. The reward for being willing to give as well as take is an ongoing friendship that strengthens with time. On the other hand, if I continually insist on being the center of attention, I may lose that friendship. What is important to me? Always having things my way or having the friendship with this person in my life?

The same applies to my marriage. While my needs and wants should be considered, so should those of my partner. We are of equal importance, and if we want these relationships to continue and be healthy, each one needs to consider what is best for the relationship. If I consider only my needs, it is likely the relationship will be weakened or destroyed. Even when I feel very strongly about something, that does not mean it is best for the relationship. In my relationships, it is as important to express my needs as it is vital to listen to others. If I always have it my way, I am in danger of damaging or losing the relationship, and what good is that?

WORKING TRADITION ONE
Our common welfare should come first; personal recovery depends upon CPA unity.

The following questions can help deepen your understanding and application of Tradition One in your recovery and in all your affairs. Use these questions with your sponsor or sponsee or your CPA group, or explore them on your own, selecting the ones that are relevant.

1. How does my individual recovery depend on CPA unity?
2. In what ways do I foster unity in recovery, in my group, in service work, and in all my affairs?
3. What does "common welfare" mean to me?
4. When and how do I place "common welfare" first?
5. How do I contribute to unity in my group? How do I cultivate unity in my personal relationships?
6. How does my self-centeredness get in the way of unity in my groups? In my daily life?
7. Do I encourage and support harmony within the group? In all my affairs?
8. When I attend a meeting, do I participate by reading, sharing, leading, or helping others?
9. Am I willing to share my experience, strength, and hope at meetings?
10. When conflicts arise, how can I be part of the solution?
11. What types of service work can I do today?
12. Am I informed about CPA as a whole? How do I support it?

13. Do I compare other CPA groups or speak negatively about them?
14. Do I speak about other Twelve Step fellowships in CPA meetings?
15. Am I compassionate and kind toward those around me?
16. Do I refrain from talking about people behind their backs?
17. Am I patient, tolerant, and respectful toward those who offend me? When am I, and when am I not?
18. Can I accept others as they are? Am I able to be flexible in my relationships?
19. In what ways do my prejudices affect unity in my groups and all my affairs?
20. Am I most often a "giver" or a "taker"?
21. What does applying Tradition One in all my affairs look like today?
22. In what areas of my life do I already practice and understand:
    - Unity
    - Shared responsibility
    - Communication
    - Equality
    - Consistent message
    - Surrender
23. How can I include these spiritual tools where they may be missing in my life today?

Tradition Two

For our group purpose, there is but one ultimate authority—a loving God as He may express Himself in our group conscience. Our leaders are but trusted servants; they do not govern.

> For our group purpose, there is but one ultimate authority—a loving God as He may express Himself in our group conscience. Our leaders are but trusted servants; they do not govern.

Tradition Two addresses the organization, governance, and authority of our groups.

Who runs the CPA fellowship? The perhaps-unexpected answer is: no one. There is no individual authority among the membership; we all perform services so the group can function. No one directs or governs. All decisions are arrived at through a majority agreement after every consideration is reviewed. We come to trust a Higher Power to guide us in this process.

SPIRITUAL TOOLS FOR PRACTICING TRADITION TWO

- A Higher Power as expressed through our group conscience
- Patience
- Participation and flexibility
- Trust and faith
- Listening
- Group inventory
- Leaders do not govern—leaders are servants
- Everyone has a voice
- Service is larger than ourselves
- A willingness to serve

APPLYING TRADITION TWO

I. In Our Groups

A HIGHER POWER AS EXPRESSED THROUGH OUR GROUP CONSCIENCE

In our personal recovery, when there are challenges, questions, or situations that are confusing, we ask our Higher Power and our sponsor for guidance.

The same goes for the group. The group is not directed by the self-interest of one individual. As we meet and work together, through discussion, listening, and group conscience, we discover we can trust the decisions we reach. We may each consult our own Higher Power as we participate and listen to one another. Through the group members showing up humbly, as equals, a Higher Guidance is accessed and expressed in our group conscience.

How does this happen? We usually have a home group, which is one group we are committed to, where we participate in business meetings and the group conscience. A business meeting is a meeting held to manage the operations of the group; anyone can attend the business meeting and share their ideas. A group conscience is a consensus arrived at in a meeting held separate from the regular meeting or during a business meeting. A group conscience raises awareness of all members, and we take the time for thorough discussions so we can arrive at an informed decision. Everyone is given an opportunity to voice their thoughts. Whether someone is a newcomer or has been in CPA for a while, all opinions are valuable.

A decision made by group conscience requires that everyone involved have the necessary information to make an informed choice. This can be a slow process, and the group conscience may need to be held more than once to come to a majority decision.

PATIENCE

To make a decision, we need to be informed. This means having all of the relevant information, which often requires including everyone's ideas. We do this by hearing all voices and giving everyone an opportunity to speak. This process can take time. We may need to stop for people to meditate or to pray, ideas may need time to simmer, or we may discover we need to do more research or gather more data. In particular, arriving at a group conscience may take many meetings. But in time, we determine the actions needed, along with ways to implement them.

In turning to our Higher Power, we ensure that we make no hasty actions. Sometimes a group recites the Serenity Prayer before taking a vote. We don't need to force solutions or decisions based on our own biases. We can accept the wisdom of the group and allow our Higher Power's will to be done.

PARTICIPATION AND FLEXIBILITY
We each participate by sharing our thoughts, respecting others, and considering what is best for the group. We recognize the value of each person and remain open to new ideas, being tolerant of ideas that are different from our own. We take the time to listen to each other and to everyone's needs so the topic is thoroughly explored, and we participate in the process with integrity and a willingness to be flexible. In this way, we arrive at an outcome that is good for the whole as well as for each of us individually.

TRUST AND FAITH
We seek direction from our Higher Power to help us reach a decision that is good for the whole. Before we speak, we can pray for guidance. We learn to trust that the group decision will be wiser than any individual's decision. We may find it takes us time to be able to trust that our Higher Power will lead us in the right direction. As we have experienced the loving care of a Higher Power in our personal recovery, we now practice experiencing this same care in our group. We discover that the group conscience is shared wisdom and unity in action, and we begin to trust both an ultimate authority and each other.

LISTENING
Coming together in a group conscience and honoring the outcome is a spiritual exercise. We learn to let go of how we want the outcome to be and our desire to control the decision. This can be challenging. When we disagree, we seek to find a way to resolve a conflict in a positive way, without judging or attacking others. We listen to others—a skill we may need to strengthen. We find it helps to separate the idea from the individual who is offering it.

Sometimes we are in the minority. When that happens, we trust that others will listen to our voices and consider our opinions. When there are major differences in ideas, both the minority and the majority voices need to surrender their positions and practice humbly listening. We maintain an attitude of friendliness toward each other, which may take practice and much patience, and we remember to practice putting "principles before personalities" (Tradition Twelve).

Coming to a decision by group conscience depends on our willingness to speak with and listen to others with an attitude of curiosity, respect, and kindness. We work to find common ground. There is always more than one direction we can take or more than one solution to the situation. Together we can listen for our Higher Power's guidance, which may come through any of us. Often, we find that creative solutions arise as we listen and include each point of view.

GROUP INVENTORY
Groups can choose to take an inventory as part of their spiritual growth. If a group finds it has fallen into dysfunctional or unproductive habits or feels a lack of ease or well-being, a group inventory is a great tool of the program. Some groups do an inventory on a regular basis, just as we do in our individual program of recovery (Step Four and Step Ten), to help keep house and maintain a healthy environment of recovery for all. In the same way we work the Steps with a sponsor, as a group we assess whether we are following the Traditions and what we can do differently to adhere to them and make our meetings dynamic, welcoming, and able to carry the message of CPA recovery.

LEADERS DO NOT GOVERN—LEADERS ARE SERVANTS
In CPA, there is no hierarchy of power. Our fellowship is based on a structure of service. Various service positions are required so our meetings can function: someone needs to be the meeting chair, for instance, leading the meeting in keeping with the format; a

timekeeper may be needed to time shares so as many people who want to share can do so; someone may set up chairs, welcome newcomers, make coffee, or monitor a website. Members who fill the various service positions fulfill their responsibilities, but they don't have power over others, and the position a member holds does not define them or their value. Every member, whether performing service or not, is as important to the fellowship as every other member. No one person has authority to make decisions for the group.

This structure of equals, in service to the whole, is specific to Twelve Step groups. It may feel counterintuitive or be new to us when we first start coming to meetings. What does it look like in practice? We cooperate and work with each other; we remember to serve rather than control. We can participate in the group conscience by offering suggestions and our experience, and when a group conscience is taken, we are all tasked with carrying out what has been decided by the group. We rely on the guidance of our Higher Power and take direction from the group conscience.

Each person fulfills their role in their own way. As we show up for our service, our self-esteem and sense of purpose may increase. It can be exciting to realize that we are fully trusted to hold a position that matters to the group. In some cases, it may be the first time we have felt that kind of trust. The group relies on and trusts us to do the vital work that supports CPA.

Because there is no hierarchy, there is no pressure to be "in charge." This is what it means to be a trusted servant who has no power over others. Whether we are chairing the General Advisory Council (GAC), a meeting or a committee, we are each responsible for contributing to the functioning of CPA and participating in the group conscience. If we think something is not working smoothly, we can speak up, knowing our voice is vital, rather than turning our attention to someone "on top" to complain to or blame.

There are no rules or laws in CPA. We don't enforce the Traditions; we uphold them. They are suggestions, not absolutes.

We practice "obedience to the unenforceable." In this way, we create a safe environment in which we serve but assume no authority over others.

EVERYONE HAS A VOICE
Our fellowship is made up of a myriad of members, each with their own unique and varied life experiences. Each is at different stages in their recovery, and each person has their own reasons for becoming a member of CPA. From the newcomer to the longtimer, we are all equal, and everyone has a voice. The very existence of the fellowship depends on our awareness that each of us is valuable, regardless of religion, social status, profession, gender, or health condition. The meetings are open to anyone who wants to learn how to find serenity while living with chronic pain and chronic illness.

The Traditions work together to support Twelve Step fellowships. Tradition One requires equality in order to create unity. Tradition Two preserves this equality by supporting a service structure with no hierarchy. We don't impose decisions on anyone whether we are speaking as a chairperson, a member, or a sponsor. As we share the bond of living with chronic pain and chronic illness, we share the work of the group and are there to contribute, not to dictate a course of action. We may have diversity in many areas, but we utilize that asset rather than letting it interfere with our coming together. CPA meetings may be the first place where we encounter this level of safety and acceptance of who we are and what we bring. We need our fellowship to survive—some members feel this quite literally. If a decision is good for the well-being of CPA, then it is good for us.

SERVICE IS LARGER THAN OURSELVES
Our service roles offer us an opportunity to grow spiritually as we learn to trust and to be trustworthy. This Tradition engenders humility. We find that we are neither more nor less than others and that none of us are special. No one speaks for anyone but

themselves, in service of the group. By being given the opportunity to do service in this way, we find we can let go of being self-centered and holding strong opinions, and instead practice selflessness, focusing on what is best for CPA. We become part of something larger than ourselves.

A WILLINGNESS TO SERVE
Service work is a vital part of our personal growth. Through our service, we give back what was given to us. When we are asked to serve, we feel like we belong and are part of the fellowship. When asked to contribute, newcomers can feel like they belong.

There are suggested term lengths for each service position. We practice rotation of service, which allows everyone a chance to serve. It is an act of humility to let go of a position and mentor others so they may step in. This helps our members to grow in the program, from those who tend to dominate to those who are hesitant to step up. We each deserve the opportunity to grow through service.

When members rotate and turn over roles, no one dominates, and no individual owns a position. This allows those who don't have experience in leadership to learn new skills. In CPA, many positions have two people sharing responsibilities, with one person who has experience in the position mentoring another member so the other can confidently assume the position in the future. This is how we can include all our members who want to contribute to CPA, and it ensures that no one person bears all the responsibility. When each of us does service, no one is overburdened.

In addition to holding office, service includes helping make decisions, sharing at a meeting, setting up chairs, or saying the Serenity Prayer at a meeting. We serve, whether in a specific role or just by speaking up during a group conscience discussion. Helping the meeting stay focused on our primary purpose and keeping it from going astray is service. Welcoming newcomers and helping them understand our meeting and the Traditions is service. Reaching out to newcomers during fellowship time or offering our phone number so they know they are not alone is service.

Serving our group and the CPA fellowship changes us. Our sense of self-worth grows as we participate by doing our best and offering what we can within our capacity. When we do service work together, we often find that we form close bonds with people; we no longer feel isolated as we develop friendships and begin to trust ourselves and others.

We all share responsibility for the operation of our groups and of CPA as a whole. We appreciate the time, energy, and dedication shared by CPA members and don't take anyone for granted. And we remember to recognize each other in our service work with kindness and to honor what each person has to offer.

II. In Our Service Bodies

CPA service bodies perform work that supports both our groups and the fellowship as a whole. This may include but is not limited to the General Advisory Council, Intergroups, committees, and task forces. These bodies help the groups stay connected and unified, put on events, create CPA literature, and help make decisions that support the entire worldwide fellowship. Just as at the group level, there are no leaders, and no single service body is in charge.

Spiritual principles are at the core of all the work done on behalf of the CPA fellowship, and every member has the opportunity to participate on a service body. Although no one controls the work, we clearly define roles and projects. We ensure that members taking on a position or a project are well supported so they can be successful and effective. No one works alone. Together, we serve the primary purpose of the fellowship.

Strong communication skills are needed to be able to work harmoniously with others. As we do service, we get better and better at this. We bring an attitude of cooperation and find that our efforts sustain and broaden our personal spiritual growth. We respect each other's skills and ideas as we work together on service bodies. We take our time to support someone when they take on a service role and help them as needed until they have confidence and are comfortable taking on the responsibilities.

III. In All Our Affairs

How do we make informed decisions in our family? In our place of work? With our healthcare providers?

Just as in our CPA groups, the conscience of any group of two or more people, when informed of the facts and issues, is often wiser than that of any one person. This gives us the opportunity to make decisions as a group after looking at all sides of an issue. When we practice Tradition Two in our relationships, we don't control others; rather, everyone involved has a voice and deserves respect, and for guidance we look to our Higher Power.

Some members have found it helpful to rewrite Tradition Two in this way: "*For our relationship's purpose there is but one authority—a loving God as He may express Himself in our group conscience. We are all trusted servants. None of us governs.*" Is the voice of a loving God being expressed in the "group conscience" of our personal, work, and healthcare relationships? Or has one person become the ultimate authority?

Tradition Two helps us remember that in any group in which we participate, whether in a family, in our community, or with our medical providers, we can each be of service. This process asks us to have unconditional regard for others and to consider the needs and desires of everyone involved. What does this look like?

We actively practice listening with respect; we wait our turn to speak and don't force our views on others. We express our opinion in a way that is fair minded, honoring, and kind, and we notice if our tone communicates otherwise. We all have the right to express our opinions without being judged.

There is an equal exchange of ideas, and we cooperate instead of attempting to control. In most situations, no one person makes all the decisions. We consider all of the aspects of a problem and come to an agreement together. This means that no individual dominates or is dominated, and we pause to consider whether we are experiencing either situation. If we are, we can turn to our Higher Power for guidance before continuing the conversation.

We do our best to make sure that everyone, including ourselves, is informed of the issues. Although there are times when some people naturally have greater expertise in an area, everyone shares responsibility, participates, and comes to a decision together, with humility and as equals.

We remember to treat others with courtesy, especially those closest to us. In so doing, we preserve the unity of the relationship.

If appropriate in our relationship, we can take a formal group conscience when making a decision. Just as we do in our CPA meetings, we take our time and think things through so we can discover what is best for all our needs. We are patient and willing to discuss all points of view. What we do not do is give up responsibility and then blame others if things go wrong.

We find we are grateful to discover that we aren't always right and that we can't always get our way. In fact, we learn that sometimes we do not know what's best and that listening to others' input while relying on a Higher Power is the very best way to reach an effective decision.

We practice listening by learning to pause rather than react right away. We turn to our Higher Power for guidance, trusting that our Higher Power will help and guide us in all our relationships and in all situations. We remember that our one authority is our loving Higher Power and not any single person's desires—even our own. No one person knows what is best for us, and we don't know what is best for others. We apply the slogan *Live and Let Live.*

Practicing Tradition Two in all our affairs helps to create safe, effective, harmonious relationships in which we feel valued and empowered and in which we can be sure that our well-being, and the well-being of all concerned, really matter.

> **ASSOCIATED SPIRITUAL PRINCIPLE:** *Trust in a Higher Power, Guided by Group Conscience*
> We trust and have faith and patience in the group conscience process and how it represents our Higher Power's will and loving care.

TRADITION TWO IN ACTION

For our group purpose there is but one ultimate authority—a loving God as He may express Himself in our group conscience. Our leaders are but trusted servants; they do not govern.

VOICES OF OUR MEMBERS

Our small, virtual meeting was tight-knit and enjoyed a comfortable, safe, sharing environment. In time, attendance grew, and the increase in members changed the dynamics of our intimate meeting. With so many people, we were running over our closing time, and we knew we needed to make a change.

Many ideas were suggested about how to keep the safe and loving space that we all depended upon. Some members wanted to remove the meeting from the website so we couldn't get any bigger. Others wanted to start another meeting and have an invitation-only group. The newcomers loved the meeting and wanted it to be longer. It was suggested that maybe we could use technology to break up into smaller groups, but people were worried about splitting up the group.

When it came time for the group conscience to discuss the issue, I was asked to run the meeting. I prayed about it and talked to some members of CPA to hear their experience, strength, and hope about handling controversial issues, which was helpful and gave me confidence to lead the meeting.

In order to make sure that everyone had an opportunity to share their thoughts and feelings about the issue, it was suggested that I call on each person once with each idea presented. This took time and worked well. The collective voice, the group conscience, was clear and decided upon unanimously. There was no one in a minority position. A true, loving, ultimate authority was guiding the way. We decided to try the technology option for breakout groups, for one month, and then come back together to see how we collectively felt. It was understandable that some members were afraid of change, and the trial period helped put our members at ease.

That was a year ago, and the changes have served the group so we can continue to have a safe, comfortable meeting for all.

I always try to attend my home group business meeting. Once, we decided to take a crucial and controversial vote at our next business meeting. We provided every member with background information showing how the suggested change would support our group's primary purpose. I was shocked when seven other people, who normally never attended our meeting, showed up to our business meeting and swayed the vote. A fellow home group member had invited several friends to stuff the ballot box so she would get her own way. After that business meeting, my home group voted that, although all attending may have a voice, only home group members can vote. I honor this when I attend other group's business meetings. I can share my experience, strength, and hope, as everybody's voice and thoughts are important, but I do not vote. In this way, I'm practicing equanimity and trust in a Higher Power, as well as the tool of participation and flexibility—all part of Tradition Two.

Every group conscience begins with a little knot in my belly. I mindfully relax as I open and lean into the opportunity to practice active, respectful, and curious listening, rather than my too-oft-practiced tightening around my rigid ideas of what I want and how things should look. This requires deep listening—not a strength for me. I'm an interrupter, a talker, an eye-roller. Listening with curiosity and an earnest desire to understand my fellow CPA members requires my full, conscious awareness and focus. Without that, I default to either judging what is shared, or more often, not listening because I am busy formulating what I want to say.

It is inevitable that individuals will disagree, that we will have varied perceptions and reactions based on our own experience and beliefs. What can be magical is watching the group conscience, guided and directed by a Higher Power and the Twelve Traditions, come to peaceful solutions, again and again. Sometimes the group's decision is in alignment with my own desires; sometimes it is not, and my feathers get ruffled. Other times, someone speaking on behalf of the minority voice changes my previous decision. In the scheme of things, it doesn't matter. In practice, I quickly forget how a decision was finally made. Our common purpose and solution are all that truly matter.

In business meetings, we need each other. When we are taking a group conscience, there is a spiritual moment in which the collective wisdom comes together. One person proposes an idea that I never would have thought up on my own. Then I contribute an idea, and we all participate and come up with a beautiful solution together.

When I began to get involved in service work on a service body, I did not really know what to expect. Sometimes I met new people as well as seeing people I knew from meetings. These members cared about the good of CPA as a whole because their program mattered to them. I found people who were respectful, courteous, welcoming, and kind. Knowing CPA's trusted servants were people just like me, and knowing they cared as much about CPA as I did, gave me confidence to participate.

Learning in service that things get done on Higher Power's time, not my expected time, helped me let go of control. I could feel how a Higher Power was guiding the service bodies, committees, and task forces in prioritizing projects. As a result, I now trust that projects I value, which may have lower priority in the service body, have the right priority given the needs of CPA. I don't have to try to control by pushing for it or trying to manipulate its priority; the trusted servants see a larger picture and have a collective, Higher Power–driven group conscience. It is so freeing to have no need to control. Higher Power is in charge in all service affairs, and I am assured this guides all of us.

The example of Tradition Two in action in our service bodies helped me progress in my Step work by helping me to let go and trust my Higher Power more.

Before becoming ill, I was the kind of person who would raise my hand to take on service and really liked to participate and keep busy. In CPA, I have learned this is not realistic, and I don't have to constantly volunteer. Things still get done, even as we live with our various limitations. When I am leading a committee on a service body and ask for a volunteer, I take my time. If there is an awkward silence, I let it be there. When that space is present, it feels like a Higher Power is filling that space. I think the pause is our One Ultimate Authority coming in to pick the right person, who might be a little shy to jump in.

I enjoy performing service work. Sometimes it is chairing a meeting, and sometimes it is as a member of a service body outside the group, such as a committee. At the group level, I try not to chair every meeting. Service is a big part of my program, and I want others to be able to experience the joy it gives me. Rotation of positions in service bodies outside the group lets me experience various forms of service work. It also helps me better consider CPA as a whole, when participating in my home group's business meetings or one of our many service opportunities. This can be a one-time event, such as attending an open forum meeting or committing to a task force formed to address a specific need.

Before CPA, I would always defer to any authority figure—especially doctors. Now, I always pray before every medical appointment. I ask my Deeper Power to guide both me and my doctors. I ask for help to be honest and have clarity and courage to speak and that my physicians be humbly guided and inspired to work in concert for my well-being.

It took me quite some time to find a primary care doctor who really listened to me and treated me with patience, openness, and respect. It's my job to share information regarding my symptoms, pain levels, and concerns, and it's her job to listen and make medical suggestions. I am so fortunate that she does not rush our appointments, and I am always welcome to follow up with her with additional questions via email. Our mutual agreement to have conversations allows our Deeper Powers to express themselves in working toward my greatest and highest good. When I pray before I go to my appointments, I feel a sense of safety and security, and I remember that it's my Deeper Power's job, ultimately, to take care of me, and that the members of my healthcare team are simply Its hands, in action.

I find parenting from bed to be really challenging. There was a time when it was easy for my voice to go unheard if I wasn't kept in the loop. And there were times when I was the only one in the loop and couldn't follow through with whatever was going on. So coming together and having a family meeting about all of us contributing to making decisions, especially parenting decisions, made it possible for me stop putting put my health in the middle of it all and then forcing the conversation around my health. In these meetings (our family's "business meetings"), I wasn't the governing body, and my husband wasn't the governing body, and my son wasn't the governing body—we all were making a decision together. And we still do that. We're doing that with a very sensitive issue at the moment of my writing this, and we had a good conversation about it today. I think it's vital to always recognize that I'm just one player. I can be right-sized and my voice counts—and we are all equal.

My husband and I were in total agreement that we needed a new sofa. I had sold furniture prior to my chronic illness, so I had lots of expertise. I have been complimented many times for my ability to decorate and make a warm and receptive home. My husband, on the other hand, pays no attention to aesthetics and is color blind. I feared this simple purchase would end in divorce. Then I applied Tradition Two.

We were a group of two, with a sofa purpose, and were both trusted servants—not one expert and one who needed to be governed. We discussed what was important to each of us. For me: style and size; for him: a supportive firmness and no prints. I set out with my expertise and our collective wishes in mind and found several options in our price range. Then I invited my husband to share in the process.

I said the Serenity Prayer as we both walked into the store. "Please keep my ears, heart and mind open and keep my voice kind and compromising. Thy will, not mine, be done," I prayed.

We moved through the store from one of my selections to another, pausing for new possibilities along the way. He liked my top choice, and we left the store both feeling mutually honored and appreciated. HP had a plan, and because I didn't force my will, a simple shopping trip yielded a treasured moment of connection and respect.

WORKING TRADITION TWO

For our group purpose there is but one ultimate authority—a loving God as He may express Himself in our group conscience. Our leaders are but trusted servants; they do not govern.

The following questions can help deepen your understanding and application of Tradition Two in your recovery and in all your affairs. Use these questions with your sponsor or sponsee or your CPA group, or explore them on your own, selecting the ones that are relevant.

1. How do I support the group's business and functioning?
2. Do I participate in the group conscience process?

3. How do I help ensure the group conscience is informed?
4. Do I trust the process of the group conscience?
5. In what ways do I accept and abide by the group conscience?
6. Can I yield to the group conscience with serenity and work well with others?
7. Can I support the group conscience even when I don't agree with it? Am I able to support majority decisions that are opposed to my own? If not, what tools can I use?
8. How do I hear my Higher Power speak through others?
9. How do I support my group's trusted servants? Do I criticize trusted servants?
10. How do I contribute to my group and to CPA as a whole with service work?
11. How does my Higher Power guide me in my service work?
12. Do I seek help when I need it from someone who has held a position before me?
13. How does being a trusted servant support my personal recovery?
14. How can I contribute to the harmony of any group in which I participate?
15. Do I look for praise or credit for my service work and ideas? Do I always want to be right, or am I sure I am always right?
16. How is a "group conscience" taken in my personal relationships?
17. How does it feel when someone tries to dominate a relationship? Do I tend to dominate others or be dominated?

18. In what ways do I cooperate with others and share responsibilities in all my affairs?
19. Do I criticize or blame other members of a personal relationship or group I belong to? If so, what tools can I use to help me?
20. Do I speak for members in my personal relationships and groups without consulting them?
21. How can I be part of the solution in my relationships when a stalemate arises? What tools can I use?
22. Do I have the courage to voice a minority opinion when moved to do so?
23. What does applying Tradition Two in all my affairs look like today?
24. In what areas of my life do I already practice and understand:
    - A Higher Power as expressed through our group conscience
    - Patience
    - Participation and flexibility
    - Trust and faith
    - Listening
    - Group inventory
    - Leaders do not govern—leaders are servants
    - Everyone has a voice
    - Service is larger than ourselves
    - A willingness to serve
25. How can I include these practices where they may be missing in my life today?

Tradition Three

The only requirement for CPA membership is a desire to recover from the emotional and spiritual debilitation of chronic pain or chronic illness.

> **The only requirement for CPA membership is a desire to recover from the emotional and spiritual debilitation of chronic pain or chronic illness.**

The only qualification for membership in CPA is that our life has been affected by chronic pain and chronic illness, and we want to recover from its effects. Our fellowship is inclusive. There are no barriers or exclusions, and we each decide if we qualify to be a member of CPA.

SPIRITUAL TOOLS FOR PRACTICING TRADITION THREE

- Inclusion
- Individual choice
- Unconditional acceptance
- Welcoming the newcomer
- Connection and belonging

APPLYING TRADITION THREE

I. In Our Groups

INCLUSION
In CPA, we come from many different cultural, social, and economic backgrounds. We have one thing in common: our physical health and well-being has been compromised. Whether this has come about through surgery, congenital or adult-onset illness, accident, or numerous other ways does not matter everyone is welcome. We do not judge or assess whether someone belongs or not. We each decide for ourselves if we qualify and if we want to pursue recovery in CPA. In our meetings, we have a singleness of purpose: to carry the message of recovery and hope

to all who live with chronic pain and chronic illness. If this is what we want, we are exactly where we need to be.

Our members have a wide spectrum of personal experience living with chronic pain and chronic illness. Some of us live only with illness and don't tend to experience much physical pain. Some of us live with physical pain and don't think of ourselves as living with an illness. Some of us have both pain and illness. For some living with a physical illness, the most significant pain may be emotional. We come together for a common purpose: to recover from the social, spiritual, and emotional debilitation that results from living with our health conditions. On this common ground, we share the ways in which these conditions affect our lives and well-being.

Our individual physical circumstances vary. There are those of us who are getting sicker and may even have a life-threatening condition. There are those of us whose condition stays chronic, cycling up and down, not worsening but not improving. There are those of us who see improvement, which can last for a day, for weeks, for months, even for years—sometimes for a lifetime. Some of us may even get cured.

We are all at different places on our health journey. Just because we feel better on any given day doesn't mean we don't belong. Sometimes our condition worsens, or we receive a new diagnosis, and then we feel like a newcomer all over again. This is why one day at a time we each get to decide that we belong.

CPA is a program of attraction. We welcome newcomers. Any person who says they have a chronic illness or chronic pain is offered a hand of fellowship and welcomed into an atmosphere of unconditional love and acceptance. Our life outside of the meeting rooms is left outside the group. We open a space for everyone, no matter their diagnosis, age, gender, race, or political or religious preferences. We tell no one they are excluded.

INDIVIDUAL CHOICE
As individuals, we seek comfort and spiritual help wherever we want. We may belong to religious organizations and may

participate in various therapy and treatment programs. In the capacity of our private lives, we can affiliate with any organization or cause, or not—it's our choice. However, as members of CPA, we don't bring our outside affiliations into our meetings. For example, we maintain the safety of our meetings by being mindful about wearing political-themed clothing or buttons or about speaking of our Higher Power in religious terms.

When we enter CPA meetings, we step into a safe place that is unencumbered by comparison, status, or any of the other circumstances that may define us in our lives. We choose to leave our other affiliations outside of our CPA group, adhere to spiritual principles, and focus on our recovery and on unity. We make this choice because we each want what CPA has to offer.

UNCONDITIONAL ACCEPTANCE

A CPA group exists when two or more people come together to practice CPA principles to aid their recovery. We may attend our meetings from our computer or other electronic device while at home, or at a care facility, or we may go in person to a physical place. Our membership in the group is not based on our age, financial wealth, profession, marital status, gender, or any other identifying circumstance other than our lives being affected by chronic pain and chronic illness. When we attend a meeting, we find we have much in common with people who may be very different from us because these people understand how we feel and accept us unconditionally. We feel, maybe for the first time, like we belong.

As we leave our affiliations outside the meeting room and keep our focus on the message of recovery, we experience an atmosphere of hope. Both newcomers and longtime members feel welcome as our similarities bind us. We don't give importance to superficial differences; rather, we feel ease and safety as we practice acceptance, love, and tolerance with others, including those with different language, culture, beliefs, or social status. We offer empathy and dignity to each person. Our focus is not on our health condition but on living in serenity and peace with the challenges of our chronic pain and chronic illness.

Because we don't affiliate with any outside entity (Tradition Six), the group name does not include the name of a facility where the meeting is being held. This helps everyone who attends feel they are part of the group.

WELCOMING THE NEWCOMER

In Twelve Step meetings, we all have a responsibility to welcome the newcomer, offering understanding and comfort. There can be times when we become familiar with our friends in program and may inadvertently exclude the newcomer. Actively practicing Tradition Three means that we remember when we were new to the group and to CPA and that we make an effort to ensure newcomers are included, know they matter, and feel welcomed just as we were welcomed.

Sharing our recovery is beneficial to longtimers and newcomers alike. When we share, we speak about how we apply the program. Each group decides how to share the CPA principles with newcomers so that they feel welcomed and comfortable. We honor and learn from everyone's experience, strength, and hope and recognize that recovery doesn't have to look a particular way. This allows for each of us to recover in our own fashion, with no person or group set as the model of recovery.

CONNECTION AND BELONGING

Being a member of CPA creates a feeling of connection and belonging, of safety and togetherness, and of being aligned with a deeper purpose. We become part of something larger than ourselves. For some of us, this is the first time we've experienced such a feeling. For others, we may have once felt like we were part of a group, but as a result of our pain and illness, we lost that connection. In CPA, we once again recognize that we do indeed belong and that we are not alone.

In CPA, we meet people that we might not interact with in other areas of our life, and sometimes we discover that we hold biases or prejudices. This is why our fellowship focuses on principles, not personalities. By consciously practicing the inclusivity of Tradition Three, we learn to let go of our tendency to judge or criticize others, based perhaps on their appearance or where they live, and instead shift our focus away from external differences and place it on how we are similar. We keep our focus on the literature, our own recovery, and our willingness to practice CPA principles. Every person who comes to CPA is just like us—a person seeking to learn how to live with chronic pain and chronic illness.

Our program is available to anyone who wants it; each person decides for themselves if CPA is where they belong. You are a member if you say you are a member. This is another way we apply the unenforceable guidance of the Traditions.

The decision to become a member of CPA is between a person and their Higher Power. Recovery is possible and available for anyone who wants it. It doesn't matter what their health or physical situation may be. We each get to decide to be a member, to connect with others and the program, and to seek a new way of life in which we discover it is possible to live peacefully, joyfully, and comfortably with ourselves and others.

II. In Our Service Bodies

The General Service Virtual Office (GSVO) manages the administration of CPA, including the website, email accounts, social media accounts, publication of literature, and the Chronic Pain Anonymous Service Board (CPASB) telephone service so those interested can find CPA and learn about our program. The website helps anyone who wants to find and access a meeting, any time of day or night, from anywhere in the world.

Our public information and public outreach committees make sure that CPA is accessible to all those who want it. These service bodies carry the message of hope to the newcomer by reaching out to healthcare and other professionals and people who live with chronic pain and chronic illness.

CPA's service bodies ensure that people who need our message of hope can find us. However, each member can help get the word out about our program. We can speak to our healthcare providers and our support groups, friends, and family. Outreach literature is available to help support these efforts to inform others about CPA.

There are many service bodies and committees that support our fellowship, and every member of CPA can use their expertise and past work experience to contribute to the fellowship through service work. This may include reaching out to a newcomer, chairing a meeting, or contributing to a new piece of literature. We take the initiative and seek out ways we can feel a part of the fellowship by sharing our time, energy, and talents. Often, we find a position that is a good fit for our skills and abilities.

Practicing inclusivity in our service bodies means that everyone in the role of a trusted servant is treated with respect and gratitude. Actively creating an atmosphere of cooperation and forging relationships based on unity, connection, and belonging enables our trusted servants to meet the needs of the fellowship and enjoy filling their roles. Doing service may require learning new skills, or it may mean growing personally and learning new ways to resolve conflicts that focus on principles and not personalities. That is one of the benefits we receive from doing service. Our own recovery blossoms, of necessity, as we practice Tradition Three.

III. In All Our Affairs

In our daily lives, we are involved in many relationships—whether between two people in a marriage, among 20 people in a support group, in a workplace environment large or small, or with our healthcare team. As we do in our meetings, we can choose to relate to others in a spirit of trust, acceptance, inclusivity, and love, creating an atmosphere of mutual support. We can demonstrate dignity toward ourselves and others, accepting our friends, family, and people we encounter in our groups "as is." Even outside the CPA meetings, we can apply the principle of Tradition Three and practice turning our focus from the circumstances or status of a person to their spiritual presence, which is always of equal value to our own. We don't "take their inventory." Instead, we let go of our expectations of others, freeing them to grow or change in their own way and time. We have faith in a Higher Power that relieves us of the need to change others.

Just as we do within CPA meetings and membership, we decide for ourselves whether we choose to be a member of our relationships, whether personal, healthcare, or professional. We find that they ebb and flow—sometimes, we feel more connected than other times; some days, others are more connected to us than we are to them. We remember to invite connection and check in with ourselves about whether or not we feel a sense of belonging. As we do this, we discover that no one person or group can be all things to us all the time and that we can't be all things to anyone. We sometimes need to step back, get ourselves on track, and reassess our goals and our reasons for being in a relationship.

We often interact with many different healthcare providers who are caring for us effectively. However, if our needs change, we may decide to seek a new person to receive the care our condition now requires. We have the freedom to make this choice as part of our program of recovery and self-care.

In our relationships, do we feel aligned with a mutual purpose and values? Do we have a desire to work together with an attitude of kindness, respect, and care? Can we practice accepting others exactly as they are, in service of our mutual direction and well-being, through the ebbs and flows that naturally arise?

Our health challenges can divert us from our unity and create confusion, hurt feelings, guilt, or shame. Many of us who live with chronic pain and illness have significant experience with the effect of illness and pain on our relationships. For some of us, physical and financial security may be an important element in our relationships, and because our needs often change, this will impact those we are close to. Sometimes issues arise that are challenging. It can be helpful to speak with our sponsor and explore "our side of the street" to find out how we are contributing to the problems and how we can practice spiritual principles (if we are not already doing so). We reason things out with our CPA friends and turn to our Higher Power for guidance.

> **ASSOCIATED SPIRITUAL PRINCIPLE:** *Inclusivity*
>
> It is comforting to know we are welcome and that it is our choice to be a part of CPA. There are no questions asked about our circumstances or status. We are a member if say we are a member. As members, we help create a safe, inclusive fellowship.

TRADITION THREE IN ACTION

The only requirement for CPA membership is a desire to recover from the emotional and spiritual debilitation of chronic pain or chronic illness.

VOICES OF OUR MEMBERS

I have found that my recovery in CPA is directly affected by my ability to vulnerably admit my powerlessness. Sometimes I can do this with patience and humor, and sometimes it gets downright ugly. I'm human. Tradition Three assures me that no one can kick me out when my journey takes a less than graceful turn. As long as I desire recovery, Tradition Three keeps my CPA seat warm.

Many times, I have thought, "I'm not sick enough, or others are in more pain than I am, I don't qualify to be a member of CPA." Compare and despair. It took Tradition Three to teach me that I'm a member because I do suffer from the emotional and spiritual debilitation of living with a chronic condition. I am a member not because of my medical chart but because my powerlessness to control and direct my chronic condition makes my life unmanageable.

Recently, I've seen some positive changes in my life as a result of CPA. I practice showing up just as I am to my part-time job with less fear, I accept more social invitations, and I travel. Just accepting powerlessness and identifying unmanageability with my sponsor has led me to gently explore my capabilities and test my fears. After keeping myself on a shelf for years to avoid canceling work or having embarrassing symptoms in public, I can experiment with making plans again and practice letting go of outcomes.

As I bridge back to life, I've worried that I won't fit into CPA and that my shares about work, travel, and a budding romantic relationship will trigger people. Or worse: I won't qualify anymore. After all, who am I to be "feeling better" in this program and to take space from those who are "worse off" than me? My sponsor reminded me that she has seen me progress from obsessively fearful to having a modest faith. The decrease in stress results in less emotional suffering and physical symptoms. Last night, I shared about my fears in a meeting and afterward received support and even identification from others who feel guilty when they feel well and are able to show up physically in new ways.

I certainly can't do as much as I used to, but CPA has helped me to slowly and carefully re-engage with the world. And I know I'm in the right place because I have the spiritual malady described in the literature. I'll continue to share honestly, and when I question my place here in CPA, Tradition Three is at the ready to affirm the value of my truth.

I love that Tradition Three says "the only requirement for membership is *the desire to recover from the emotional and spiritual debilitation of* chronic pain or chronic illness," not that the only requirement is that you *have* chronic pain or chronic illness. There's a very big difference.

I have met some people who have chronic pain who don't seem to need a fellowship because they have a support system that is really profound in their lives. That might include church, family, friends, whatever—but they don't struggle with feelings of inadequacy or overwhelming fears, or with emotional and spiritual debilitation.

I have also met people outside of our program who have chronic pain and chronic illness and don't seem to have a desire to change; they seem to want to only complain about their illness and don't express a willingness or desire to stop being miserable. I believe these people are not really candidates for CPA unless, deep down, they really do have a desire to recover from the emotional and spiritual effects of chronic pain and chronic illness.

It is often said that Twelve Step programs are for those who want them, not those who need them. When I am in a CPA meeting, I can trust that all who are present either have or are willing to invite the desire stated in this Tradition.

There is a culture in CPA—our Steps, Traditions, and Concepts guide us to discuss our conditions and our solutions in different ways. This was all foreign to me as a newcomer. I cried a lot, spoke of how unfair life was, what my doctors were telling me, how afraid I was, how it would never improve, how I didn't understand how anyone could be happy or joyous or even kind to others who clearly didn't understand.

The fellowship members were patient with me, gave me time to consider what CPA was offering me. And then, one random day, I started to hear the message of hope, and my language began to change. I let go of the specifics, which didn't seem so important anymore.

What became important was: CPA offered a way out of the dark hole I was in. I began to work the Steps and Traditions, really listening to the experience, strength, and hope being shared in the meetings.

I came to working the program in my own time. It is my goal to give every newcomer the same time and space I received. I was so broken when I came to CPA, and it was the acceptance and tolerance of the members that carried me. I want the newcomer to feel comfortable; their transformation will happen as their Higher Power handles it. There is no need to force; the program wasn't forced upon me. I want to pass on the CPA solution so others have the same chance at recovery I was given by those who came before me. I welcome the newcomer. I see in them the hope that one more person may find the peace and serenity I have found in CPA.

During my early years in CPA, I was impatient and judgmental. I wanted my recovery, and while I was still miserable, I didn't want to hear too much of other people's misery; I wanted to hear about recovery. I was particularly annoyed by people who didn't seem to be working the Steps and had no signs of spiritual or emotional improvement. These people seemed to say the same things over and over. And as I became less depressed and hysterical, I didn't want other people's depression to bring me down.

I wondered why these people were allowed to go on and on, and thought that if a person was not sharing a solution, they should not share in a meeting. I thought they should quietly listen and talk to their sponsors. I was very impatient and marveled at the patience and compassion of the meeting chairs and of other group members.

But just as I have grown in spiritual and emotional health, I have seen improvements in some of those people I thought were hopeless. Others who don't seem to change do seem to receive some kind of hope and strength from coming to and participating in meetings. Seeing this has led me to consciously work on reducing my judgmental attitudes and expanding my compassion. When these critical feelings arise, I now remind myself that each person is also in spiritual and emotional pain and has every right to be in CPA and to work the program at their own pace.

I will never forget the day I first came to a virtual CPA meeting. I could not stop crying, seeing CPA members reclining on pillows just like me, some with braces on, just like me. They were laughing and kindly reached out to me with delight and generosity to welcome me and answer my questions. I had been living two lives up to that day: an inside life with one me, disheveled, despairing, unable to read the telephone bill without crying, unwashed in pajamas and in bed; and the other me, who would gather all my stubborn determination and put on my colorful clothes and be with others in a desperate attempt to appear fine, until I got home and collapsed again. Nobody but my husband saw the "inside" me. As a newly diagnosed condition worsened, my outside life got smaller and smaller, and because I wanted nobody to see my inside life, it got smaller too.

In those first few meetings, I listened to the format carefully as it described that in meetings, in CPA, we refrain from discussing the specifics of our illnesses, medical community, doctors, symptoms, and so on. When the CPA preamble was read, I heard the words: *"The only requirement for membership is a desire to recover from the emotional and spiritual debilitation of chronic pain or chronic illness."* I turned my camera off because I'd begun to weep when I heard what my soul had been longing for—mental, emotional, and spiritual relief.

Yes, the sense of physical pain and illness was devastating, but it had been going on for decades, and I knew it was my relationship with it that caused me to suffer and to lash out at those who most loved me. Here it was: a promise that by working the CPA Steps and living the CPA program—regardless of what my body did, regardless of the amount or duration of a sense of pain and illness—my relationship with that pain and illness could change, and therein, I could be relieved of the hell I had endured and exchange it for one of joyful acceptance. I bought the package then and there, and it did not cost me the tens of thousands of dollars I had spent on miracle cures. What it cost was willingness—nothing more, nothing less. This program was a tried-and-true experiment I could apply, with the help and guidance of a loving Higher Power and a fellowship who understood in depth what I'd only begun to comprehend.

To me, it's not a responsibility to welcome newcomers—it's a joy. My heart is so full of gratitude for CPA saving my life that welcoming and volunteering to answer any questions or simply be a friendly ear is an honor and a privilege. I get to give back what was so freely given to me. It gives me great happiness to see returning newcomers and witness the renewal of hope and peace on their faces and in their shares.

I am so grateful for our Intergroup service bodies who have worked diligently to create ease and accessibility on our various platforms.

At first, I was afraid to attend videoconference meetings and only went to phone meetings. It wasn't until another member encouraged me to explore something different and offered to help me access the videoconference meetings that I took the risk and went. Now, I can benefit from the recovery on different platforms and from all the Intergroups have to offer—whether it be speakers, special events, or workshops. I'm so grateful that with just a little bit of guidance from a friendly CPA member, my limitations and fears do not limit my recovery possibilities, and because members do service at the Intergroup level, all these ways to access recovery are available to our fellowship.

In most of the other fellowships I've been involved in, the longer you are involved in the fellowship, the more service jobs you are able to do. In CPA, because some people have physical debilitation that gets worse as time goes by, I discovered I was able to do more service in the first three or four years, which I can no longer do due to the reduction of my cognitive abilities. I am now aware of the importance of not taking too many service jobs. It's easy to volunteer for a service job just because no one else has, but sometimes, if I just wait, someone who otherwise had not considered it will step up and do it. We are truly in this together. What works for me today is to have one periodic regular service job, one regular recurring service, and one I do on an occasional basis.

Once I began to participate in CPA service work, I began to understand the importance of the GSVO. It is run by volunteers and special workers who maintain the CPASB website, oversee the process of publishing our literature, coordinate the graphic design and layout of our books and brochures, send out thank-you letters for contributions, and handle calls from those seeking hope. I am grateful for all the trusted servants and special workers who address the background tasks of CPA, ensuring the message of hope is shared with all who may benefit from it.

By the time I discovered the CPA website, I was eager to learn how to live with this new thing called "chronic pain and chronic illness." On my first visit to the site, I downloaded and sometimes printed the materials I found. I added meetings to my calendar and ordered the books. As I read the literature, I began to experience hope that I would be happy again. I could not wait to attend my first meeting. Today, I regularly visit the CPA website to find a brochure, check the meeting calendar, and send in my Tradition Seven contributions. It is such a comfort to know I can connect with the fellowship at any time, day or night, and find the hopeful voice of CPA.

Tradition Three reminds me that I am an equal and valuable member of my family and that although my contributions look different from my other family members due to my chronic pain and chronic illness, I am still a contributing member. I really struggled with this in the beginning of my recovery journey. I complained to my sponsor about the things I could no longer do for my family, and she challenged me to make a list of what I can do. It was an amazing experience, and I shared what I wrote with my husband. My husband was experiencing his own grief about the changes in our life, and he was grateful to be reminded of all my contributions, such as my positive and lighthearted attitude, my gentle honoring of his own journey to adjust, and how I live the CPA program. He even pointed out some contributions I had omitted, which helped shift both our attitudes and focus.

I am so grateful for my sponsor helping me shift my perception. I learned that limitations do not mean I have no value or purpose. Today my self-worth is based on so much more than how many times I can do the dishes. I feel my family's version of Tradition Three in action: we each, and all, are valued and belong.

When I became a person with chronic pain and chronic illness, I assumed people wouldn't want to be with me. And after time in CPA, I realized I didn't tell them how they could be with me. It wasn't until I felt included in the fellowship of CPA that I got clear that I could communicate with the people in my life with whom I shared the fellowship of friendship. And I saw that some of my friends really did want our friendship to continue. They just didn't know how; I didn't know how. For some of us, this process takes a while to work out.

Being a member of CPA has helped me understand what it is like to communicate clearly and to experience the value of inclusion, both in the program and out.

I am an auntie to an amazing 11-year-old. We have a special bond, and we talk about anything. When chronic illness struck, I knew it would dramatically affect our relationship. I could hear the disappointment in her voice every time I needed to cancel an outing, even though she said she understood. Time and time again, I had to cancel our fun plans. I was afraid to explain the realities of my illness, and I certainly didn't want to "scare" her on my bad days.

On one such occasion, my Higher Power stepped in. Instead of cancelling, I asked if she wanted to come over and simply watch a movie with me. I told her that I was not feeling well and that I understood if she had other fun things to do. Her response amazed me. She said, "Just being with you *is* fun. We don't have to do stuff. We can just *be*." She went on to tell me that she already understood my situation and could even see my crashes coming on. We now have movie dates with popcorn and chocolates (her favorite). We laugh and we share about our lives, all from the comfort of my bed.

I thought I knew how my illness affected others, and it took this amazing girl to remind me that there is more to life than what I can or cannot do. I am fun and lovable regardless of my physical condition. This child's insight has not only affected how I view all my relationships but led to my own self-acceptance and self-love. It took an 11-year-old to teach me to become a human being not a "human doing."

WORKING TRADITION THREE

The only requirement for CPA membership is a desire to recover from the emotional and spiritual debilitation of chronic pain or chronic illness.

The following questions can help deepen your understanding and application of Tradition Three in your recovery and in all your affairs. Use these questions with your sponsor or sponsee or your CPA group, or explore them on your own, selecting the ones that are relevant.

1. What does CPA membership mean to me?
2. Do I leave my other affiliations outside the meeting?
3. How do I help create a safe and caring environment in my meetings?
4. What was my first meeting like? What was helpful that I want to pass on to others?
5. What made me decide that I belong in CPA?
6. How do I welcome newcomers? What can I do specifically to help them feel welcome?
7. Am I tolerant of a newcomer's inexperience at sharing?
8. Do I accept newcomers unconditionally? Or do I prejudge them?
9. Are there ways in which I judge others in my meetings?
10. How am I tolerant and accepting of others, no matter how different they are from me?
11. Do I treat all members of CPA with kindness, compassion, and respect? Do I do the same in all my affairs? What are some specific ways in which I can do this?
12. Are there members I reach out to for support? If not, what would help me to do so?

13. Do I let differences in our health challenges interfere with my carrying the message?
14. How do my health issues affect the relationships in all my affairs?
15. Do I judge people I encounter by details of their personal life, such as religion, politics, domestic arrangements, or work? What biases and prejudices have I discovered in myself?
16. Are there ways I can work with others to take a relationship "group conscience"?
17. Am I able to share my feelings and needs with people I am in relationship with at home or at work, or with healthcare providers?
18. Am I able to listen attentively and with an open mind to the people in my life?
19. In what ways am I taking responsibility for my part in my relationships?
20. What does applying Tradition Three in all my affairs look like today?
21. In what areas of my life do I already practice and understand the need for:
    - Inclusion
    - Individual choice
    - Unconditional acceptance
    - Welcoming the newcomer
    - Connection and belonging
22. How can I include these spiritual tools where they may be missing in my life today?

Tradition Four

Each group should be autonomous except in matters affecting other groups or CPA as a whole.

Each group should be autonomous except in matters affecting other groups or CPA as a whole.

Each CPA group is free to make decisions about the matters that affect their own group: things like choosing a meeting format (Speaker meeting, Step Study, etc.), where to meet, or whether the meeting will be open or closed (open to anyone interested in CPA or limited only to people seeking their own recovery from chronic pain and illness). Groups can manage their affairs however they choose.

Along with this freedom comes the responsibility for the group to be aware of how their choices affect CPA and to not make decisions that will infringe on other groups or the fellowship as a whole. Much like the principle of unity as expressed in Tradition One, in Tradition Four, individual groups are asked to consider if what they are doing is good for the fellowship. Autonomy means the right to make decisions for and to govern ourselves. This Tradition balances that right with our responsibility to the fellowship, to our group, and to each other.

SPIRITUAL TOOLS FOR PRACTICING TRADITION FOUR

- Autonomy
- Boundaries
- Balance
- Responsibility for unity
- Interdependence
- Participation in service

APPLYING TRADITION FOUR

I. In Our Groups

AUTONOMY

Each group manages its affairs to fit the people it serves, and each group has its own character so it can be of benefit carrying the message. Naturally, this looks different for different groups of people.

There are many choices for a group to make. A group meeting needs a location and a time to meet. The group decides what kind of a meeting it will be, such as literature study or Step study. Each group decides how to allocate funds, what structure is best for their meeting, how long the meeting will last, if shares are timed or not, and what topics to discuss. The decisions the group makes need to serve the members who attend. The meeting also needs to determine how it can attract others who live with chronic pain and chronic illness and to carry the message of recovery in its unique community.

Autonomy allows us to adapt our group to its community, as needed—for example, having a meeting that is chemical-free and fragrance-free or choosing to mute members as they enter a videoconference. Specifics like this are up to the members attending each meeting and decided by the group conscience.

BOUNDARIES

Although autonomy may not have specific rules, it does come with boundaries. We must remember that we are always part of a greater whole. What does this look like in practice?

No group has the power to tell another group what they should do. Each group makes decisions that best support its members. However, to maintain the integrity of CPA, we each have a responsibility to uphold the Traditions, and members may speak up if they think the boundaries that support our fellowship are being ignored. For example, if a group actively promotes a healthcare treatment and suggests other groups do so as well, this would adversely affect CPA as a whole. When we practice Tradition Four, we maintain the boundaries suggested by the Traditions, in service of the best recovery for all.

CPA meetings use only literature endorsed by the fellowship, referred to as Conference Approved Literature (CAL). We are unified when we read the same literature, thus eliminating confusion and providing clearly spelled-out support for our recovery. CAL conforms to the principles of our program, with consistent language and concepts approved by our members. Our literature helps us stay aligned with our primary purpose and is not diluted by other programs of care. If we were to simply read any of the myriad self-help, spiritual practice, or latest healthcare approaches in our meetings, we would soon lose our focus, our faith and our progress in the very program we have come to trust. By using only CAL in our meetings, we know we are working the CPA program together, in a manner we've agreed upon. At any time, we can turn to our literature for support and clarity we can count on. CAL ensures the meetings stay consistent in their message so that anyone who seeks CPA, wherever they may be, will find the program they recognize that supports their recovery from living with chronic pain and chronic illness.

In our meetings, we are free to act how we choose as long as it doesn't affect another member or the group as a whole. On a videoconference meeting, we may attend from our bed; at a physical meeting, we may lie down on the floor or stand. However, we don't act in ways that distract and block the message being shared by a fellow member or that would disrupt the meeting or disturb other members.

BALANCE

Our groups turn to the Traditions for guidance so that we don't compromise our principles, which help us in recovery and need to be sustained. There is no authority, and we have freedom—yet we also are aware of how we affect the whole fellowship. We value autonomy, but not at the expense of unity or of the very program that is the source of our recovery, serenity, and well-being. Tradition Four proposes that balancing autonomy with group harmony is vital for effective and continued recovery. The other Traditions remind us of specific limits within our autonomy as we fulfill our responsibilities. They guide us in our interactions as a part of a greater whole, which can include how we interact with groups outside of CPA.

Our connection extends beyond our group, and so we remember that what we do affects others. Each member is responsible for helping their group maintain the Traditions. Since no one person has ultimate authority in CPA, we each need to take responsibility. As we balance freedom and responsibility, we actively choose to obey the unenforceable. The Traditions provide a structure that works to create freedom with responsibility balanced in a sustainable, long-lasting way. We are all part of the greater whole, and each member has responsibility for the fellowship.

Sometimes, we may find our behaviors affect our interactions with others in harmful or disruptive ways. When this happens, we can stop and reflect and return to our Step work to help us see our part more clearly. In this way, we can strengthen our ability to contribute to the group in a constructive way, which supports the balance between autonomy and responsibility.

RESPONSIBILITY FOR UNITY

The Group Representative (GR) brings information from the larger fellowship back to their group and takes information from their group back to the fellowship. In this process, we recognize that the service structure goes beyond our meeting and that we are linked into the whole.

Regularly scheduled business meetings improve the likelihood of group unity and help create an environment in which members can thrive. Another way a group stays strong and maintains its responsibility to uphold this Tradition is to take a group inventory in the same way an individual would take a Step Four inventory. A group inventory involves sharing what is working and not working at the meeting and allows for the ultimate authority, a loving God, to be expressed in the group conscience. As in applying the Steps, when we err, we take responsibility, correct our course, and move on. Through the process of group inventory and taking our group conscience, we can become aware of how our choices affect the group and the welfare of CPA as a whole. It is valuable to be reminded that we all can attend to our primary purpose: to carry the message of recovery.

It is useful to remember both what is and is not our responsibility. What others are doing is none of our business unless it affects us directly, our group, or CPA as a whole. We welcome different methods, formats, cultures, and personalities as we reach out to others who suffer and carry the message of hope.

We learn how to achieve harmony by following the Traditions, and there is security to be found in this process. If there are problems in our group, we may have moved too far from the Traditions. When this happens, it may in fact affect the larger fellowship. So when there are difficulties in our group or service body, turning to the Traditions helps guide us toward unity.

There is no government in CPA. Changes come from the members, not from the top. If you feel strongly about something, it is up to you to raise the issue with your group and change it via the group conscience. A group may choose to ignore the Traditions; they have the right to make that choice, and no group can be coerced. However, groups that don't abide by the Traditions rarely last.

When a group is making a choice that will affect other groups or CPA, this needs to be addressed, just as we would address a member who was breaking a Tradition during a meeting. The group may need to take action to protect the welfare of CPA members, the service bodies, and the fellowship as a whole. However, we have no authority, only a commitment to the unity and well-being of the fellowship.

On a personal level, we take responsibility for sharing our recovery and carrying the message in meetings and in our interactions with others in CPA. One way we can do this is to become self-aware: Do we go on and on when we share or speak about topics not related to our recovery? Do we give advice to others or offer guidance on medical issues? *WAIT: Why Am I Talking?* is a good slogan to remember—it can help us examine our motives before we speak.

INTERDEPENDENCE
We are independent, yet we cooperate with other groups and are connected by our shared principles. We depend on one another to balance autonomy with working well with others, both in our groups and with the fellowship as a whole. Because we are part of the group, the best interest of the group is also our best interest.

One way we experience the vibrancy of CPA interdependence is by creating a welcoming atmosphere in our meetings and being thoughtful and kind toward each other, knowing we are all vital to the membership. Our meetings are where we can grow and flourish. It may take effort. Certainly it takes conscious intention. And we find it is well worth it. If we are divisive, exclusive, or rigid, we may no longer be an attractive group, and we will not contribute to CPA unity or be a place conducive to recovery.

We need each other to sustain our recovery, and we choose to participate fully in CPA when we follow the Traditions. No one forces us to follow them, and they are neither rules nor laws. No person or group can overrule the rights of another person or another group. Instead, we take it upon ourselves to understand the guidelines of the Traditions. We share the Traditions with each other, and particularly with newcomers, so that we all understand the same principles of recovery, which help us individually and as a group. When we do, we experience a new level of recovery that is only possible when autonomy is interdependent with unity.

II. In Our Service Bodies

PARTICIPATION IN SERVICE
Work that would divert energy from carrying the message is often done by our service bodies. They sell literature, manage the daily business of CPA, and support our groups as needed. Just like the groups, they autonomously make decisions on many practical matters. In doing this, they consider how any decision will affect the whole fellowship as well as the groups.

Our service bodies help us stay in communication with each other and with CPA as a whole. We need open communication to build consensus and make sure the needs of the fellowship are being met. Through clear communication, we can support unity across groups. These bodies (which can be found in the *CPA Service Handbook*) and various committees work regularly to ensure that channels of communication are available to every member of our fellowship.

Service work beyond the group level starts with each meeting's General Representative. However, each one of us is responsible for CPA, and our strength as a fellowship increases when all of our voices are heard. In order for our service bodies to truly meet the needs of the fellowship, the service bodies need to know who the fellowship is and what is needed. By speaking up and participating, we make it possible for our service bodies to serve the membership well.

III. In All Our Affairs

"We are autonomous as individuals except in matters affecting the relationship as a whole." Some members of CPA use this rewrite of Tradition Four when applying it to personal relationships.

In order to thrive, we need both independence and unity. We learn the importance of caring for our individual selves as we strive for balance between freedom and responsibility in relationship with others, and we learn to act autonomously while keeping an eye out for harmony with each other. We balance these opposites by always turning to the guidance of a Power greater than ourselves.

Here is an example. We may wake up and feel clear that it is not going to be a day when we can help our spouse with yard work, as was planned. Rather than ignore our body's need and push ahead without saying anything, we communicate with our spouse. We know our spouse needs help to do the job, so together we decide what is best for us as a team. Do we hire someone to help that day? Do we decide to put off the job till a better day or hire others to do the job entirely, while we spend time relaxing as a couple? We talk it over and ask our loving Higher Power for guidance. When we bring this Tradition into our lives, our relationships evolve, and unexpected solutions become possible.

We are autonomous, and we consider how the decisions we make may affect our relationships and our well-being. We can have different interests and continue to maintain respect for each other. That is to be expected and is even essential to healthy relationships. We have our own opinions and do not attempt to control the opinions of others; we don't need to impose our perceptions onto another person for our perceptions to be valid.

Through trial and error, we learn how to apply autonomy and responsibility in our relationships. We become more skillful at clear communication and respectful exchange of each person's needs and ideas. We recognize that our choices impact others, and we learn to consider their feelings as they consider our feelings. We become more aware of how our actions and behaviors affect others. Finding a balance may mean making compromises, or it may mean that everyone doesn't have to agree and can have different preferences. What doesn't support our recovery is maintaining conflicts.

Here are some of the skills and behaviors we learn:
- Rather than being self-serving and holding on to selfish demands in the name of autonomy, we become self-caring and turn to our Higher Power for guidance.

- We accept the consequences of our actions gracefully and allow others the same opportunity.
- We recognize that we are responsible for our actions and reactions, not others'.
- We allow others to take responsibility for their own actions and thoughts. We come to understand that what someone else does is none of our business unless it directly affects us or the relationship as a whole.
- We focus on ourselves and recognize our individual actions as our own choices; we don't have to wait for the other person to change before we change and don't have to wait for someone else to make our life happy.

Even as we depend on others for our care, we always have autonomy. We are responsible toward others and stay on the lookout for when we become self-centered. It does not serve us to do whatever we want without concern or considering the needs of others.

When we interact with our healthcare providers, we remember that we have goals to achieve together. We all do our part, and we can all be wrong at times. Especially in this area, we remember to turn to our Higher Power for guidance and remember that no person, even a family member or an expert in a given field, is our Higher Power. At times, we will find ourselves returning to Step One, recognizing what is not in our control and surrendering to our current reality. That is one way to practice autonomy.

Discovering the balance between autonomy and unity is one of the greatest gifts of Twelve Step recovery. Being a healthy, thriving individual while being in relationships with others means taking responsibility for one's own choices while assessing how these choices affect the relationships that matter to us.

> **ASSOCIATED SPIRITUAL PRINCIPLE:**
> *Interdependent Autonomy*
>
> Each group needs to make necessary choices for its functioning and to protect and support the fellowship as a whole. When we realize how our actions and that of our group have consequences for others, we then consider them in our decision-making process.

TRADITION FOUR IN ACTION

Each group is autonomous except in matters affecting other groups or CPA as a whole.

VOICES OF OUR MEMBERS

I love the different flavors to each of the CPA meetings I attend. We have so many options for literature, topics, and formats and a whole fellowship of CPA speakers to share their experience, strength, and hope. Each group gets to be as creative as it pleases, provided the group's choices do not dilute, distort, or distract from the CPA message. Adherence to this Tradition and obedience to our unenforceable meeting etiquette assure a compassionate and safe environment where recovery can flourish. For example, in our meeting we have three-minute shares to allow as many people as possible the chance to speak. In other meetings, shares are not timed. Our meetings experience equanimity in their individuality.

Autonomy balanced with responsibility matters in my CPA group. Sometimes I find outside literature that helps me, and I think it could help others and consider bringing it to my CPA meeting and sharing it. It could be a self-help book or a book about my illness, or some type of spiritual literature. The question I ask myself is: Will bringing this literature into my group dilute the CPA message, thus reducing the ability for CPA to help in its own unique way? CPA is helpful to so many people, and if members started to change its unique message by bringing in outside literature, the effectiveness of CPA could be diminished. When I thoughtfully consider my desire to share outside literature with my group, it's clear that ultimately the right decision is to not bring this literature to my meeting. There may be some other way I can share the material with others on an individual basis, as opportunities come up. This seems to me to be a balanced solution. My love of this literature is not wrong and does not confuse or dilute the CPA message as long as I don't bring it into a meeting. And I can still share it with others.

Balanced autonomy brings harmony, security, and unity. It feels good to learn to be strong in ourselves and in the ability to express needs and wants, but to also be considerate of others and our program—to consider how our choices may affect them.

I think it is really important when group decisions are made that they be announced ahead of time, or that there be a regularly scheduled business meeting, so members know when suggested changes are to be discussed. I went to a meeting that I used to attend regularly, and I wasn't there one week, and the next week when I came back they were using literature that is not on the list of CPA-approved books. They had decided that any literature from another Twelve Step followship was okay to use in our meeting. I wasn't comfortable with that, but the group conscience hadn't been held at a preannounced time, so I couldn't voice my opinion or vote.

In order for members and groups to put Tradition Four into practice—taking responsibility for our autonomous decisions, as they affect other groups and CPA as a whole—clear communication and dependable structures are essential. We're all in this together. Our group conscience may have come out exactly the same way, even if I had been present, but at least my voice would have been part of the discussion, and Tradition Four might have been taken into consideration.

When I first raised my hand to volunteer to be Group Representative (GR), I truly had no clue what I would be doing other than it was "service." The group conscience voted in the affirmative for me to be the GR. I was delighted. For my program, service is essential. As I receive, I give. As I give, I receive. My service is manageable when I remember I can do it as I am able and not let it become harmful to my physical, emotional, or spiritual well-being.

Being a GR in my meeting is a two-year service commitment. In time, I understood that the role of the GR is to maintain the lines of communication between the group and the larger fellowship. Much information is communicated in both directions. I attend the monthly General Advisory Council meeting, where all the CPA GRs meet as a whole. I am an autonomous representative of our autonomous group, among all the other GRs, who are there in the same capacity. I am honored to represent my group.

I have one voice and one vote as a CPA home group member. As my home group is autonomous from other groups, I do not vote in other business meetings, thereby having undue influence on specific fellowship matters. My home group's informed group conscience is shared at the World Service Conference via my home group's delegate. I trust my delegate to carry our group's desires, yet I also honor my delegate's autonomy to practice their right of decision when more is revealed on any given topic. I trust our trusted servants' pledge to do what is helpful for the entirety of CPA, not just what is best for my home group.

I have been to a few General Advisory Council (GAC) meetings as a member-at-large, and I really enjoy going to them and believe it is an honor and a privilege to be there. I can attend and witness how much work our members do in their effort to keep running everything that we tend to take for granted or are not even aware is going on. Often, on the group level, members just show up at a meeting and think that is all there is to CPA—reading documents you can get off the CPA website and sharing our recovery. Attending service body meetings beyond the group level has given me a chance to appreciate that those materials are there because of all the work that is done by volunteers to support the fellowship. As a member, I can participate in the discussions at the GAC that affect our members, and I like how all members are included.

Tradition Four reminds me that I am not just a wife, employee, or friend. It is healthful for me to have individual interests and autonomous hobbies apart from my other roles. Most importantly, it reminds me that my happiness is not dependent on another's mood and behavior. I am free to be me, and to live and let live.

Tradition Four is also a signpost. It warns me that although I am my own person, I am in relationships with others, and my choices may directly affect those I love or have made a commitment to. Part of my CPA recovery is about being mindful of how my chronic pain and chronic illness affect not just me. Just because I am in pain doesn't mean I have to be a pain.

Autonomy is the right to make decisions for and govern myself. I can do whatever I want to do, I can decide things for myself. The caveat is that I also need to consider how choices I make affect other people in my life. The trick is finding the balance between freedom and responsibility.

An example would be if I wanted to purchase something that would be very beneficial and helpful in my life, but this item is not a necessity. Autonomy tells me that I am able to choose to make this purchase if I want to, but because I am married, responsibility tells me I need to think about how an expensive purchase affects our household finances. This responsibility to consider others varies, depending on the situation.

A personal challenge I have around this is that I have a difficult time maintaining my autonomy because of being overly concerned about others. My response to wanting to purchase something somewhat expensive but very beneficial to me and to my husband would be to never bring it up because I am afraid to cause conflict or disharmony and I don't want to displease him. In this case, I think I need to be stronger in the freedom of my autonomy, to learn to speak up for things that are important to me. Autonomy works both ways.

No person is my Higher Power. When I was first dealing with my injury, I saw every doctor as the person who would fix me, and then I'd be well again. I'd follow the suggested treatments and go through the procedures, thinking these health professionals were my Higher Power and could make the problem disappear. Now that I've been in CPA for a little while, I see this pattern and instead apply Tradition Four. I accept my autonomy and my responsibility to turn to my own Higher Power who will bring healing to my whole being while I maintain relationships with those who are helping to make that happen, however that looks. It's a great way to be more peaceful with my care and its outcomes, and a more empowering way to live.

I've been with my wife for 26 years and often, on days I was hurting, I would "push through and pay later." Or I'd make a decision to stop taking a medication because it had stopped working. Or thousands of decisions like these. I would always defer to myself, asking whether my choice was worth it to me. I would never consider that my wife was so affected by those decisions that I shouldn't make them by myself. I've realized I've got to make decisions like these jointly with her because she has to pick up the pieces, and she's affected. Over all these years, I missed seeing my self-centeredness—the shadow side of autonomy. She recently brought to my attention that not only was my life in peril when I found CPA, but our marriage was too. Our relationship is greatly improved now that I am in CPA and working the Steps and Traditions. I'm growing as a person. Tradition Four is a wonderful support to my happy marriage.

WORKING TRADITION FOUR
Each group should be autonomous except in matters affecting other groups or CPA as a whole.

The following questions can help deepen your understanding and application of Tradition Four in your recovery and in all your affairs. Use these questions with your sponsor or sponsee or your CPA group, or explore them on your own, selecting the ones that are relevant.

1. How does my group consider the impact of its decisions on other groups and CPA as a whole?
2. How do I keep the focus on the primary purpose of my group?
3. Am I available to help newcomers understand the importance of this Tradition?
4. Does my group take responsibility for our actions? Do I do this in my own life?
5. How do I accept the consequences of my actions? Do I offer this chance to others?
6. In what ways do I balance independence and responsibility?
7. How do I practice autonomy in my group? In my life? How does my autonomy benefit the common welfare?
8. Am I familiar with other CPA groups and keep open lines of communications when making decisions?
9. How does my group consider the welfare of CPA as a whole?
10. Do I recognize I am seen as a representative of the entire fellowship by outsiders who know I am in CPA? How does this impact my behavior?
11. How do I practice "obedience to the unenforceable"?

12. How often do I turn to my Higher Power to help me make decisions? Do I do this within my group?
13. Do I seek to understand the many different ways there are to look at an issue? How do I do this?
14. Are there circumstances where I believe there is only one right way of doing things? What are they?
15. In my personal relationships, what is important to agree on? When is it okay to have differing opinions?
16. In what ways do I focus on not harming others emotionally, physically, mentally, or spiritually when I make choices?
17. How do I have autonomy in my relationships with healthcare providers? Family? Caregivers?
18. Do I understand that just as I have rights as an individual, so too do others in my relationships? In what situations have I specifically recognized this?
19. How do I practice *Live and Let Live* for myself and other people with whom I interact regularly?
20. What does applying Tradition Four in all my affairs look like today?
21. In what areas of my life do I already practice and understand the need for:
    - Autonomy
    - Boundaries
    - Balance
    - Responsibility for unity
    - Interdependence
    - Participation in service
22. How can I include these spiritual tools where they may be missing in my life today?

Tradition Five

*Each group has but one primary purpose—
to carry its message to people living with
chronic pain and chronic illness.*

Each group has but one primary purpose—to carry its message to people living with chronic pain and chronic illness.

We have a singleness of purpose in CPA. The focus of our fellowship is to share our recovery with both newcomers and each other.

Recovery is defined as the ability to live peacefully, joyfully, and comfortably with ourselves and others. We each have the ability to recover and to pass along what we have been given to those who want it.

SPIRITUAL TOOLS FOR PRACTICING TRADITION FIVE

- Primary purpose
- Giving it away
- Carrying the message
- Message of hope and recovery
- Self-compassion
- Group responsibility

APPLYING TRADITION FIVE

I. In Our Groups

PRIMARY PURPOSE
The foundation of the group is grounded in our primary purpose: carrying the message of recovery to those living with chronic pain and chronic illness. This Tradition reminds us what is important and how to keep it in focus. Our purpose holds us together, and our message is simple and clear.

This shared purpose creates loving connections and a deep bond between members, formed when we set aside any differences and come together to recover from the emotional and spiritual debilitation of chronic pain and chronic illness. People arrive feeling despair and hopelessness, just as we did. And just like us, newcomers soon realize they are no longer alone and there is a new way to live.

It is comforting and motivating to know we have a primary aim of carrying the message of hope to others, and together we fend off anything that interferes with our purpose. This singleness of purpose guides all our choices as we reach out and help those who are suffering. We support each other in keeping this focus and avoid anything that diverts from it. For example, if our meeting ever veers into discussions of specific healthcare techniques or devolves into understandable complaints about care providers, we can each make an effort to bring the focus back to CPA recovery.

Each member participates in upholding our primary purpose. Because we welcome newcomers and offer our friendship and compassion, people who enter the meetings of CPA, whether physically or virtually, no longer feel isolated and misunderstood. We all need a safe place in which we can share about personal matters, where people are patient and listen uncritically. When we each make an effort to make this place available, we are supporting our primary purpose. We don't offer medical advice or treatments. Instead, we share how recovery is found in the Steps and Traditions.

GIVING IT AWAY
The survival of the program depends on our choosing to carry the message of hope and recovery through the Steps and Traditions. Therefore, we all need to participate and share with others; as we do, our own recovery deepens. This is a lifelong journey, and it is a joyful one as well. Once we have worked the Steps, we know something of that joy, and we find that we have to give it away to others in order to keep it. We do this by attending meetings, listening to others, sharing, sponsoring, doing service—being an example of recovery in action. When we help others, we also help ourselves, and we continue to grow spiritually.

Our experiences in recovery—working the Steps, Traditions, and Concepts around living with chronic pain and illness—are our inner resources. We have suffered, we have found a new life, and we have something to pass on to others, who can find hope and comfort in our words when we share. Just as others helped us, we help people regain sanity and serenity. We provide encouragement, just as others provided it for us, and we share our experience, strength, and hope.

The best way to support the primary purpose of CPA is by taking care of ourselves and working our own program of recovery. Our group can't carry out its purpose if the members are not willing to commit to their personal program and to serve the group. Our recovery depends on CPA unity, and that unity depends on aligning ourselves with our primary purpose.

Each of us matters in CPA. Each of us is important and valued. When we share at a meeting, talk to our sponsor, or communicate with friends, family, and healthcare providers, we are working this Tradition. By being an example of recovery, we are carrying the message. When we share how we have been resilient in the face of our health struggles, others can learn from our experiences. We use our pain and illness to help others, and this gives a deeper purpose to our lives. By "giving it away," we are enriched.

What we have lived through in our health and recovery journey provides us with a way to reach out and help those who are suffering. The challenges that led us to seek CPA and our own recovery are not wasted: they are our experience; they are our strength; they are our hope. Our story inspires us and deepens our recovery as we share it with others. As we carry the message, we can experience a spiritual awakening.

Giving it away looks different for each of us; however, for others to see how the program works, we need to share our experience and our transformation. If we don't, people won't want to stick around to find their own miracle.

CARRYING THE MESSAGE

"Carrying the message" means we bring the path of recovery that is available in CPA to those who need and want it. We do this by sharing in meetings, by welcoming newcomers, by being a sponsor, and by making sure CPA is available, accessible, and attractive.

Our own lives are transformed when we practice Tradition Five. As we carry the message, we hear the message. As we share our story and our experience, gratitude for what we have received and what we can offer to others becomes part of our daily lives. We are responsible to newcomers and to each other so we can all hear a message of hope. We come to a meeting to give as much as to receive—when we give what we have received to others, our self-centeredness is transformed and we become less fixated on our needs.

We all struggle occasionally. But in CPA, we have found that a time when we are struggling may be exactly the time to help someone else. By reaching out, we can free ourselves and interrupt our own self-obsession over our condition. It doesn't matter how far along we are in our recovery or how long we have been in CPA—at every point in our journey, there is the potential for spiritual growth and a new way of life.

On any given day, we will find ourselves at different stages of our recovery. As our life situations change, so too will our recovery. Everyone has a different desire for growth and capacity for recovery, and these will fluctuate for each of us over our lifetime. But by keeping our primary purpose in focus, we can accept that recovery is not a linear process while continuing on its path. Through sharing, we identify with each other, and by sticking with CPA and carrying its message, we support ourselves and one another, even at times when we are uncertain if the message is having an effect. We all need to hear stories of hope through honest sharing so we can witness how the program positively changes us. If we keep showing up, sharing, listening, and carrying the message, we'll see positive results naturally arise.

MESSAGE OF HOPE AND RECOVERY

Because CPA really works, our message is one of hope.

We each have something to offer newcomers. As a group and as individuals, we have an obligation to reach out to the person who still suffers. By sharing our experience, strength, and hope, we offer a way out of the misery that is often part of living with chronic pain and chronic illness.

Newcomers need to hear our messages of hope and recovery. We share with them how life was before recovery, the tools we have used in recovery, and what life is like now. We share with them areas in which we struggle and where we have found serenity. Through these messages, newcomers understand that recovery is available to each of us and that we all can discover a new way of life.

It's important to remember that we are each responsible for carrying the message. If we whine and complain in our shares, our recovery is not attractive, and we offer no hope. This doesn't mean we cannot share our struggles, of course. Our meetings are safe places to do this. However, it is vital that we share the message, not just the mess. When we make an effort to consciously practice this Tradition by sharing our progress in recovery, we offer strength and spiritual solutions to each other. Newcomers need these solutions, perhaps desperately, as do we all. When we are willing to be vulnerable and open our hearts, we invite others to do the same. We may have lost a former purpose in our life due to chronic pain and chronic illness. But as we carry the message of CPA to others, we discover a new purpose, one that is valuable and can have long-lasting positive effects.

Carrying the message is about communication, and so we use language that the person who is suffering (who may have no prior recovery experience) can hear and understand. Our message is powerful not only through what we say, but also how we say it and how we behave. Our groups will be safe and amiable when we treat each other with dignity. People can't hear us if we are not treating them (and ourselves) with respect, compassion, and kindness.

Carrying the message happens when we share during a meeting; it also happens through our actions, such as when we interact before and after the meeting. Thus we ensure that our actions and messages are consistent, genuine, and always welcoming toward those who need and want our program. This can look like offering someone a hug, saying hello to a newcomer, or including a newcomer in fellowship.

SELF-COMPASSION
Just because we are in the CPA program doesn't mean we don't still struggle. No matter how long we have been around and how much we've experienced, we all need to hear the message so we can continue to grow and become whole. Spending many years in CPA doesn't mean we won't experience uncomfortable feelings such as fear, sadness or shame, and it is important to share these along with issues we are wrestling with. Speaking our truth is an act of self-compassion and courage and keeps our recovery strong. No one is beyond need of help. We each share about our difficulties and how we apply our program, and in this way, we all benefit from focusing on our primary purpose.

GROUP RESPONSIBILITY
Our group is a place to find the message of recovery. Some groups in CPA are small; however, the size of a meeting is not what determines its success. A meeting is working well if its members feel safe, share honestly and openly, and keep coming back. When the recovery is clear and reflected in the member shares, a meeting carries the message to those who need and want it.

Each member has a responsibility to the group and to the fellowship to uphold this Tradition, and our groups have numerous ways to support our efforts to carry the message. They may provide literature to sell or may direct members to the CPA website where literature can be found. Groups may offer phone lists so members can reach out to each other when they need help outside of meetings. In speaker meetings, a member shares what brought them to CPA, how they have worked their program, and how their life looks today. There are newcomer meetings that help people learn about the Steps and Traditions. Meetings may have greeters to welcome newcomers and answer their questions. Virtual meetings often offer time for members to get together after the meeting ends and offer socialization and a way out of isolation.

II. In Our Service Bodies

All the service work we do on behalf of CPA, in our groups and our service bodies, and all the priorities we set are grounded in the primary purpose: to carry the message of recovery to those living with chronic pain and chronic illness. There is a lot of behind-the-scenes work that goes into running our meetings, as well as the fellowship, which means that we each need to do our part to carry the message. When we do service work, whether in our group or for a CPA service body, we are strengthening CPA—for ourselves, for our fellowship, and for all those who suffer but have yet to come to a meeting. We find we also increase and deepen our own recovery, strengthening our self-esteem and general well-being.

As trusted servants in CPA, we are not only people who live with chronic pain and chronic illness—we are human. We deserve dignity and respect when we err or when we can't fulfill our responsibilities. Sometimes we discover that we need to step back. Sometimes we find we may need more recovery before we can be accountable in a position we've taken on. Even when we realize we are unable to follow through, we carry the message by how we deal with the challenge. We do not condemn ourselves but rather hold ourselves with compassion; we share honestly with our fellows what is and is not possible for us. We work our program of recovery as we address the obstacles and problems that show up in our service work, particularly when they are due to our health conditions. We speak with our sponsor and program friends and pray for guidance. These situations can help us build useful skills and teach us loving ways to communicate that create harmony rather than disharmony. Having a safe place to practice being imperfect while still showing up helps us in ways we might never have expected when we started this journey.

Working with our fellow members in service often leads to a deeper love for our program. We feel like we belong and develop an abiding respect for each other. Some of us never thought we would feel that we have value, and in CPA we find that we always have something to offer others and that our life has meaning. This is all possible because we are unified by carrying the message of our primary purpose.

III. In All Our Affairs

In our personal relationships, we share joys and strengths and face challenges together. We may have come together for a specific purpose, stated or unstated. The reasons the relationship came into being shape it and guide its course; they underlie the message we share between one another in the relationship and form how that message will be shared with those outside the relationship. In any relationship we have with others, we can align with a deeper purpose that we can choose to name, or not—a primary purpose that all involved agree on and that can be empowering and effective and can create harmony in all our affairs.

We can turn to the Fifth Tradition for guidance. In recovery, our primary purpose is clear, and when we focus on it, we more easily interact with love, respect, comfort, and encouragement for all members and newcomers. We can utilize these very ways of being in all our relationships, providing comfort to others with our words, with a soft touch, with our ability to listen and not judge or criticize. Just as we do in our meetings, in all our relationships we can practice by not gossiping or repeating what was said to us in confidence and by giving advice only when asked. When we agree on our primary purpose, we honor each person as a valuable human being and treat them with dignity and respect. We discover that we each have experience, strength, and hope to share.

Just as we need to take care of ourselves in our meetings, we find we can only be a trusted partner in a relationship by taking care of ourselves first. This may mean we need to focus on loving ourselves so we can become a more loving person to others. All of us are capable of this, no matter our physical condition, and we begin by offering compassion, forgiveness, and gentle love to ourselves.

What might this look like? As an example: We may be famous in our family for preparing a special holiday food that all are looking forward to, but this year our chronic pain or illness is making it impossible for us to make the well-loved dish. We know the "primary purpose" of our holiday meal is to celebrate the love and joy of being together at this special time. We turn toward ourselves and our Higher Power first, and then perhaps our sponsor, before communicating with our family. We feel what we are feeling about the situation—sadness, disappointment, maybe even anger or fear of being rejected. We ask our Higher Power for help to forgive ourselves and forgive our bodies and to hold ourselves gently, the way we might hold a child or animal we love dearly. When we are ready, we are honest with the members of our family about what is true for us. In this way, we increase intimacy, respect, and love between everyone involved, starting with ourselves.

Sometimes, in order to get practice with this, we first need to receive this kind of love and support from our program friends so we can bring it into our hearts. After a time, we can begin to offer similar love and compassion to those we care about. We can each be an expression of love.

> **ASSOCIATED SPIRITUAL PRINCIPLE:** *Primary Purpose*
>
> Our primary purpose is to carry the message of recovery and give comfort to those with chronic pain and chronic illness. In order to keep our recovery, we need to understand CPA's purpose and share our experience, hope, and strength with others. We are all part of the whole.

TRADITION FIVE IN ACTION

Each group has but one primary purpose—to carry its message to people living with chronic pain and chronic illness.

VOICES OF OUR MEMBERS

I always pray before each CPA meeting that my words and attitude be as welcoming and inclusive as possible. I pray for my voice to be guided by my Higher, Deeper Self so that someone may find comfort in my share. I genuinely wish to give more to a meeting than I get from it. It was suggested to me long ago that I can briefly share my "mess" only if I share what Step or Twelve Step principle I am applying to said mess. CPA has taught me to show up authentically while carrying the CPA message of hope and recovery.

I've noticed that people who only want to complain often leave CPA. Although it is suggested that we don't talk in detail about our illness or pain, those who need to share in this way are not stopped or interrupted, as that is not the culture at a CPA meeting. The culture is to welcome people who want to live life more effectively, with chronic pain and illness—even though they may be struggling as they learn to apply the solutions found in our program. We don't "police" people into carrying the message; over time, members start experiencing recovery, and they discover that receiving and carrying the message of CPA is how that recovery happens.

We are all at the meeting because of chronic pain and illness. We encourage newcomers to attend several meetings before deciding if CPA is for them. Lately, I've been making a point of reaching out to newcomers.

Sometimes we reach out, after they introduce themselves, by saying, "Oh, I'm so glad you're here." On our videoconference meetings, I've seen a lot of members putting their phone numbers into the "chat" box, making themselves available for outreach calls. Members also make sure newcomers know other ways to stay connected to CPA—making sure that they know what literature is available and what's a good place to start with the literature. We encourage them to hang out for a while after the meeting to participate in fellowship.

One of the things that's hard for me, though, is that when people first come in, if they do call…it's always exciting when they do call…but sometimes in the beginning they want to talk a lot about the specific illness issues, and sometimes I'll listen a little bit, but usually I say, "You know, I've found it doesn't matter that much what our specific illness is, it's the way it affects us that we can help each other with, so much." And then I share a recent example about how recovery looks in my own life. That's my way of carrying the message, one-on-one.

During fellowship, before and after meetings, I make a point to not just hang out with my friends. I notice who's new and take time to welcome them personally and ask if they have any questions. It was so helpful to me when I first arrived at CPA. When I felt welcomed, I stayed, and was able to receive, and now I carry the message of CPA recovery.

I was reintroduced to the importance of singleness of purpose when I came to CPA, something I had never understood before so deeply. I had worked all Twelve Steps, formally, in two programs, with two different sponsors who did not have chronic pain and illness. And although I did get relief, I did not get freedom. That's because they didn't understand; they didn't have the language; they didn't have the literature; they didn't have the problem. Singleness of purpose means I don't have to explain to anyone here what it feels like to be chronically ill or in chronic pain, nor what that does, spiritually and emotionally. I never have to explain it because you have it. I now understand more deeply what it means to carry the message of *this* program, and why there are so many Twelve Step programs—the Steps work, but each program is distinct unto itself. The significant fact that I don't have to explain but can recover with you by focusing on our primary purpose has really hit me. I just never understood how important, how essential it is, to be clear about and carry the message of our program only.

Tradition Five is honestly one of the main reasons I kept coming back to CPA. After several years of obsession, fear, guilt, and anger from trying to figure out how to live with chronic pain and illness, I felt alone. I stumbled into CPA. I saw a variety of people on videoconference meetings yet could not figure out what their pain or illness was. Weren't we here to talk about that? I so wanted to talk about my conditions; maybe *this* group would finally understand and give me the pity I thought I deserved, since family and friends did not.

I was surprised that nobody talked about health conditions. Instead, they focused on how their lives improved because of applying CPA principles, by discussing how they were growing emotionally and spiritually, compared to where they were. I knew I was home. I now had hope. I heard about how to apply the Twelve Steps and Twelve Traditions to living with pain and illness. Meeting topics included "One Day at a Time," readings from our Twelve Step study book, *Recipe for Recovery*, or the Serenity Prayer. Even in fellowship time, after the meeting, nobody talked about their physical ailments. Members answered specific questions about how they applied the CPA recovery program to their lives. It became clear that the only thing all members have in common is the CPA program of recovery.

I can still see the smiling faces of those at my first meetings. I now understand it is a certain sacrifice to ensure our sharing is only about the primary purpose of CPA. I believe it is a way of being of service. What if those at my first meetings had not focused on carrying the message? I would not have been able to sort through my personal confusion to hear what the CPA program of recovery is all about. Because other members surrendered to the guidance of Tradition Five, I have a new life! I am now honored to be one of the members who also carries the CPA message to people living with chronic pain and chronic illness.

Whether I choose to do service by sponsoring or hold a position in my home group, a committee, or any other service body, carrying the message to those who still suffer is one way I work my

CPA program. If I want all the benefits CPA recovery has to offer, I must work the whole program. I practice the Twelve Steps and Traditions in my daily life, I attend meetings, I communicate regularly with my sponsor and fellow members, and I do service. The Steps teach me how to live with myself and my chronic pain and chronic illness. The Traditions teach me how to live and work with others while living with chronic pain and chronic illness. CPA service allows me to practice these new skills in a safe place, with others who are doing the same, before I take them out into the world at large.

When I am moved to volunteer, I trust my Higher Power and my fellow CPA members to gently guide and support me. I simply trust and rely on our Twelve Steps, Traditions, and Concepts to support our primary purpose and give myself permission to take a risk. I let go of the outcomes and remember that carrying the message of CPA is a journey, not a destination or qualification.

One of the first things that happened when I became ill was that I had to stop doing Twelve Step work in another program because I was going into a locked facility—taking the meetings into a jail. It's not a place where they can respond to, "Oh no, I'm having pain, I have to leave right now." I didn't realize how much that service was contributing to my self-esteem until it was no longer possible for me to do. And then, a few years later, I had to completely leave work. I had cut back, cut back, and cut back, until I simply couldn't do it anymore. My body just wouldn't do it. It was really difficult to feel worthy. Even being able to enjoy getting things done around the house or run errands…a lot of things were just no longer possible.

Being able to do some of the service that we do for each other in CPA was really good for my self-esteem. I was able to take phone calls, even sometimes chair a meeting. At the same time, I was learning that my value comes from my existence, not from my achievements, so I practiced balance. Although I have a degenerative condition, as technology has advanced, it has gotten easier to contribute in small ways, and I'm grateful for that. I do what I can and accept that my presence is the greatest service to all. In this way, I get to be a living example of the message of CPA.

I've been a member of CPA for a short time. Sometimes I can speak, and sometimes I can't. I was grateful to find out that there is more to CPA than just meetings, that there's actually this larger structure that supports all of us. I can offer that I'm a writer and an editor—I can type, and I can edit. That was exciting to me because I love that kind of service.

And as I offer to participate in service, I appreciate that in CPA, if I can't carry out my service, there is no punitive action. I'm free to pass it on to the next person who's able. It was such a relief to me at the time I found this out—first, that I could really share about what was going on in my body, and secondarily, that I have a Twelve Step outlet where I can continue to grow, continue to do service, and continue to contribute.

I get teary about that because I need this. I know to keep the recovery I have, I have to give it away. Honestly, even to *get* it, I have to give it away. In my experience, in recovery we start with giving. We don't start with taking.

My husband and I both had Twelve Step experience before we met, and we took our decision to marry seriously. We sat down, inventoried our motives, and determined that our marriage's primary purpose was to be a vehicle for spiritual growth.

We decided to make praying together each morning and at mealtimes a habit. We each are committed to our respective Twelve Step programs, and when our individual human edges create conflict in our relationship, we always fall back on this primary purpose. We trust we are each working our Steps on our own issues, and if we were wrong in any given situation, an amends will be coming. When my chronic pain and chronic illness threw our marriage a curve ball, our primary purpose, plus the principles of the Twelve Steps and Twelve Traditions, were there to guide us. I am so grateful for my chronic pain and chronic illness, as it has brought us both increased emotional and spiritual maturity.

I was amazed to find that once I was practicing the skills of being kind and compassionate to my body and myself, how differently I acted in the outside world. This is how I carry the message of CPA—by enjoying my life and practicing my recovery, one day at a time.

I think my primary purpose is self-care. Even though sick, I was a live-in caregiver for my aging mom for several years. It's important for me to set a good example of self-care. When I was not physically well, I would only take care of her most basic needs. If she asked more of me, I would say, "I can't do that today, maybe another time." If she had an emergency that was serious, in spite of my condition, I would contact the paramedics, communicate with them, and then go back on ice or whatever I needed to do for my own well-being. For one hospitalization, I went with her, and for the other two, I did not. It became necessary for her just to go with the paramedics, and for me not to follow her. In CPA, I learned how to balance taking care of myself with taking care of someone else. This is one way I carry the message of our program—I practice self-care.

I kind of hate to complain about the pain I'm in. I hate to tell people about it. But then, they don't know about it, and they're surprised when I'm not able to do things. They think I'm not doing things with them because I don't want to or I'm just being rude. My way of "carrying the message" of CPA is to create a balance between telling people just enough about my condition, and inform them of my intentions, while also practicing recovery-based conversations. I hate to just be complaining because that drags me down too.

I've realized there's a difference between complaining and explaining. When I hadn't described what my limitations were to my family, it was hard to go anywhere besides doctor appointments and physical therapy. My family didn't want to do things unless I joined them. I didn't want to be the reason they would miss holidays and family trips with other family members. But when I did go, often I would just lie in bed and not be able to participate in the activities. Or I would push myself and then I would pay for it for days.

Now I know how to explain what I need rather than complain afterward. In CPA, I've learned how to balance the difficulties presented by chronic pain and chronic illness with the easeful approach that recovery language and behaviors can provide.

My wife has a concept of what my primary purpose is. My friends have a concept of what my primary purpose is. Even my cat has an idea of what my primary purpose is. And before CPA, my primary purpose was fulfilling their concepts of my primary purpose. Thanks to CPA, and inventory work, and fellowship work, my primary purpose today is to discover and practice how to live peacefully, joyfully, and comfortably, regardless of what my body's doing. There is so much that I am powerless over. But for me, my primary purpose is to be paying attention to my thoughts, my attitudes, my actions, and what's coming out of my mouth. I have turned my primary purpose over to my higher, deeper self, and I have found the ease of living that comes with making that decision.

My primary purpose as a patient is to listen carefully to the information I receive and defer to the expertise of others, as appropriate. There are times when I've had to say no, particularly to physical therapists who don't fully understand my chronic situation. Sometimes they want me to do more than what is appropriate for my body. I have to remember that I'm the one who's going to experience the pain the next day. (And it can be excruciating pain.) My pain is sometimes the result of the amount of movement, but it can also be the result of the wrong kind of movement.

I recently had an experience with a talk therapy counselor who was helping me quite a bit but wanted to explore how exercise could help me, which is an interesting topic, but the combination of the chronic conditions I have puts a severe limitation on exercise. He wanted to discuss it a great deal, and I finally said to him: "This is not realistic for me and not a conversation I am willing to have today." Sometimes carrying the message of my CPA recovery means being courageous and saying, "No."

WORKING TRADITION FIVE

Each group has but one primary purpose—to carry its message to people living with chronic pain and chronic illness.

The following questions can help deepen your understanding and application of Tradition Five in your recovery and in all your affairs. Use these questions with your sponsor or sponsee or your CPA group, or explore them on your own, selecting the ones that are relevant.

1. How do I understand the primary purpose of CPA?
2. What does it mean to me to "carry the message"?
3. How am I welcoming to newcomers?
4. How do I carry the CPA message? When I share and interact with others, what is the message I carry? How can I strengthen it?
5. How do I consciously connect my sharing at meetings with the message of CPA's hope and strength?
6. How do I help my group fulfill our primary purpose?
7. How do I share my experience of CPA tools with others?
8. Do I remember that everyone in CPA suffers, from newcomers to longtimers, and that I can learn from and be of service to everyone?
9. What do I believe I have to offer the member who is suffering?
10. How do I give comfort as well as receive it?
11. What is my primary purpose in personal areas of my life? In relationships with others?

12. Would any of my relationships outside of CPA benefit by naming and agreeing on "our primary purpose"?
13. Am I patient, and do I listen to others with compassion and kindness?
14. Am I critical of caregivers, family, friends, or medical personnel? If so, how can I communicate differently?
15. Do I do my part in relationships? Do I know that Higher Power will do for me what I can't and will help me do what I can do for myself?
16. How am I helping my relationships fulfill their purpose and attain their goals? Am I living the program to the best of my ability in all my affairs?
17. Am I giving comfort and encouragement to the other people in my personal relationships?
18. What does applying Tradition Five in all my affairs look like today?
19. In what areas of my life do I already practice and understand the need for:
    - Primary purpose
    - Giving it away
    - Carrying the message
    - Message of hope and recovery
    - Self-compassion
    - Group responsibility
20. How can I include these spiritual tools where they may be missing in my life today?

Tradition Six

A CPA group ought never endorse, finance, or lend the CPA name to any outside enterprise, lest problems of money, property, and prestige divert us from our primary purpose.

A CPA group ought never endorse, finance, or lend the CPA name to any outside enterprise, lest problems of money, property, and prestige divert us from our primary purpose.

Although there are many excellent organizations that can support those suffering with chronic pain and chronic illness, CPA does not endorse or use its name in conjunction with any outside groups. We keep our attention focused on our program. In this way we support unity and avoid controversy and problems that will distract us. Tradition Six guides us to make this clear so there is no confusion.

SPIRITUAL TOOLS FOR PRACTICING TRADITION SIX

- Keeping the focus on the primary purpose, as an individual
- Cooperation with other organizations while maintaining boundaries
- Singleness of purpose
- Focus of service

APPLYING TRADITION SIX

I. In Our Groups

KEEPING THE FOCUS ON THE PRIMARY PURPOSE, AS AN INDIVIDUAL

CPA is a spiritual program that applies the Twelve Steps to recovery from the debilitating effects of life with chronic pain and chronic illness. Any outside organization, whether it is related to politics, religion, healthcare, or other spiritual practices, is not an element of our message. We need to make it possible for the greatest number of people to have access to our program, so it is essential that we not dilute or divert our message by bringing other resources into our meetings. As an individual, we can support and be part of any organization we choose; however, we leave these choices out of CPA meetings. By keeping our affiliations outside our group, we protect the group from conflicts that can impede our recovery. We can endorse any group, but we don't do it specifically as a member of CPA.

It is common for us to belong to other organizations. There are many emotional and physical resources outside of CPA that can support us, and we often find spiritual guidance in other communities we belong to. All of these outside associations remain unnamed when we share our experience, strength, and hope in a meeting. When we get together with our friends, even if they are fellow members, we can share about whatever has benefitted us. We just don't do this in meetings.

When we share in a meeting, we are mindful of whether what we are sharing is in accord with our primary purpose. Because our groups are made up only of fellow CPA members, each of us has a responsibility to keep the meeting a place of recovery for all. Though there are many beneficial groups we may have found helpful in our lives—for example, we may belong to a group that is focused on our particular health issue—we don't bring this into our CPA meetings. This includes literature and specific terminology from other groups.

We do not name outside enterprises of any kind in our shares. For instance, we do not mention names of social media sites, search engines, or product brand names. If our group usually goes out for fellowship after our meeting at a particular restaurant, we can invite everyone to join in without naming the restaurant in our share or announcement. We can merely say, "If you are interested, please see me after the meeting to find out where we'll be." This may seem like overkill, but keeping to Tradition Six across the board in this way creates a sense of safety, security, and non-endorsement. It protects our primary purpose and does not detract our focus from our recovery.

COOPERATION WITH OTHER ORGANIZATIONS WHILE MAINTAINING BOUNDARIES

We want to maintain cooperative relationships with outside institutions, as this is important to support the functioning of our fellowship, and we do so within the boundaries of the Traditions. For example, we pay rent to use rooms for our meetings. Whether we meet at a facility or via a digital service, we don't affiliate with the facility or service where our meetings are held, but we do cooperate with and abide by the rules of the facility or service. We may rent a space at an institution, health facility, or medical office, but we don't endorse it. This means we don't promote the institution in our meetings, announcements, or posted information online. We do not suggest that CPA is a part of the facility, or vice versa.

Boundaries create healthy lines of separation. By making clear agreements, we ensure the organizations we are involved with understand. We don't want there to be any misunderstandings, so we clearly define our relationship with outside organizations and do so in a way that is respectful and direct, so there is no confusion about affiliation. Every interaction with an outside group is public relations. By being honest and transparent, we are living the principles of CPA and protecting the integrity of our program.

We have found many benefits to having a cooperative relationship with other organizations, and this is something we want to continue. If any organization wants to list the CPA meeting in their newsletter, local mailing, or website, this would be within the guidelines of the Traditions. However, they can't use CPA to promote their own programs. For our survival, it is important that we stay aligned with our message and our principles. We don't endorse other groups or list them on the CPA website, but we maintain a relationship that is friendly, cooperative, and respectful.

SINGLENESS OF PURPOSE

Our only purpose is to carry the message of recovery to those who suffer with chronic pain and chronic illness. CPA is a simple program of one person sharing their experience, strength, and hope with another. Anything that doesn't support this focus is a diversion for our group. Our clear spiritual aim guides us, and we don't let anything interfere with our primary purpose.

We know that our program works, and we want to *Keep it Simple*. It can become confusing, to longtimers and newcomers alike, if we bring outside enterprises into our program. It can also lead to controversy, which in turn can interfere with our unity. By not endorsing, funding, or lending our name to outside enterprises, we maintain our focus on our recovery from the emotional and spiritual debilitation of living with chronic pain and chronic illness and are better able to carry the message of CPA.

Our CPA groups do not need a large amount of funds or materials to operate. We just need a few supplies and rent for our meeting location or a fee for our virtual meeting space. Money is solely a means of supporting our primary purpose, not a goal in itself. CPA as a fellowship has no need to gain money. This is a very freeing concept. We maintain only the funds that cover our expenses, along with a prudent reserve, and this is all that we need to support us in our recovery.

Property and prestige are not our focus, individually or in our groups. By following the example of Twelve Step groups who nearly floundered before this Tradition was in place, we uphold CPA's survival. The desire to hold property or to feel the warm glow of social status when we are admired, as a member or as a group, can be a strong pull. But if we were to own property, who would manage it, derive profit from it, sign the legal papers? We would be taking on a myriad of organizational details and responsibilities that would easily divert our attention from our recovery.

Similarly, and more insidiously, we find that when our focus shifts to prestige, our recovery takes a back seat. Focus on prestige invites comparison between members and groups. When this happens, whether as an individual or as a group, feeling our value as "more than" or "less than" is a diversion from what we are joined together for and destroys our unity. Our focus is on personal recovery, and so long as we keep this simple concept in our sights, our groups and fellowship will thrive.

It is imperative for us to keep CPA a safe place where people of all walks of life and with any kind of chronic pain and chronic illness feel comfortable and included. We should never feel pressured to purchase anything. During the meeting, we don't make announcements about any program outside of CPA. We concentrate on CPA's solutions and not that of other programs, organizations, or treatment programs.

II. In Our Service Bodies

FOCUS OF SERVICE

When our groups and our members practice Tradition Six, it naturally folds into all of our service work, at every level. It becomes a "no-brainer" to do service, making our commitments feel easy and rewarding. When our group has negotiated within our Traditions with the facility or digital service we interact with, for instance, we feel clear and competent when paying the fees. When we have taken in only the funds we need to meet our expenses and have a prudent reserve, we do not feel pressured to manage large amounts of money.

When we are doing service for CPA and have no affiliation with other products, practices, or institutions, we relax into supporting our recovery and that of our fellows. When our service boards do not affiliate with outside enterprises, there is no pressure on CPA as a whole to compete with or compare itself to any other healthcare or chronic pain or chronic illness program. Tradition Six gives CPA, at every level of its organizational structure, the freedom to focus solely and successfully on our primary purpose.

III. In All Our Affairs

When we practice Tradition Six in our personal lives, we choose to stay focused on what is important in our relationships. As mentioned in Tradition Five, we may need to identify a primary purpose, discussing our needs and wants. We don't let outside issues and the routine problems of day-to-day living divert us; instead, we cooperate with friends, family members, and healthcare providers, working together toward a shared common good.

In this process, we are responsible for our own spiritual, emotional, and physical well-being, not that of others. This is one way we do not "endorse or lend our name to outside enterprises" at a personal level. We can only truly know our own needs, and we need to share them with the members of our family, fellow workers, and healthcare providers with clarity, compassion, and non-comparison. We protect our serenity by balancing the establishment of clear boundaries with the willingness to include the needs of the whole.

We keep in mind the importance of communicating our needs, especially as our needs may change. We may notice that we are asking others to do things we can do for ourselves or that they are doing things we want to do for ourselves. When this becomes a problem, we can take the time to reassess and discuss what requests might be helpful in the situation so we can make alterations.

Sometimes, our daily needs are dependent on care received from others. It is important to communicate clearly and succinctly, saying what we mean without being mean, keeping in mind the dignity of all concerned. When we look at our caregivers as fellow participants in our primary purpose, we accept they may make mistakes, and we ask them to do the same for us. When tensions occur, we can pray for guidance. It is possible we may need to forgive and let go.

This Tradition reminds us that we can't be all things to all people—no one can. We are separate entities working together with a common aim. One primary purpose in a relationship may simply be to love and care for each other to the best of our ability. In other cases, our primary purpose may be to make sure the best decisions possible are being made to support our well-being. We do not get involved in affairs that do not concern us, and we don't ask others to get involved in concerns that do not involve them. We each have our own ideas and feelings, and we share them as necessary; we don't need to focus on anyone else's opinions.

Relationships are reciprocal, and we are mutually dependent on each other. We offer support to and receive support from spouses, partners, children, other family members, friends, support groups, and members of our healthcare team. Each member of a relationship contributes their part. When we practice Tradition Six, we have no need to compare the value or status of each contribution. We recognize that we are all in it together, that each of us has value and something to give. Each individual has something to offer the whole. In all our relationships, Tradition Six reminds us that, in a very tangible way, money, property, and prestige are not measures of worth when we are focused on our primary purpose.

> **ASSOCIATED SPIRITUAL PRINCIPLE:**
> *Non-affiliation*
> We have a unique purpose and do not affiliate with outside enterprises. We practice *Live and Let Live*. CPA is a clearly defined, discrete organization, focused on our recovery and on respecting those we interact with as distinct entities themselves.

TRADITION SIX IN ACTION

A CPA group ought never endorse, finance, or lend the CPA name to any outside enterprise, lest problems of money, property, and prestige divert us from our primary purpose.

VOICES OF OUR MEMBERS

I was at a telephone meeting once, and someone was carrying on about a bad experience that they had with a particular computer program (which they named), and the company had gotten involved.

I want to be at meetings where the CEO of any company would feel safe coming if they had problems with pain or illness; the leader of any religion; the leader of any country. That they would feel safe coming to a CPA meeting to hear the message of recovery and would not have to hear their family, organization, country, or company bashed. By not naming outside enterprises in our meetings, we ensure they are safe places where recovery is the focus—and recovery happens.

When I go to meetings, I am there as a member. I am not there representing whatever positions I may hold in CPA. These do not define who I am. I am equal to each and every member, and so are they, no matter how long anyone has been in CPA.

Even as a longtimer, I get permission to be a mess. I remember when my first sponsor, who had been in recovery for a long time, was struggling in her program. I asked, "How can *you* be having a hard time?" She replied that she was always a newcomer, that she is always working at her program and is never done. I think about that now, years later, when I go to a meeting. I can cry, I can be lost and confused. I appreciate the permission that we have to share our entire selves, no matter what position we fill or how long we have been around. Whatever "prestige" others may attribute to us, we are all equals on the path of recovery.

I don't like cliques, and Tradition Six addresses this. When we make an announcement in a meeting, it is relevant to our program. We practice inclusion, not exclusivity. We are all equals in CPA. It does not matter what we did or do in the outside world. It does not matter whom we know. We are all here, right now, to share our experience, strength, and hope, and recover together.

When I first chaired a meeting as a newcomer, it was the only meeting I had been to at the time, and I knew most of the members. That very day, new people came, some of whom had been in CPA for a while. I judged them as "CPA professionals" and thought they knew far more than I did. I made it difficult on myself because I was not treating them as equals. I felt insecure and "less than." I am grateful that I know now that we are all equals and that newcomers are a vital part of every meeting. Now I know that members who have been around for a while show newcomers what recovery looks like. And *they* learn from newcomers, as they are reminded of what they felt like when they first came in and of how far they have come in CPA.

A new member joined our group. It was clear she had Twelve Step experience when she shared. When it was time for announcements, she raised her hand. I was surprised when, given her apparent experience, she proceeded to give a long-winded sales pitch on a new supplement she was selling. The chair finally broke in and reminded her that we do not promote, sell, or discuss outside treatment options. The saleswoman got defensive, saying she only wanted to share that which had helped her so much. We thanked her for her kind intentions and reminded everyone of our group's primary purpose. The woman is now a valued member of CPA and has never mentioned her product again.

My CPA friends are finding many ways to socialize together, even though we live in different states and countries, such as having a movie night or a virtual dance. When we have these virtual gatherings, we don't announce them during our meeting. If there is a flyer, it says, "This is not an official CPA event, it is a social event."

When we first started showing movies, I was afraid that we needed a disclaimer, like, "The opinions expressed here do not reflect CPA as a whole, etc." I was afraid that if we didn't, it might imply something about the movie. Then someone pointed out to me that it was just like other fellowships having a dance. It does not mean that you endorse the band but are just having a get-together that is not a meeting. So, we make it really clear. We announce these get-togethers after meetings, on social media, and we make them available to everyone.

In CPA, the Board of Trustees of CPASB manages funds and sets a budget every year. That budget is transparent and is found on the CPA website so that anyone who wants to can see where the income comes from to support CPA and what the expenses are for CPA. Everyone can see how the Board balances the budget. As part of the fiduciary responsibility, the Board establishes a minimum amount to keep as prudent reserve to cover operating expenses, should any problems affect income. This kind of financial transparency—showing that CPA is not relying on outside enterprises—does not need funding from outside the program, and does not accept or own property, reminds me of the freedom, clarity, and safety generated by applying Tradition Six.

A member of the Board of Trustees learned of a national organization that was planning a major campaign to help educate people about chronic pain and how it affects millions. It seemed a perfect opportunity for our fellowship to reach out to the public and let them know about our program of recovery. However, in order to participate with the dozens of groups joining together, CPA was asked to put links for other treatments and healthcare providers on the CPA website. We explained that we could not endorse any outside enterprise and chose not to be included in the campaign. The organizers were understanding, and even though we could not reciprocate, they elected to include a link to CPA on their website. In this way, we were able to cooperate with an organization while maintaining our Traditions and spiritual principles.

This Tradition reminds me to mind my own business. My husband is self-employed, in a service-based job. My friends sometimes say, "Ask your husband," how to deal with an issue he has expertise in. I became a third-party messenger service, and this created many problems. As a result, I have drawn a self-loving boundary. Now I say, "Thank you, he would love to hear from you. Here is his phone number. Thank you for your business." This Tradition teaches me I don't need to meddle or take on responsibility that is not mine.

When I talk about my health situation with friends and family, they often want to rush in and help. They have good intentions, but sometimes they are not helpful, and their "help" undermines my ability to do things on my own. I am responsible for me, and I am responsible for outreach and for asking people for what I need. I don't need others to do for me what I can do for myself. And I like that there is clarity: I am responsible for myself, and I can say, "No thank you." I don't have to receive help just because someone wants to give it to me.

I went to a healthcare provider, looking for treatment, and by the end of the appointment I realized that all they were interested in doing was selling me unnecessary services and supplements, seeking to make money. I felt angry because I was seeking relief from pain, feeling hopeless and desperate, and it seemed they were taking advantage of my need. I chose not to return to the practice. When the name of this provider is brought up, I have suggested to people to be mindful, do your research, and take someone with you. For me, there is no greater offense than people who prey on those who are vulnerable. This is another reason that "we do not endorse." Non-endorsement protects CPA's reputation and integrity.

Medical professionals don't have a lot of time. So I make a list of the three most important things that need to happen in my appointment, along with a few other items, if there is time. I respect my healthcare providers by not taking up a lot of time with unnecessary information, so they can listen to what I have to say. By keeping it simple, I get what I need, and the providers are appreciative of the way I treat them and are responsive to my needs.

This is one way I practice Tradition Six—by keeping my primary purpose in focus and keeping things less important to my care out of my medical appointments.

It's easy for me to take up a lot of space in my relationship with my partner—filled with my doubts about my worth and contributions as a chronically ill person—despite loving support and kindness from my partner, every day. When I'm not right-sized about my value, I take precious energy away from intimacy and the joy and serenity of the partnership. After "coming up short" in my own mind, I can easily find myself scorekeeping and building resentments. The more I can rely on my program and Higher Power for a sense of self-worth and self-esteem, the less pressure there is on my partner and relationship for validation. Keeping the concepts of "power and prestige" out of my relationships can be difficult for me. Tradition Six reminds me that they are not part of the primary purpose of my relationships—at all.

WORKING TRADITION SIX
A CPA group ought never endorse, finance, or lend the CPA name to any outside enterprise, lest problems of money, property, and prestige divert us from our primary purpose.

The following questions can help deepen your understanding and application of Tradition Six in your recovery and in all your affairs. Use these questions with your sponsor or sponsee or your CPA group, or explore them on your own, selecting the ones that are relevant.

1. What is CPA'S primary spiritual aim?
2. What does it mean to not "endorse, finance or lend our name"? How do we apply this in our group? What does that look like?
3. How does the use of literature other than Conference Approved Literature divert us from our primary purpose?
4. Do I leave outside affiliations out of my sharing? How am I mindful of this as I share?
5. What can I do if someone tries to promote their business or an outside enterprise in a meeting?
6. How do I keep my involvements outside of CPA separate from my group and service involvements?
7. How do I help keep the group from being diverted?
8. What is the aim of my primary relationships at home, at work, and in my healthcare?
9. In my personal affairs, have I been diverted by money, property, or prestige?
10. Do I compromise values and boundaries to reach goals?

11. What does applying Tradition Six in all my affairs look like today?
12. In what areas of my life do I already practice and understand the need for:
    - Keeping the focus on the primary purpose, as an individual
    - Cooperation with other organizations while maintaining boundaries
    - Singleness of purpose
    - Focus of service
13. How can I include these spiritual tools where they may be missing in my life today?

Tradition Seven

Every CPA group ought to be fully self-supporting, declining outside contributions.

> **Every CPA group ought to be fully self-supporting, declining outside contributions.**

CPA's groups have expenses and need money to operate. We create financial independence by taking on the responsibility of supporting ourselves and not receiving funds from outside sources. When members give money, time, and talents to our group, we have the funds and resources to take care of our needs and to reach out to others who still suffer.

SPIRITUAL TOOLS FOR PRACTICING TRADITION SEVEN

- Being self-supporting
- Supporting the whole
- Building spiritual strength
- Willingness to give
- Honesty about finances
- Independence and unity
- Compassionate participation

APPLYING TRADITION SEVEN

I. In Our Groups

BEING SELF-SUPPORTING
We want CPA to be available for our current members and to be sustainable for the future members that have yet to find us. We are each responsible for supporting the fellowship as an individual, as a member of our group, and as part of the worldwide fellowship. We do this by attending, sharing, and listening at meetings; contributing funds to support the meeting's expenses; donating money to the larger fellowship; doing service at the group level and beyond; and by carrying the message.

Financial support ensures that we can continue to operate, and so we are asked to offer a voluntary donation, either at a meeting or by mailing a check or sending money electronically. When we are self-supporting—meaning that we "pay our own way"—we don't need to affiliate with other groups. We need our meetings to be there, and only we, the members, can make that happen. Being able to meet our group expenses, such as paying rent or service fees for the spaces we meet in, is the sign of a healthy program that is valuable to its members.

Being self-supporting is not just about money; it maintains CPA's unity and the survival of the program. In order to thrive, CPA needs the willingness of its members to provide service in many ways. This begins with a commitment to our own recovery. We contribute vital resources by giving our time, energy, and attention. We attend meetings. We share our experience, strength, and hope; we share how we practice our program; we listen to and sponsor one another.

Service specific to our groups is also needed. There would be no CPA if we did not all take responsibility so that our meetings can function and be there for us. There are many service positions available, and because we are living with chronic pain and chronic illness, most service positions are shared by more than one person. We support the group when we volunteer for jobs such as chairing a meeting, being a Group Representative, being a greeter or treasurer, and (if we are meeting in a physical space) setting up or cleaning up. When members assume these positions, the group runs smoothly.

When we volunteer, we enrich the program and make it stronger. We don't often arrive at our first CPA meeting feeling great about ourselves, and we may believe there is nothing we have to give. However, we soon learn, even at our first meeting, we can contribute. Sharing at a meeting or reaching out to a newcomer is an act of service. As we grow in our recovery, we find new ways to put our skills and talents to use to support our group and CPA as a whole.

Being fully self-supporting implies that all members support and are supported by our program. It is sustainable when everyone contributes what they can. We need balance so some don't feel left out and discounted and others don't feel overwhelmed and underappreciated. So we all participate. All service positions are of equal value, and we rotate so everyone gets to contribute.

We all have talents and can do our individual part as we are guided by our Higher Power.

Although each group is self-supporting, our groups help each other and get assistance from CPA as a whole, and Intergroups work on projects together. As CPA grows, these combinations will continue to evolve, and we will discover new ways to bring CPA recovery to our members, some of whom are unable to attend a physical meeting.

In all that we do, we evaluate how what we are doing supports our primary purpose. Groups hold meetings, but they also offer recovery workshops, speaker meetings, and reach out to local healthcare providers. Being self-supporting means we each commit to keeping CPA strong. We contribute our money, time, and energy, along with giving our trust, respect, compassion, and support to our fellow members. This ensures CPA will be there for those of us who are part of the fellowship now and for those who will need CPA in the future.

SUPPORTING THE WHOLE

We are members of a worldwide fellowship, and we communicate and stay connected through our service structure flow. CPA provides many services that we may take for granted as individuals and as groups, such as the website, telephone service, or the publication of literature. We need the worldwide service structure to provide these services as well as to manage the day-to-day operations and necessary activities such as replying to inquiries about the fellowship and helping new groups get started.

The non-profit corporation Chronic Pain Anonymous Service Board (CPASB) is the clearinghouse for our fellowship. It provides many services to the groups, such as coordinating and publishing our literature, which is written by our members. When we donate to CPASB, individually as well as a group, we help support the entire service structure.

Some of us attend meetings by telephone, videoconference, or online. There is no basket to pass in these virtual rooms; however, this does not absolve us of the need to be fully self-supporting. The monies that are collected at our meetings support our group and CPASB and help the worldwide CPA fellowship fulfill our vision to reach all who suffer. If we attend a non-physical meeting, it is important to give our service bodies the resources they need to carry out their responsibilities on our behalf.

When we understand the service structure of CPA and consciously practice Tradition Seven, each group takes responsibility for supporting the whole. This interdependence allows us to sustain CPA and preserve our unity. Our fellowship benefits from our money, our time, and our enthusiasm, and our service bodies function through the direction and support of members and groups. In this way, CPA can continue to offer new literature and other resources that support our primary purpose, which in turn supports us all.

A unified fellowship requires communication. One way we support the whole is by making sure our voice is heard in the service structure. Each meeting has a Group Representative who represents their group at the General Advisory Council. Also, the World Service Conference is an annual meeting held so the worldwide fellowship can participate in a yearly group conscience. Sending a delegate from our group lets our voice be present at the World Service Conference. This unifies our entire fellowship and lets the groups have their say in how resources and funds are utilized. The members are the foundation of the groups, and the groups are the foundation of the CPA fellowship. In this "trickle-up" model, our membership has the final say in all matters.

BUILDING SPIRITUAL STRENGTH

Generosity, gratitude, willingness, faith, trust, and humility are some of the spiritual traits that we develop as we actively apply being fully self-supporting in CPA, declining outside contributions. It is a profound and transformative process.

Being generous is a powerful spiritual practice. When we use our money, time, and energy in practical ways that make it possible for all to benefit from CPA, we are building our spiritual muscles. Being self-supporting gives us a feeling of dignity. Seeing that we can take care of our own needs gives us hope. However, we don't do this alone, and as we each do our part, together, a deep sense of capability and self-worth and a new sense of calm grows in us. Through knowing we are each responsible for the survival of CPA and applying ourselves by practicing Tradition Seven, we find that our spiritual strength increases.

We express our gratitude in the action of giving to others in CPA, whether through time, service, or money. Gratitude and giving are well known and even scientifically proven to increase self-esteem, serenity, and well-being. In recovery, we don't depend on others for our happiness. This is a practice of giving rather than taking. As we discover that doing service is a way out of isolation and that giving helps us, we start to feel truly good about ourselves.

Our faith strengthens when we are willing to be self-supporting. We trust the process of recovery and that our Higher Power will help us determine what we need and what we can offer—whether that means money, time, energy, or other resources. As a group and as individuals, we need tangible things that require our talents, time, and attention. We rely on our Higher Power and trust in the ultimate authority that is expressed in our group conscience in order to receive the support we need. We trust each other in this process and have faith that we are being shown how we need to grow. We find we are gently guided as to how we need to contribute, individually and as a group. Time and time again we see that when we are willing, our Higher Power gives us the courage and capability. Soon, we are able to fully trust that as we work together, with our Higher Power, our protection and the protection of our groups are in good hands.

We need to practice our program in supporting CPA. Is what we are doing sustainable and realistic for us? Over time, our health conditions change—sometimes improving, sometimes getting worse. At an individual, group, and larger CPA fellowship level, we review the commitments we already have and decide, based on our conditions, if we can take on more or need to take on less. Humility keeps us honest and living within our means and limits, whether with money or service. Sometimes it means we need to ask for help and let others know when we require assistance. Doing so fosters self-respect and strengthens our relationships with others, thus deepening our own spiritual development.

WILLINGNESS TO GIVE
Our groups need to take care of their responsibilities so they can function and be available to all who need them. Members voluntarily choose to accept the responsibility to contribute. While there are no group dues or fees, there are financial obligations, such as paying a fee for the space where the meeting is held. Each group's survival depends on the members joining together in service of the whole.

We each decide what we can give to our group. Our contribution is not measured by an amount of money—we can give our experience, strength, and hope; we can chair the meeting; we can sponsor others; we can reach out to someone who is struggling. Through acts of service, an attitude of kindness, and a willingness to share how we have applied the program and what works for us, we give to others.

We decide what is reasonable for us to contribute in energy, time, and finances. Contributing can consist of attending a speaker meeting or listening to another member who is having a difficult day. We contribute what we can and when we can, and we choose to give financially, or to give our time, or to give compassion, or whatever is called for and we have to offer. We freely choose to support the services and people that support us.

No matter how much we contribute in money, time or talents, we are all equal. Contributions won't be the same for each individual across time, or from person to person. We mutually share responsibility for CPA to be there for us so we can recover, and we realize that if we don't participate and don't ensure CPA is self-sustaining, we jeopardize our recovery. Contributing becomes something we want to do, contributing both to our unity and to our own recovery.

When we are self-supporting in CPA, we develop confidence and gain the courage to be self-supporting in all areas of our life, whatever that looks like for each of us. We begin to feel like we can thrive, no matter our situation, and don't have to hold ourselves in the role of victim. In being self-supporting, however we define it, we experience empowerment, honor, and a sense of value and self-worth. This new sense of freedom and personal power is one of the results of working Tradition Seven.

HONESTY ABOUT FINANCES
We give away our message freely; however, money is essential for our services to be provided to our groups and the global fellowship. We never fundraise outside of the fellowship; rather, we are self-supporting through our member donations, along with literature and book sales. We see our contributions making a difference as new brochures and books are published, as our website provides information and resources, and as our General Service Virtual Office operates to support our fellowship. These services help us reach out to those who suffer from chronic pain and chronic illness and ensure that CPA is a vibrant program that is there for all those who need it.

In recovery, honesty and accountability are vital. We keep our agreements with the people and places that make CPA possible. When we pay the company that hosts our online meetings, we are being self-supporting. When we pay the rent on time and abide by the rules of the physical space where we hold our meeting, we are being self-supporting. If the location will not accept payment, we can seek another way to maintain balance and create agreed-upon terms. In this way, our group follows our Traditions.

Our groups don't need a lot of money to provide the necessary resources for our meetings. We don't amass and hold funds we don't need—an excess of funds will divert us from our primary spiritual aim. Instead, we make sure there are sufficient funds and raise more, as needed, for CPA events, literature, or other needs. We discover as we go how much money is necessary to run both our group and CPA as a whole, and then we maintain a prudent reserve to ensure we don't have too much, nor too little, money to manage. Our success in CPA is measured in recovery, not by our financial wealth.

INDEPENDENCE AND UNITY
Each of us decides how to step up and meet the responsibilities of supporting the well-being of our group and CPA as a whole. Our groups make choices based on their own resources, which include money as well as energy, experience, time, and talents. This is how we can all thrive as we meet our needs together. We are independent, and we are unified.

A vital, counterintuitive part of being self-supporting involves asking for help when we need it. Those of us in CPA know this well. It is possible at times that a group may need to ask for assistance from its membership. When we give within the fellowship, the bonds that are formed increase our unity. When we take care of our own needs, we are free to run the fellowship as we wish, with no one controlling us. When we have charge of all our resources, our survival is in our hands.

II. In Our Service Bodies

COMPASSIONATE PARTICIPATION
Our service work builds the structure of CPA that supports us. This service may consist of helping with literature,

organizing Intergroups, performing public outreach, or leading a committee.

Our energies in supporting the service structure are always focused on supporting our primary purpose. This requires that we attend to our own program of recovery. There are times when our enthusiasm is greater than what our bodies can manage; as individuals and groups, we need to allocate and balance not just financial resources but our energy and our cognitive and physical resources as well, so no one feels overwhelmed. Our human resources need to be mindfully considered along with our financial ones.

We pay attention to what we can and can't give in service work. We apply our program tools and don't make time and energy commitments that will not serve our own well-being and may not be realistic. Just as we have a prudent reserve of monies, we are cognizant of energy expenditures. When we plan projects supporting our service structure, we want to be sure we have the resources to carry them out, which includes people with the skills and energy to complete them. We need to determine what kind of commitment is required and whether it is prudent for us, individually and as a service body.

As contributing members of CPA, we focus our energy, our time, and our hearts on supporting the primary purpose. In doing this, we want to be sure we do not harm ourselves. Our efforts should strengthen our program, our personal recovery, and our sense of self-worth. If we find we are struggling, we need to speak with our sponsor, pray for guidance, and determine what changes need to be made. We each work our own program and take responsibility for what we are capable of contributing. Since this can change rapidly and unexpectedly for some of us, we keep in mind to ask for help when we need it. When any person needs to turn over their responsibilities or delay completion of a task, we meet this with patience and understanding.

III. In All Our Affairs

Tradition Seven, when applied to our personal lives, invites freedom and empowerment. Some members of CPA rewrite it this way: *"We are self-supporting, caring for our well-being, physically, emotionally, and spiritually. We ask for help when we need it, turning first to a Higher Power for support, instead of expecting others to be responsible for us."*

When we are self-supporting, we don't depend on other people for our happiness. We recognize that our moods and attitudes are something that only we can manage. When we interact with others, we do not seek to control one another to get what we think we need or want. We don't have that power, nor do they. Being self-supporting means we are not victims. We take responsibility for our feelings rather than blaming others. We look at our own behavior and reactions, remembering to stay focused on our choices and our own recovery.

We are responsible for ourselves, even if we need others for our daily functioning. We are responsible for our emotional and spiritual growth. As we actively practice being self-supporting and invite our Higher Power into this process, we more easily focus on our own needs and wants while cooperating with others. We recognize our equal status in all our relationships. Being responsible for ourselves makes this equality possible. It is not the quantity of what we can do, it is the quality. Honesty with ourselves and others about what in fact we can offer can create harmony and clarity where there may once have been discord and confusion. We can have a healthy dependence on others and still be a giver, not a taker.

We trust our Higher Power that we will receive what we need to keep growing and be safe. We trust ourselves and have faith in our abilities and our self-agency. As we identify our needs and authentically express them, we are supporting ourselves emotionally. We can stay connected with others while knowing each of us is a separate person.

Taking care of our well-being means we need to be aware of our feelings and motivations. We often need to request help, and when we do so, we choose to be fully honest and direct. Are we being manipulative in any way? Are we respectful of the other person? Are we feeling like a victim? Are we victimizing someone else? These questions help us to find clarity when our goal is to be self-supporting and stay connected. Our experience working Tradition Seven in our program gives us an understanding of how satisfying it is to relate to others in this way.

We participate in our relationships within our personal parameters. These parameters are dynamic—our needs and capacities may change, and we adjust as conditions shift. There is no formula that says we all have to contribute equally. In fact, we have found that having a "balance sheet," keeping track of who has done what and when, perhaps measuring our own and others' worth by this accounting, is detrimental to unity. It is important to our self-esteem and to our recovery that we share responsibilities and do our part. We are self-supporting, and we must each define that according to our life circumstances.

Resentments can occur in relationships when we are living with pain and illness. We may feel we've lost our identity when we can no longer contribute financially. There are times we need to depend on others. This is the counterintuitive piece of being fully self-supporting, in action. It is a significant, spiritually wholesome act to ask for help and receive with gratitude. We still, however, need to find what our contribution can be. We may need to re-examine our role in our relationships and discover new ways to contribute, financially or otherwise. How can we be self-supporting, emotionally and spiritually? How do we have dignity and respect, even if we are physically and/or financially dependent on others? We are valuable members of our relationships, and our recovery—while specifically practicing this Tradition—can make this evident to ourselves and others.

In money matters, just as we do in our groups, we practice honesty and clarity. It is our responsibility to manage our finances.

We make sure our spending does not exceed our ability to pay. We look at ways we may be accruing debt or fearfully amassing large sums we don't intend to use, and we ask for help.

> **ASSOCIATED SPIRITUAL PRINCIPLE:** *Being Self-Supporting*
>
> We accept no outside contributions to protect our spiritual foundations. This gives us a sense of freedom and empowerment. We support the fellowship as a whole, financially and through service.

TRADITION SEVEN IN ACTION

Every CPA group ought to be fully self-supporting, declining outside contributions.

VOICES OF OUR MEMBERS

Groups have expenses: rent, literature, and costs associated with public outreach. Supporting my group can take many forms. I can hold a group position, I can assist with setup and cleanup, I can volunteer to read our Steps or Traditions, or I can simply remember to take CPA brochures and flyers to my next doctor's appointment...but my group also needs my financial support. The amount I give isn't important. It's the tangible expression of gratitude and knowing that I am doing my part to carry the CPA message of recovery. CPA has taught me that changed attitudes can aid recovery. I practice shifting my thoughts from lack and limitation to grateful abundance every time I make a Seventh Tradition contribution.

When I came to CPA, I could no longer work, and fear of financial insecurity set in. My once-energetic life was grounded due to extreme fatigue. I was frightened even to do the dishes for the potential consequences of expending the energy. Even something as simple setting up a Seventh Tradition auto-draft at my bank to contribute seemed too taxing. As I began to recover in CPA, I came to believe that my Higher Power knew my physical and financial needs. I experimented with putting this new attitude to the test. Time after time, often in the most unexpected ways, my Higher Power provided for me, sometimes just in the nick of time. Today I'm able to serve and contribute financially to CPA from a grateful heart instead of a fearful mind, trusting that Higher Power will continue to support, guide, and know my needs better than I do. This trust supports my well-being, as my contribution supports my group—it's me, putting Tradition Seven into action.

I had to leave work because of my illness and had to fight for a long time to get benefits. During that in-between time, my checking account would literally go down to nothing, so I couldn't have any automatic payments—no matter how small—going out of my account. I would occasionally make a donation to my meeting because I was grateful for how CPA was making my life better in many ways. I was able to do some service, but rarely could I contribute financially. When I finally received my benefits, it was satisfying to set up a monthly donation to CPA from my bank. Chronic Pain Anonymous is making my life so much more livable. It's important to me that it continue to exist. I know that the money I contribute is well used. I appreciate the accountability we receive from the Board of Trustees because I want to know that my money is being spent in ways that carry the message and make the fellowship strong.

I've turned my life and my will over to a Power greater than myself, no matter how limited my resources are. I'm not trusting my Higher Power if I'm not willing to give up a dollar for a meeting. When I give that dollar, it's my way of saying, "I trust you to take care of me," even when that's some of my grocery money. I find that really powerful.

Sometimes I feel a little reluctant. When I do, I tune in to my HP and follow the guidance I receive. In this way, I contribute what and when it is reasonable for my situation and never see recovery as a free ride. I am part of my meeting—as a giver and a receiver.

We have a group that meets in a facility in which their policy doesn't allow them to receive funds from other organizations. So instead of paying rent, occasionally we give them a gift card to the office supply store. They have a library, so we provide them with our CPA books. Sometimes, we just buy them flowers. When a facility has a policy of not taking rent, we can create "terms of gratitude." It was definitely received as a show of gratitude, and we considered these gestures the expenses of holding our weekly meeting.

When I volunteered for the role of Group Representative for a CPA meeting, I was unsure if I was the right person for the job. I was encouraged to step up to take the role and try my best—just as every other member with a service position does. Then I became a delegate and attended a World Service Conference. I was thrilled by how much detailed work and preparation is involved in the support of Chronic Pain Anonymous and how much care is taken to preserve the Traditions as the fellowship grows. It's not easy. Sometimes there are no immediate, clear answers as to how to apply the Traditions to the evolution and sustainability of the program, and it can be slow work to make changes. Time was always taken to consider carefully the many aspects involved before making a decision. Taking time to pause and care allows for Higher Power to be a part of the process. This reminds me that I don't serve myself by rushing through feelings for an outcome, even when I'm uncomfortable. When I wait, I allow my Higher Power in. Pausing and caring is one way I practice being fully self-supporting, in my own life and in service to my group and CPA.

Our service bodies exist to perform tasks that our individual groups cannot, such as publishing books and responding to inquiries about CPA from around the world. These services require fiscal support. So I not only contribute to my local group, but I have set up a monthly bank auto-draft contribution to CPA. Not only do I personally benefit from all that Chronic Pain Anonymous service bodies offer, but I wish to ensure the future of CPA for those who still suffer.

I also ensure our service bodies are self-supported by actively participating in them. All members' voices are equally valuable, and sharing my unique experience, strength, and hope is vital to the health and wealth of our collective group conscience. I (not "someone else") am responsible for the future and unity of CPA.

One of my mother's favorite sayings was: "If you don't vote, you don't get to complain." That's really how I feel about service in CPA. If I do not contribute my voice, my time, my thoughts, and my heart to our service bodies, to literature development, to decision-making, then I don't get to complain. I can disagree but still honor the group conscience, with gratitude, but if I am not contributing my time and energy and if I'm not appreciating those who do, then I have no right to complain. I can be so willful—"I'm going to do what I want to do when I want to do it. And if I don't want to contribute, that's fine." That is an unskillful attitude. If I have done my very best, if I have done my part, then I can rest, knowing that my side of the street is clean. It still doesn't give me license to complain. In fact, if I've contributed my part, even when things don't go my way, I find I'm less inclined to complain. I feel serene because I've been of service.

My sanity is deeply invested, deeply reliant on CPA. I'm being self-centered when I don't contribute.

I am so grateful for the service I do on our service bodies. It's a spiritual experience for me. My program is strengthened as I show up for opportunities to cooperate with others. My fear is challenged, my faith is tested, and I engage in tasks and behaviors I have never done before. Doing CPA service is being fully self-supporting—of my recovery. According to Step Twelve, I'm responsible for doing service as part of my recovery plan. If I want all the benefits CPA has to offer, I have to be willing to work the whole program—not just the Steps, not just fellowship in meetings, but also giving back through service or financially. I am practicing my whole program, and the benefits have been enormous.

At my phone meeting, it is necessary to arrange ahead of time who is going to chair, but none of us know what condition we will be in when our turn comes up. So, for every time slot we fill, we have backups so the meeting will flow smoothly if the first person is unable to step into the role. Recently, I was leading a meeting, and during the meeting my cognition got worse, and so I asked, "Is there someone here who can take over for me?" It helps me to say yes to service when I know that if I can't complete it, someone else is willing to step in.

I'm so grateful for service because it stretches me. The paradox is that asking for help and being fully self-supporting are the same—when I ask for help, I am being fully self-supporting. And those who offer backup are too. They support a fellow member, their own recovery, and the meeting as a whole. It's so clear that we are all in it together. It's beautiful. Knowing my limits and honoring my body are being fully self-supporting, and so is asking for help.

Although I had a lot of experience doing service at many levels in another Twelve Step program, when I arrived in CPA, I felt that I had nothing to give. I was beaten down from trying to figure out how to live with chronic pain and chronic illness on my own. The self-esteem I had gained in my other program had disappeared, causing me to question if I would ever be able to competently contribute to the world.

After attending many CPA meetings, I knew it was time to give back and to get involved. I had learned that service is important for personal recovery. Since the meetings were virtual, a way to serve was more challenging than I was used to—like arranging chairs or picking up trash in a face-to-face meeting. A meeting I regularly attended was seeking a member to chair one meeting per month. I had not done this in CPA, nor in a virtual meeting. I was concerned that I might not feel well on that one day each month, or my brain issues would cause problems in following the format. Yet I knew I was responsible to do my part in keeping CPA going; why should it "not" be me? Tradition Seven tells me that it is up to all CPA members to ensure the program continues functioning—financially and also at all service levels.

CPA members encouraged me, offering compassion and kindness. Most important to me was their assurance that one of them would substitute for me if I had a hard pain day. I signed up! I fumbled a bit the first few times but discovered that I still had the necessary skills. I only heard appreciation! My confidence, self-esteem, and gratitude for being able to contribute all grew. Now, a year later, knowing that others believed in me enough to give me that responsibility still brings a smile to my face! This confidence has carried over into my life outside of CPA as well. Service has helped restore my whole life. I can feel my ability to be fully self-supporting and grow every day.

Before chronic pain and chronic illness, I was indeed fully self-supporting. I prided myself on my independence and my ability to contribute financially to my family. I was a go-getting only child, and this was the source of my self-worth. Tradition Seven took on a whole new meaning once my illness took hold. I could no longer identify myself as being fully self-supporting, as I was physically dependent on my family. With this loss of identity, depression set in, and I found myself seeking not only physical support but emotional support as well.

CPA has been invaluable on my healing journey from the emotional and spiritual debilitation of living with chronic pain and chronic illness. It gives me tools that allow me to be emotionally fully self-supporting. I can self-soothe with slogans and apply the Twelve Steps to that which is troubling me. I surrender the belief that self-supporting means it is all up to me, that I have to do it, "buck up," "pull myself up by my own bootstraps," and, "if I don't do it, it won't get done." Reliance on my Higher Power is now a way of life, not only for my emotional needs but for my financial needs as well. I have come to believe that there is a Power greater than my own best efforts that not only cares for me but is actively supporting me—financially, emotionally, and physically. When I am frightened, CPA reminds me that my Higher Power is just a breath away, and I am never truly alone.

At first it was so hard to maintain my dignity when I stopped being able to make my own meals and shower on my own. I felt like I was too young to be dealing with this and wondered how I would maintain my sense of self as parts of me slipped away. Tradition Seven is about being self-supporting…about how I contribute to supporting myself and my family, even with *this* body.

As I worked the Steps, I began to see how my pride was getting in the way. For me, the solution lay in the Serenity Prayer words "the wisdom to know the difference." I got over my reservations about using mobility aids, as my disability is invisible and I was afraid that I would be judged for being lazy or too young to be using them. But they give me independence and freedom. My mobility aids have helped me in just about every task and allow me to have more autonomy.

The other main struggle that stood between me and being self-supporting was my lack of communication about my needs. I had to stop feeling like a burden and letting this belief get in the way of asking for help. I realized that being too vague about what I need assistance with only caused confusion for me and for those trying to help me. My contribution is to be specific about what I am asking for, and I've learned to say it calmly and lovingly. There's no need to be harsh. The wisdom I've gained is about being humble and practicing honesty in the interactions with my caregivers. I may rely on others to get through my day, but I do so with the understanding of "the courage to do the things I can."

The Serenity Prayer is an important tool for me as I apply Tradition Seven in all my affairs.

One of the things I have learned is that when I ask for help, it is always okay for the other person to say, "No." And in fact, I have to count on them to be able and willing to say, "No." If they do something for me and resent it, it's going to harm our relationship, and I'm not going to want to ask them for help in the future.

Before I became ill, I really enjoyed helping others. I had an elderly neighbor, and when it would snow, when I scraped off my car, I would do hers too. When I took out my trash, I would take hers out too. And that felt good. Now I am not able to do those things, and sometimes I'm not able to do them for myself. It took a while to get good at asking for help, but someone pointed out to me that if no one receives, then no one can give.

When each person involved in requesting or offering help honors their own boundaries, both the giver and the receiver are being fully self-supporting. And this strengthens the relationship.

Communication is the most useful tool that I have on this journey of self-support. I used to hide my flare-ups and pain, and then I would develop resentments because others had expectations of me and I was not clear about what I could or could not do. I wasn't communicating honestly and directly with those around me. I have to be responsible for doing my part in my relationships. Being self-supporting is not about what I can do or how much I have. For me, it's about remembering to include clear and honest communication and support the give-and-take that is part of any healthy relationship.

For instance, there are many times I need to turn to my husband for help. However, there are times when I get stronger and more able to function, and it can be hard for him to step back. I want to ask for care and for help, until if possible, I can do it myself. This is a new way to see my need for assistance and an opportunity for clear communication: I can ask for help until I can do it myself. My situation changes as I cycle between getting stronger and weaker. I need to let him know that part of the quality of my life improving is that when I can, I need to do things for myself. It's also important for me to see that he sometimes needs time to adjust to the change.

I have periods of time in which I am much more functional than other times, when I'm less functional. Financially, I live on a fixed income. Someone suggested to me that if I was accepting funds from my mother to help me out, that I wasn't in alignment with Tradition Seven. However, I am learning a deeper lesson: that by reaching out and being willing to receive help, I am acting in humility. This gives me a sense of self-esteem.

For two years, I lived with a friend, rent-free, and I had the hardest time accepting that this arrangement was okay. It was a gift to me that the person generously offered. I have a few friends right now who are offering to help me move; each of them has said, "I understand you're trying to practice your Tradition Seven, so I'd like to offer you moving expenses as a gift." I cried with gratitude because I genuinely need extra help.

It's been good for me to be honest and to accept help so that I can live. Deprivation and scarcity are not good for my heart, my soul, or my well-being. My Higher Power wants me to be as healthy as I can be, as well as I can be, and to participate in sharing, and in service—as I am now—in a recovery program that serves others.

It is important for me to engage in service. If these gifts allow me to do that work, I will gratefully receive support from others.

I very much wish I could make the income I once did in my prior career, but that's not possible now. I am accepting my situation as it is, being honest about it, and praying for help from my Higher Power. Answers always come. Someone will show up and drive a truck right when I need it, without my knowing where it came from. Sometimes, it's a total stranger. I need to open my heart to receive these gifts. When others are in need and I have services that I can offer, I offer those. Or, when I do find myself in a place where I'm financially flush for a moment and can help someone else, I do that too. We don't have to hurt ourselves to be fully self-supporting. That's not the point of Tradition Seven at all.

When fear about an unknown situation comes up, and I think, "Oh no, what if this terrible thing happens?" I find it helpful to switch my thinking to, "What if something amazing happens?" Recently, when I was in a situation where I did not know where I would be living in the upcoming months, I started thinking: What if I get a phone call from a friend who says, "I need someone to babysit my mansion in the tropics and call the pool boy when I'm gone for a while." If that were to happen, I would be like, "I'm there!" I try to practice that. "What if something incredible happens?" Changing my mind-set from one of fear to one of faith in possibilities is one way I'm being fully self-supporting today.

WORKING TRADITION SEVEN
Every CPA group ought to be fully self-supporting, declining outside contributions.

The following questions can help deepen your understanding and application of Tradition Seven in your recovery and in all your affairs. Use these questions with your sponsor or sponsee or your CPA group, or explore them on your own, selecting the ones that are relevant.

1. What does being self-supporting mean in our group?
2. Since we decline outside contributions, what are some examples of these? How can we decline graciously?
3. How do I help my group and CPA remain self-supporting? Can I be generous in new ways?
4. What role does gratitude or fear play in my willingness to give?
5. Do I respect the group treasurer and the job they do?
6. Do I contribute to CPA when there is an appeal?
7. How does my group manage finances, such as rent, literature, or donating to CPA?
8. Does my group hold business meetings? If this does not happen, how can I help encourage this practice?
9. Does my group have a Group Representative? If not, how can I help encourage this position be filled?
10. How do I regularly participate in service and encourage others to do so as well?
11. Do we rotate positions in my group? In my service bodies?

12. How do I see my Higher Power providing for my needs?
13. How do I contribute to and support my own well-being?
14. Do I take responsibility for my health needs, such as diet, exercise, and self-care?
15. How do I know when I am giving too much or too little?
16. In what ways do I ask for and accept the help of others?
17. How am I responsible for myself even though I may depend on others for daily functioning?
18. How am I self-supporting emotionally?
19. How do I take responsibility for my feelings and not blame others or see myself as a victim? If I do find myself feeling like a victim, what program tools can I use to shift my attitude?
20. Is there anyone in my personal life I am making my Higher Power?
21. Do I give only on my own terms? How do I practice generosity? Am I able to do this unselfishly (and what does that word mean to me)?
22. Do I manage my personal finances responsibly?
23. What does applying Tradition Seven in all my affairs look like today?
24. In what areas of my life do I already practice and understand the need for:
    - Being self-supporting
    - Supporting the whole

- Building spiritual strength
- Willingness to give
- Honesty about finances
- Independence and unity
- Compassionate participation

25. How can I include these spiritual tools where they may be missing in my life today?

Tradition Eight

Chronic Pain Anonymous should remain forever non-professional, but our service centers may employ special workers.

> **Chronic Pain Anonymous should remain forever non-professional, but our service centers may employ special workers.**

We don't sell our experience, strength, and hope. We freely give what we have received as members in CPA. However, we pay professionals to work in jobs that provide specific services to CPA, such as bookkeepers, lawyers, and technical support, so we can function. There are no paid professional CPA members in Twelve Step work.

SPIRITUAL TOOLS FOR PRACTICING TRADITION EIGHT

- Freely sharing the gifts of recovery
- Recovering together
- Non-professionals doing service
- Leaving our professional roles outside
- Accountability

APPLYING TRADITION EIGHT

I. In Our Groups

FREELY SHARING THE GIFTS OF RECOVERY
This is a fellowship of reciprocal support. We recover using the Twelve Steps, and we do this together, finding joy in sharing what we have received in the fellowship. Our own recovery is strengthened and maintained when we give away what we have learned as part of our spiritual growth and so that others may also recover. As we share CPA recovery with each other, we create deep bonds. This may happen one-on-one, with a sponsor or another CPA member, in our groups, and as we do service. The spiritual

alchemy of the Twelve Steps is dependent on this fact: we do not recover alone.

We practice a loving exchange of help and encouragement with each other. We identify with each other's stories and learn that we are not alone in our problems. We share experience, not knowledge. There are no CPA experts. This is a program of mutuality, and each of us is part of its blessings.

Imagine what would happen if, instead, we had to pay one another to receive the gifts of recovery. Immediately, expectations and demands for specific results might arise. We would not be taking personal responsibility for our recovery but would instead feel that since we were paying for it, we'd better get the results of someone else's efforts, knowledge, and skill—and quickly, too. As many of us in CPA can attest, there are numerous therapies, healthcare avenues, and groups we can pay to help us.

Recovery is a safe haven. It is uniquely effective because it utilizes each participant's willingness to become humble and shake off the bondage of living with chronic pain and chronic illness— together. It invites the guidance of a Higher Power, defined only by our own understanding. It is not possible to charge money for this. And if that were done, who then would be "in charge"? The entire structure of CPA would fall apart, and recovery would become just another possible solution to our pain and illness, offered by a hierarchy of individuals, that we can afford for a short time until we tire of it or run out of money. Keeping recovery non-professional means we have access to it at any time of day or night, forever. It is literally priceless.

When we realize the value of our recovery and how it works, it becomes clear that we are all responsible for carrying the message. All we need is to be willing to do so. Our experience, of both our struggles and our release from them, is useful to others, and as we share, we keep the program vital and keep CPA a source of strength and wisdom. When we share our program experience with another member, we often hear what *we* need to hear, either in what we say or in what the other person shares with us—sometimes, this may be something we have forgotten. Participating in this process of giving it away is how recovery works. We grow and learn together.

CPA recovery is a spiritual gift passed from one member to another, from one heart to another. We don't sell what we have—we give it away. There are no strings attached to our service to each other, and Tradition Eight holds this tenet of our program in place by specifically naming it.

RECOVERING TOGETHER

In CPA, we find people with whom we can identify, people who understand us and the challenges of life with chronic pain and chronic illness. Although we share freely, we do not counsel. No one earns certification in CPA, and there are no credentials to achieve. We are equals, and we recover together as equals.

We place our dependence on our Higher Power, not on each other. No one person has answers for another. Instead, we share with each other our experience—how we have worked the Steps of recovery and how our Higher Power may have guided us. This can often be deeply helpful and may even be exactly what another person needs to hear. But we share it because it is our experience, not because we are telling someone what to do or not do.

No matter what professional training we may have, there are no professional CPA members. As we help one another by sharing our experience, strength, and hope, we maintain humility and value each other as fellow members on a journey together. As members share solutions that have worked for them, we can begin to feel encouraged that if others can find happiness and serenity, so can we.

Because there are no authorities or experts, we can relax into a space of unity and collaboration where no one feels pressured to "know more" or have it all together. We don't focus on what we do outside of the meetings, how long we have been in CPA, or what service we have done in the fellowship. In every meeting, one day at a time, we are always just one member in recovery who is sharing with others. We don't hire anyone to speak at our meetings. No one gets financial rewards for carrying our message. We have found a way to be free of the obsession of living with chronic pain and chronic illness, and we want to pass it on to others. We simply tell about our own lives.

We are present for each other and listen to one another as equals. This is one of the ways we practice anonymity (Tradition Twelve). We share our names but not our titles or associations. We recognize the humanity in each of us, and we connect through the suffering we have known and the program we are working today. We each have something to bring to others: a newcomer's experience can be just as valuable and life-altering to hear as a longtimer's share.

In our meetings, we are willing to ask for and to offer help, as equals. We share our recovery, our wisdom, and our compassion. We are one person living with chronic pain and chronic illness helping another. When we have disagreements and challenges, we remember that we are brought together for the same reason. We are grateful for CPA and endeavor to reach out to those who still suffer.

NON-PROFESSIONALS DOING SERVICE

Our service work is an investment in our own spiritual healing and transformation, and it deepens and enhances our recovery. We are freely given the gifts of experience, strength, and hope that are passed down by others who came before us. All we need to do as members is pass it on as well. This is how our fellowship grows. The most important service is welcoming the newcomer, extending the hand of kindness and compassion we received, and passing it on to others.

The service work we do is spiritually fulfilling and expresses our gratitude through action. We take on service roles as volunteers—we are not paid for our Twelve Step work, whether we are serving as our meeting's Group Representative, giving a talk in the community, or chairing a meeting. We are focused on our primary purpose—carrying the message—and not on personal ambitions. We are one among all the others who came before us, volunteers dedicated to sustaining and growing CPA. Our service is offered with humility and anonymity.

The sponsor/sponsee relationship is at the heart of working the Steps and the program of recovery in CPA. Sponsors are not paid professionals. A sponsor is just one person who is recovering, sharing with another member. As a sponsor, we are passing on what was given to us. We don't control others or outcomes and don't give advice.

Likewise, trusted servants—members volunteering in service positions—are not paid for their service. Our fellowship supports, trusts, and respects them. We may request specific standards of performance, yet we know they have other obligations and their own health conditions that affect their service. We know they need to set priorities and boundaries as a valuable lesson in their service work. As trusted servants we know our limits and ask for help as we need it; we also remember that we are not in charge, but in service.

As we do service, we can grow and learn new skills. We may discover new areas of interest as we try different positions or work in different service areas. For example, we may keep the books as treasurer for our group, and this may be brand new for us. It is good for our fellowship when we accept a new role, and it is also good for our personal recovery. We don't expect perfection; this expectation inhibits our ability to grow. As we rise to the requirements of a particular position, we develop new capabilities and grow in confidence. We learn we can be accountable. As another example, we chair a meeting for the first time, and although it may seem daunting, we learn we are quite capable of this leadership role.

Learning on the job in this way is possible and fruitful because we are all equals, freely giving our time and attention to service. Again, imagine if each necessary service position had a salary attached to it…the entire fabric of equality, humility, and unity would be unraveled, and with it the strong program we rely on for our recovery would fall apart.

In our service, we are dependable and conscientious. Whether doing service in our group, on a service body, or in the community, the way we act and the manner in which speak are part of being a trusted servant. Our behavior, not our training or our status, is the way we carry the message.

LEAVING OUR PROFESSIONAL ROLES OUTSIDE
Some members of CPA might be professionals in healthcare. But in our meeting, we do not offer service in the capacity of our professional roles. We are here for our own recovery. We introduce ourselves by our name, not by our title in the outside world, leaving our work identities outside of the meeting. In our program of CPA recovery, we share our experience, not our professional knowledge. This frees us and allows us, just like everyone else in the meeting, the opportunity to let go fully into the safety of anonymity and equality and seek the recovery we need.

Practicing Tradition Eight means we go to our meeting for our recovery, not to promote ourselves or our professional programs. It is recommended that we don't offer our professional services to members of our meetings so we can keep our roles clear and have no confusion. We leave our credentials outside the fellowship. We don't advise or consult, and we don't diagnose or treat.

II. In Our Service Bodies

ACCOUNTABILITY
As an organization, Chronic Pain Anonymous Service Board (CPASB) is structured as a U.S. non-profit 501(c)(3) corporation and is maintained by the Board of Trustees. This body of Directors is delegated to manage the legal and financial responsibilities of CPASB. They oversee the publishing of books and other literature, they work with the lawyers who make sure that CPASB is in alignment with legal requirements, and they hire and interact with our website provider and other business entities to support the primary purpose of CPA, the fellowship.

The business organization of CPASB makes it possible for the fellowship to function. This structure requires orderly procedures for maximum service to our groups and members. Volunteers help us keep our costs down; however, we need to hire people for some of these activities. To remain effectively operational, we may pay graphic designers, editors, technical support experts, and people with legal and accounting skills.

As the fellowship grows, it is not practical for it to be run solely by volunteers; we need paid workers to help make our Twelve Step work sustainable and operational. We pay for some services, such as managing the website. We need continuity and consistency to keep the organization able to support our members and to reach out to others who are in need.

If someone in CPA is hired as a special worker in their professional capacity, they need to be paid for their work. We might hire someone for a specific time period, such as to edit a book, or for long-term roles, such as bookkeeper. All the tasks are done to serve the primary purpose, carry the message, and to help CPA be sustainable and grow. If we are paid for our skills in some capacity, there are distinct lines between our paid professional role and any volunteer service work we are providing as a member of CPA.

Our paid special workers are paid not for doing Twelve Step work but for specific jobs. Paid positions in CPA, in which the decisions may affect the members and the direction of the fellowship, are held by CPA members whenever possible. For instance, a graphic artist would not need to be a CPA member. Although the design skills are valuable to us, the artist's work does not directly affect the fellowship.

We employ professionals to support our service efforts and compensate them with appropriate wages for their field. We budget accordingly for special workers and pay for what we deem necessary. We practice prudent use of resources to make it possible for our fellowship to run effectively. We pay a fair rate and have clear accountability and clear descriptions of the job we are filling. We pay for time and expertise. We treat special workers with integrity, respect, and honesty. We include the Traditions in our relationships with all people we interact with in our business interactions—practicing the principles in all our affairs.

The special workers are accountable for carrying out the will of the fellowship when they support our service efforts, and we ensure they carry out their tasks aligned with the Traditions. The Board of Trustees, a body of members and non-members who volunteer their time and skill, oversees all paid service work. The Board is guided by the fellowship through the World Service Conference and through abiding by the Twelve Steps and Twelve Traditions. At times, the Board may delegate some work to the Executive Director or a CPA service body.

III. In All Our Affairs

One possible way of rewriting this Tradition, as it applies to all our affairs, is this: *"We are non-professionals in our relationships and relate as one individual to another. When we have a need of interacting with an expert, we continue to have self-agency for our individual decisions."*

In all our relationships, we are equals who share our experiences in order to reach our goals together. This may not always seem true in the world outside the meeting rooms of CPA. But spiritually speaking, it is always true. In fact, being in the meeting rooms gives us practice discovering this as we interact as equals with people of significantly varied backgrounds from our own. Just as with our fellow members, we don't seek to fix others or expect them to fix us. We each have areas of knowledge; we respect and listen to others, allowing ourselves to reap the benefits of their expertise, as we share our own. We learn we can rely on the skills of others as well our own. Our relationships in all areas of life are improved as we focus on sharing our experience, strength, and hope with each other as equals.

The challenges of life don't have to be faced alone. We learn in recovery that we can receive help and maintain a sense of independence. We can get help creating structures that support us in our finances, health, and personal life. We don't have to know how to do everything; we can hire others and ask for their expertise. We learn to trust others to help us and to do a "good enough" job.

Practicing Tradition Eight in all our affairs means we recognize that when we give to someone, we don't have to expect them to return it—we do not need to be compensated for what we give away. When someone gives to us, we can find ways to pass it on rather than feeling that we owe them something for it. We practice a natural reciprocity instead of holding transactional expectations. We trust our Higher Power with the "balance sheet."

It is possible that members have lost avenues in which we experienced self-worth, possibly from our work, a title, or our role in our family. This doesn't mean our self-worth has to be in any way diminished. We can participate in our relationships in new ways, within our capacity, knowing that we are all fellow travelers on this unpredictable journey.

> **ASSOCIATED SPIRITUAL PRINCIPLE:** *Integrity*
>
> Recovery is a spiritual gift, not a transaction. "You have to give it away to keep it." Our fellowship is non-professional, and we avoid professional titles. We are a membership of equals: one member, sharing with another member. When necessary jobs need filling, we accountably pay our special workers in accordance with the principles of the program.

TRADITION EIGHT IN ACTION

Chronic Pain Anonymous should forever remain non-professional, but our service centers may employ special workers.

VOICES OF OUR MEMBERS

I have had a tendency to give other people in my life too much power. One of the most important gifts I've received from CPA is experiencing Tradition Eight in action.

When a member of CPA freely shares with anyone suffering with chronic pain or illness, what they say is motivated by a desire to share what they have received and a desire to work Step Twelve. When a health professional charges a fee to provide services, the motives and dynamic change into specified roles. This can be helpful to me of course, but it is not the work of one CPA member freely sharing their experience, strength, and hope. One important change that happens when there is no profit involved is that the giver can receive an enormous spiritual experience, while the one receiving experiences a gift of personal empowerment and choice.

Tradition Eight helps me to know that everyone else in the program, whether they're my sponsor, someone I might have a crush on, or someone holding an authoritative-seeming service position is just "another person in the rooms." I have learned that when I allow others to be an expert on my life or put them on a pedestal, it only harms me.

I am grateful that my fellow CPA members and I don't give medical and mental health advice, as I learned the hard way to leave that to those who are much more learned than I. Before coming to CPA, I believed I had to be my own dietician, doctor, physical therapist, and mental health expert. I had extreme prejudice against all Western medicine, especially pharmaceuticals, which my condition now demanded. I fought my mental health team for a year and a half, stating that, "I can't be depressed and anxious because I have a Twelve Step program." It was only when I surrendered my self-will and admitted the reality of my emotional powerlessness that the amazing trifecta of professionally guided medication and counseling plus the wonders of CPA led to my current ability to live peacefully, joyfully, and comfortably with myself and others.

I have a doctorate and generally use letters after my name. However, I don't put them up on a videoconference meeting. We are all equals in CPA. I do sometimes, at a meeting, say I am a former professor. It is important to me to share that I was a professor, how far from that career I am right now, and how much I am grieving the loss. I need to share about this loss in my life in a way that is caring and compassionate toward myself. For some of us, it is important that we continue to identify with our lost professional roles as we recover and grow toward acceptance. Sometimes this means naming those roles in our shares, as part of our CPA recovery stories.

Tradition Eight is a reminder to be right-sized. Can I be a member among members? Am I contributing from my ego or from my heart in meetings? When I come from a place of what I've done, what I've accomplished, I set myself apart from others. And it can be subtly divisive. When I respond as a member among members, it creates unity. I am so grateful for CPA—that we greet each other with unconditional kindness. I just want to be human. Not a human doer, a human achiever. Just a human lover.

I went to my first Twelve Step meeting at 15, and I am now 42, so I have been very attached to my identity as a recovering person over the years. I think this is because I do not have a lot of professional accomplishments to speak of, and I also have difficulty committing to and following through on things I start. So the fact that I have committed to recovery for so many years has become very important to me.

Recovery has been a place where I have always felt welcome, and once I got over the initial shock of whatever brought me there, it became a place where I could excel, achieve my goals, and even surpass my own expectations of myself. Family and friends, in and outside of the program, noticed changes in me and gave me recognition and praise, which made my attachment to my recovery identity grow. As positive as this has been for me, it has also contributed to me acting and feeling like I am an expert on recovery. I have often gotten carried away with this feeling and told myself that I *was* a kind of expert, since I have so much experience…forgetting all humility. I have caught myself "explaining" recovery to a newcomer or even to my sponsor instead of just sharing my feelings and experiences as honestly as possible.

I need to remind myself that I always have more to learn. This is the attitude that will bring me recovery, healing, insight, and growth. As long as I am telling myself I am an expert on something, I am blocking anything new and beneficial from getting in.

When I had to leave my job on a newspaper due to illness, I came to understand how deeply my self-identity was attached to what I did for a living. I had to ask myself, "Who am I?" and "What is my purpose in life?" I learned in CPA that I did not want to know how someone earned their living or what their political affinities were, nor was any conversation about this in a meeting appropriate. I did want to know the nature of recovery, and the answer to the question, "How did you do it?" I have learned that the measure of someone is their walk, not their talk. And this includes me. I am not measurable by my profession, affiliations, or titles. I am a human among humans.

I am so grateful for the apprentice concept we use in CPA. It provides safe waters for me to test my abilities and to take risks in a new position that my Higher Power has inspired me to undertake. I have received excellent mentorship, with CPA members sharing their skills with me. Rewarding relationships and friendships have developed. I may not have known these folks if I had not set aside what I thought I could and couldn't do based on my own work history. My life is more enriched, and my self-esteem has increased.

I am so grateful that social class, career paths, and diplomas lose their importance when we gather together in CPA service. We meet as equals, and our individual voices are important to CPA's future. My unique skills are celebrated, not required.

I am grateful to know that our fellowship practices the spiritual principle of recognizing our limitations and asking for specialized help when needed. We always pay a competitive wage when we employ special workers. How tempting it could be to cry poverty or "noble cause" to justify reduced wages, yet we practice the spiritual principles of honesty, faith, and integrity in all our business affairs.

In my service on the CPASB Board of Trustees, I learned much about our legal and financial responsibilities. I worked with trusted servants and supporters of CPA who were focused on CPA's primary purpose, on outreach to professionals, and on ensuring CPA "kept the lights on." It allowed me to be involved in ways I never imagined and gave me a new understanding of all the people who work in the background. Just as in any meeting, those on the Board are no greater or less than any other trusted servant. They are directed by the World Service Conference, which represents the fellowship. The Board is entrusted with the administrative tasks that ensure CPA can provide the services requested by the fellowship. None of us are "professionals"; we rotate in and out of service positions as is necessary and healthy for ourselves and for CPA. There are positions that cannot practically be held by volunteers, and we pay a fair wage to those special workers.

There is so much going on "behind the scenes," and I am proud to be a trusted servant in a structure of such integrity.

Am I paying my housekeeper appropriately? Just because I am disabled doesn't mean I should get a break. I had pled poverty and therefore exception from paying a standard rate. It damaged a relationship and made me feel awful about myself and perpetuated my victim mindset. Today, I pay what people ask, or, if I do not wish to pay their rate, I search for someone else. I don't negotiate salaries using my disability as a justification not to pay someone what they think their work is worth.

When I was in dire financial circumstances, between leaving work and getting benefits, some friends helped me out and were very generous. When my situation was resolved, I called and let them know I was doing okay and offered to pay them back. One said nothing was needed, or I could pay it forward. And the other person said that that would work as well. Paying it forward, I helped someone who had a problem with their phone at the phone meetings. I contacted her and said, "I would be honored to buy you a telephone," and she accepted. It felt nice to be able to do this.

Practicing Tradition Eight in "all my affairs" isn't about owing the people I receive from; it is about practicing integrity and reciprocity, which feels so good.

There were many years when I couldn't grocery shop, cook, or do laundry or any household chores. At the time, I thought I was worthless, with everyone doing everything for me. Those were hard times. Now that I am at this healthier stage in my life, I enjoy giving to people, knowing it was given to me. I can pass it on. There is a story arc we are not aware of, a larger narrative of our life. Receiving from others was a gift to them, they felt good, and now when I have opportunities, I can give to others. My self-worth is not dependent on how much I give or receive. This exchange just looks different at different times, and I am always a person of worth.

Tradition Eight releases me from the overwhelm of trying to do everything myself. I can ask for special help when I need it. Chronic pain and chronic illness dramatically changed my family life dynamics. I balked at the idea that I could no longer drive anywhere I wanted, at any time I wanted. Things that I could once do with enthusiasm and consistency became but a fading memory. As I grieved my multiple losses, I made the unskillful choice not to go anywhere.

The day came when I had to travel, and my husband was unavailable to take me. I cried, ranted, and then pouted. Finally, I prayed, and HP reminded me that despite my feelings of shame, I had best ask for help. I timidly called a girlfriend, explained the situation, repeatedly apologized for the late notice, and practically begged for a ride. What she said next has stayed with me to this day. "Thank you for giving me the opportunity of good karma." Wow! She made me feel as if I were doing her a favor instead of being a burden. I will be forever grateful to this "special worker," sent straight from Higher Power, who gave me permission to reframe my negative thinking around asking for help.

WORKING TRADITION EIGHT
Chronic Pain Anonymous should remain forever non-professional, but our service centers may employ special workers.

The following questions can help deepen your understanding and application of Tradition Eight in your recovery and in all your affairs. Use these questions with your sponsor or sponsee or your CPA group, or explore them on your own, selecting the ones that are relevant.

1. Do I remember I am a member of CPA and not an expert? Do I treat others in my group as experts?
2. Do I remember I am not in CPA as a professional, no matter the training I have had?
3. Do I remember I am not an expert on recovery?
4. Do I know I don't have to be a perfect model of recovery?
5. How do I know what is the appropriate amount of service for me?
6. How do I find balance between taking care of myself and reaching out for assistance?
7. Do I assess others based on their outside affiliations, titles, or professional roles?

8. When do I need to call on professionals for help? Are there times I should call on professionals and don't?
9. In what ways do I give freely without expecting anything in return? In what ways do I receive and not feel obligated to give back?
10. What does applying Tradition Eight in all my affairs look like today?
11. In what areas of my life do I already practice and understand the need for:
    - Freely sharing the gifts of recovery
    - Recovering together
    - Non-professionals doing service
    - Leaving our professional roles outside
    - Accountability
12. How can I include these spiritual tools where they may be missing in my life today?

Tradition Nine

CPA, as such, ought never be organized, but we may create service boards or committees directly responsible to those they serve.

> CPA, as such, ought never be organized, but we may create service boards or committees directly responsible to those they serve.

Some organization is necessary for effective functioning, and in CPA we keep this simple. Our service structure flow provides the minimum organization needed to comply with legal statutes and accomplish practical administration tasks. Titles don't bring authority, and positions are rotated so we can all share the responsibility of serving the fellowship. We create committees and service bodies as needs come up and dissolve them when they are no longer necessary. We are all accountable to the fellowship in our service roles. We operate in the spirit of service and offer suggestions—we don't dictate, individually or collectively.

SPIRITUAL TOOLS FOR PRACTICING TRADITION NINE

- Most participation, least control
- Clear flow of information
- Trusted servants
- Fellowship of equals
- Structured service bodies

APPLYING TRADITION NINE

I. In Our Groups

MOST PARTICIPATION, LEAST CONTROL

Groups are the core of CPA, as this is where most people first enter the fellowship and begin their recovery journey.

Groups need some structure so they will run smoothly and create an environment that supports recovery. We decide as a group how we want to be organized and which group policies to establish. For instance: How long will we meet for? Will there be a speaker, or will we read literature as our main focus? Groups need a meeting format and for members to take on specific tasks. We keep the structure simple and ensure we practice rotation in the positions. If something is not working, or if we decide we'd like to try something new, the group can make a change.

Groups hold business meetings in which all members are invited to participate as we make choices that keep our meetings strong. This is group autonomy in action. We each have our own opinion, and together we come to a group conscience. Everyone has a voice. We don't need to move quickly or force solutions in this process; instead, we take our time, concentrating on placing our common welfare first, ensuring decisions are beneficial to all.

The more people who participate and the more voices that are heard, the more effective the meeting will be.

No one person or small clique should have all of the responsibility. We need to share the tasks involved to make our meetings function. Practicing Tradition Nine means we do this with a light touch, inviting everyone's input and willingness to serve, without urgency or demanding that things go one way or another. When a majority of our members expect to rotate into and out of service positions, we find our meetings are healthy, with vibrant recovery. Each person can know how to chair the meeting, how to say the Serenity Prayer, or how to sign into a videoconference room. Since there are occasions when a particular member may not be able to attend, the meeting won't fall apart if someone is too ill to fulfill their role; there are always others who can step in for them. We can all learn how to perform the functions that keep our meetings strong so a meeting is not dependent on any one person.

Some groups and some members will be more consistently involved in service; however, each of us has a part to play. Everyone can welcome newcomers. Everyone can share their experience, strength, and hope. Everyone can carry the message.

It is always possible our Higher Power will direct us to fill a position of responsibility. As this happens, we learn to balance our responsibilities with taking care of ourselves. We can always say no at one time and say yes later on. If we can't fulfill a task, we ask for help.

Our groups need to be willing to devote resources of energy, talent, and time to CPA as a whole and participate in decision-making for the worldwide fellowship. The groups *are* the fellowship of CPA, so as a group we look for ways we can be part of the process. Group members choose representatives to speak for them on service bodies such as committees or Intergroups, and at the World Service Conference (WSC). These representatives bring to these service bodies the issues and ideas that matter to their members. There is an exchange of ideas and experiences so that our groups can be helpful to each other as well as the whole.

By suggesting that we have the least possible organization while still making choices that keep us intact and healthy, Tradition Nine allows us to trust our group to a Higher Power and to trust each other. No one is forced to comply with stringent rules. We have only suggested guidelines, such as how to conduct the group business meeting. Not only are there no rules, there are no rulers. Common sense and respect for each and every member—as well as our Higher Power—guide us in our CPA functioning. This Tradition helps us to practice Step Three as a group, turning our will and our lives over to a loving Higher Power.

Some of the ways CPA is not organized are: We don't organize how one person helps another. We reach out and share what is in our experience, but we don't organize what someone says. We don't assign sponsors or mandate Step work. We don't demand that the Steps be studied in a precise way. We don't organize our collective spirit.

By exercising non-organization and freedom of choice, working together, and being guided by our Higher Power, we grow, recover, and thrive.

CLEAR FLOW OF INFORMATION

In order to create an atmosphere that supports recovery and keeps our meetings and fellowship strong, we need a free flow of information that supports our goodwill and passes along necessary data. We operate with transparency rather than creating a hierarchy of those who know and those who do not. We note what needs to be communicated and create systems to share the information. For example, we may keep a notebook or online document and note details of decisions that have been made via group conscience, or any issues that need to be discussed, so whoever is chairing the meeting will have that information available.

Groups and service bodies can communicate between each other at any time. We have trusted servants whose positions are specifically focused on communication between the groups and the rest of CPA. Group Representatives, Intergroup Representatives, and WSC delegates, are some examples of service positions that support the service structure flow in this way. At the meetings, members are informed of the worldwide news by the Group Representative (GR). The GR is responsible for bringing timely, accurate information to their meeting and bringing any issues from their meeting back to the larger fellowship.

Clear communication is needed for groups to function in harmony and unity. We need methods to discuss plans and to allow for changes. We figure out systems that work best in each situation so we can communicate openly and invite discussion. Open communication, utilizing a system that all members understand and can participate in, helps us realize and affirm accountability in service. We are trusted with the tasks we have taken on and report regularly to the body on which we are serving.

Communication requires listening. We listen carefully to each other, practicing mutual respect and honor. We remember to be kind, even when we don't agree. We are all working together in service of our primary purpose, and we allow everyone to participate in the process. When we listen, we stay connected to the group conscience and to our Higher Power.

Committees and service boards are made up of members from many backgrounds, with many different styles of communication. We practice patience, tolerance, and curiosity when we find ourselves surprised by someone else's approach or point of view. We are flexible in our interactions, keep an open mind, and rely on the spiritual guidance of the Traditions and our Higher Power. As we discuss issues together, we may discover new solutions and ideas we had not considered, and we find we can release our preference for a distinct option. It can be a slow process to make decisions in this way, and we do not rush. We take the time that is needed so that we each get a voice.

When we come together beyond the group level, we will be working with people we do not know well and may be challenged by differences. When this happens, we need to put aside our ideas and urge to control and be receptive to new information. At times, new suggestions may enhance our service work, both individually and as a group. We remember that we serve in a spirit of generosity and humbleness. Surrendering to the group conscience reminds us to keep service separate from our need to be right or to be the one with the answer. Sometimes, in order to surrender, we may need to return to the Steps to deepen our own personal recovery.

One significant way we communicate in CPA is through our literature. Written by our members and published by Chronic Pain Anonymous Service Board (CPASB), the resources we have created together can support us all, and we can turn to these resources to help resolve conflicts. Our literature makes certain the message we carry is reliable and consistent, from place to place, year after year. This includes our books, brochures, and informational documents for our fellowship as well as public outreach.

TRUSTED SERVANTS
Our groups and service bodies have roles to be filled. These roles give a framework to the meeting and service bodies and enable them to function effectively. As trusted servants, we have specific

tasks, such as treasurer, timekeeper, or secretary; we don't control, govern, or direct others. The term "trusted servant" was coined by A.A. when it created its literature, and it is apt. It clearly names the great value the fellowship places on each person taking on a service position while also defining their role as one purely of service, not authority.

How does this look in practice? Leadership is given to the membership, not to any one individual. There are no bosses. We derive no authority from our titles. We take on service positions for a limited time period so we don't identify ourselves with any role we are fulfilling. This keeps us right-sized and allows everyone in the fellowship the chance to share responsibility. We pass the job on to someone else, which helps us to participate equally and averts the possibility of any one person exerting control.

Each person performing the duties of a role for a set period of time creates a healthy flow of energy and participation. Doing service is an important component of one's personal recovery, and rotating service allows everyone to have a chance to practice this part of the program. There are opportunities for new people to get involved and for longtimers to try something new. Rotating leadership keeps our fellowship dynamic and prevents dominance and rigid organization in any area of service.

Tradition Nine helps CPA to maintain equality, unity, and an effective recovery environment. We are committed to not be "organized" in a formal, rule-bound way. In CPA, service bodies and roles are open to all members, and anyone can volunteer for a position. There are job descriptions with suggested qualifications for each service role, and as new people contribute, we may learn different and better ways of doing things.

We cooperate with each other and support each other as we learn new roles. We practice mentorship as we rotate positions, which supports constancy over time. We help each other learn the required tasks for each position. As we serve, we listen to feedback with patience and open-mindedness, allowing others to have input so our work can be improved. We don't get caught up in perfectionism in our roles. Nor do we criticize each other's efforts, as each person does a job differently. For example, there are many different ways to hold a business meeting or lead a recovery meeting.

We stay informed. We listen to reports from trusted servants and ask questions to increase our understanding. We participate in the process to ensure tasks have the necessary resources and can be completed. We pay attention because we care about the effectiveness of our program and know we may be the next person doing service and will need the help, attention, and support of our fellows.

We give our trusted servants freedom to accomplish their tasks. Across all levels of service, we are trusted servants with responsibilities and the capacity to use our judgment after conferring with our fellow members and a Power greater than ourselves. We are all custodians of the Twelve Traditions, serving the person who is still suffering as well as serving our group, the fellowship, and our Higher Power. We perform our duties in the spirit of love, giving without expectations, understanding that service is appreciation and fellowship in action.

The Traditions are a set of guidelines that support one another—like the beams of a well-made house. Tradition Nine, upheld by all the others, makes it possible for CPA to function with as little organization and control as possible.

FELLOWSHIP OF EQUALS
We are a fellowship. In CPA, all members are equal, and when they hold titled positions, they are merely trusted servants; titles are not badges of authority. There is no one to give orders, and there is no one to obey. We are united by our common purpose and our common welfare—to recover from the debilitation of living with chronic pain and chronic illness. The recovery of every member depends on this. We offer service without concern for status, and our authority comes from our Higher Power as expressed through our group conscience.

We are never alone in our service. Our groups function and make decisions through an informed group conscience. And we always have, and can ask for, help. When we serve as equals, we are practicing anonymity. There is no ego involved as we work with each other. As trusted servants, we are guided by the group conscience, not the will of individuals. As equals, no one has moral or spiritual superiority, and no one person is in charge. This can be very freeing, creating a fun and non-pressured work environment. We may not have had this experience in any other part of our lives. Discovering what it is to be part of a fellowship of equals is one of the most powerful and unexpected gifts of the program.

The fellowship's principle of equality is demonstrated by our rotation of service. This practice keeps us equal and humble and allows everyone an opportunity to serve and contribute to the membership. It is beneficial for our personal growth to turn over tasks and learn new ones. We may feel inexperienced and uncertain at times, but CPA members don't expect perfection, and in staying open, we can discover new directions for our life we had not previously considered. We honor each other and the fellowship when everyone turns over their position so others can serve and flourish.

II. In Our Service Bodies

STRUCTURED SERVICE BODIES

Some areas of service, especially those beyond the group level, need planning and predictability in order for our fellowship to function and run smoothly. We need service bodies to support us, and this requires a service flow. Groups delegate some responsibilities to the service bodies so they are not diverted from their primary purpose. Service bodies derive their authority from the groups and adhere to the principles of the Traditions.

We have no bosses, but we do have a system to get things done. Service bodies need to be sufficiently organized to function well.

We have scheduled times for meetings, due dates and agendas to guide us. Bills and our special workers need to be paid. We need committees to get projects accomplished. For example, the WSC needs planning and organizing. Creating and publishing new literature takes a lot of coordinated work.

Though we plan and organize in our service bodies, the final authority and decision-making resides in the hands of the groups. Our service bodies, such as boards or committees, are also trusted servants, responsible to those they serve. All of our service bodies maintain the spirit of unity and are dedicated to carrying the message of hope to those who suffer, thus helping to keep CPA strong for the future of the fellowship.

Our boards and committees fulfill necessary and specific tasks. For example, they may hire and supervise paid workers who are involved in website design or literature publishing, or they coordinate conferences and events. The service bodies listen to and carry out the will of the fellowship as expressed in the group conscience. For instance, the fellowship requested a Public Service Announcement at a WSC; as a result, a committee was formed to implement this project. As trusted servants, our service bodies are diligent in following the group conscience of the fellowship and at times may be delegated the authority to make decisions. They have heard our voice and are doing business on our behalf. We trust them, knowing they are acting responsibly and to the best of their abilities, in service to the groups.

The service bodies are responsible to the groups, and the groups have a different but vital responsibility: they need to be attentive to the service bodies and to stay involved. In this way, we hold each other accountable. Staying informed and involved as members brings us together in unity and keeps the fellowship on track, fulfilling its primary purpose—carrying the message of recovery to those who live with chronic pain and chronic illness. Being responsible to those we serve means we practice surrender to the voice of the group conscience, and we learn to participate and to be steady, accepting, and patient. These are skills that serve us in our personal recovery and support the ongoing continuity of our fellowship.

There are many different service bodies. You can learn more about them in the CPA Service Manual, found on the website, that describes our service flow, bodies, and roles.

Here are descriptions of just a couple of them:

WORLD SERVICE CONFERENCE (WSC)
Every group has the opportunity to be represented and can send a delegate to the annual World Service Conference. At the Conference, literature is approved, policy decisions are made, and the fellowship comes together in unity to support our primary purpose. Between conferences, the Board of Trustees and General Service Virtual Office (GSVO) oversee the day-to-day operations of the worldwide fellowship.

CHRONIC PAIN ANONYMOUS SERVICE BOARD (CPASB)
In order to carry out business as a non-profit group, CPA needs a legal entity. Chronic Pain Anonymous Service Board (CPASB) is incorporated as a non-profit 501(c)(3) corporation in the U.S. and is managed by the Board of Trustees. They have no authority over the groups or other service bodies. CPASB has a separate structure with required duties to perform for the corporation. The Board observes legal bylaws and guards the legal rights of the CPA fellowship. CPASB is responsible for publishing our literature so it reflects our message and preserves our unity. The Board does this as trusted servants to the fellowship, with input from the membership.

It is the responsibility of the Board of Trustees to provide CPASB with sound governance and fiduciary and strategic oversight. They oversee the health and growth of CPA under the guidance of the WSC, and they safeguard the CPA Steps, Traditions and Concepts. They manage CPA service funds, assuring the financial integrity and solvency of CPA according to the Concepts. (See Appendix for the Twelve Concepts of Service.)

III. In All Our Affairs

All our relationships contribute to our spiritual growth. When we practice equality and a commitment to freedom of choice and togetherness, rather than being uncompromising, we are bringing Tradition Nine into our daily lives. Our personal relationships, and even our relationships at work or in our healthcare community, do not necessarily benefit from being overly organized.

Just as in the program, we all have an opportunity to serve others. We can put our abilities to use, put status and ego to one side, and take our share of the responsibilities in service of the best outcomes for all involved. Our relationships may look different than they did in the past, before we were affected by chronic pain and illness. No matter what structures are now in place, we all have something to contribute to the relationship.

We can make a point of bringing compassion and kindness to all our interactions. We learn this in the safety of CPA—in the meetings and by doing service—and we practice our program when we bring this Tradition into the rest of our lives. We don't give orders or expect obedience from our family, friends, coworkers, or healthcare providers. We each have a voice, and in some situations, no one person is in charge. We are responsible and accountable, with realistic expectations. We consult with our Higher Power and trust and follow the guidance we receive.

There are times when we need to delegate responsibilities, sometimes those we once managed. We treat others who work for us and on our behalf the way we would treat a trusted servant; we give support and gratitude to others for doing their best for the good of the relationship. We practice trust and flexibility by letting others do their tasks without our input. Practicing this Tradition means we have faith that we don't have to micromanage to be safe. Others don't have to do a job in a certain way—we trust them to accomplish it because we trust our Higher Power is taking care of us.

As we release the idea that we must control situations around us, we begin to accept reality as it is. Tasks won't get done on our timetable and exactly as we would do them. We accept, respect, and can even enjoy this. We trust that others will be able to step up to the challenges in front of them, especially when they need to take over some of our responsibilities. We discover that everything doesn't have to be in perfect order for us to feel comfortable and content. We do our part and allow others to do theirs, while remembering to have gratitude for the talents and time of the people helping us.

We learn to communicate clearly. We understand the value of transparency and can identify what is reasonable in any relationship. Not everyone is able to support us in ways we need. We make sure we don't have unrealistic expectations of others when it comes to our care. We ask our Higher Power for guidance, and we may speak with our sponsor to help us get clarity.

We are equal with others in our relationships, and we keep equality and fellowship in mind as we decide what kind of structure, based on service, is best for each of our relationships. For instance, with a caregiver, we can determine mutually agreed-upon guidelines regarding acceptable conduct. We make sure these are communicated plainly and understood, and we hold one another accountable for honoring them. We practice mutual trust, honesty, and respect.

In order for each of us to be "responsible to those we serve," we must be honest about what we can and are willing to give. We may be fearful of confrontation and conflict; however, in the spirit of our primary purpose and mutual respect, we are honest when these situations arise. When we openly communicate about our needs and protect our serenity, our safety, and our well-being, we are being responsible not only to ourselves but to people in our relationships.

No one person is responsible for everything. We do our part and let others do theirs, letting go of perfection. We see whether we can rotate responsibilities so no one person carries more than their share or has more control. We trust others to fulfill their responsibilities without interference. We can offer our ideas and not force them on others, and we enjoy trusting each other and don't force compliance. No one in our relationships need have power or authority over another. We can ask someone to take on a responsibility, but they are free to decline or suggest an alternative. We practice *Let go and let God.*

> **ASSOCIATED SPIRITUAL PRINCIPLE:** *Flexible Structure of Service*
>
> We are one of many trusted servants. We are all equal and contribute our share to support unity and the primary purpose without applying stringent organization or control.

TRADITION NINE IN ACTION

CPA, as such, ought never be organized, but we may create service boards or committees directly responsible to those they serve.

VOICES OF OUR MEMBERS

This Tradition reminds me of the importance of keeping a group history and archiving business meetings. As my group grows and changes, having the history and archives helps us learn from past challenges and reinforces unity.

In my personal recovery, my past doesn't dictate my future, but it does offer valuable lessons that can make my life easier. And it shows me just how far I have come.

With a little bit of simple organization, group archives give us a sense of our past, remind us of our group conscience, and reveal the growth of our group as a healthy recovery environment.

I don't yet have a clear understanding of what service work I can do in CPA. I'm just now learning what I can do without hurting myself. The idea that I can try something, and if I find it to be too much (which I didn't know when I agreed to it) that I can hand it to someone else, is so freeing. I was asked to work on a document, and I didn't know I couldn't do it until I tried. Having the freedom to be able to try something, and not being able to do it, and that not being a big deal, then trying something else, is a positive experience in my recovery program. I'm so grateful CPA does not need stringent organization in order to work beautifully.

I have seen a lot of new members chair meetings. They each have their own style. Some are quiet and straightforward, and some are warm and talkative. But nobody ever cuts in to say, "You are not doing it the way that I do it." There is so much patience for someone new learning a position, and there is so much acceptance for how each person handles a position differently. It gives me the courage to one day to step up and take on more service roles.

I have found that when I regularly attend a meeting and don't actively participate in the life of the meeting, I feel like an outsider looking in. Participation feels like stepping up to the plate of responsibility and recovery. I enjoy being a trusted servant.

One role I took on was to be a Group Representative. In this position, I am representing my group, not making decisions for my group. Matters requiring a vote of the group must always come back to the group for discussion. My responsibility was to be thoroughly informed on an issue in order be knowledgeable during the discussion and decision-making. Serving as an equal member of our fellowship, in service to all of our recovery, has been truly satisfying and deeply supports my own recovery in CPA.

I am the public outreach chair for my group. My perfectionism and self-imposed expectations of myself almost stopped me from taking the position. At first, I put unreasonable and unhealthy demands on myself, until my sponsor reminded me of *Easy Does It*. She reminded me that my group had placed their faith and trust in me, and this was an opportunity for me to contribute to the group while still honoring my realities of living with chronic pain and chronic illness. I was still living from the place of being a human "do-er," needing to prove my worth. I was answering to my ego and not respecting the group I served.

Thanks to CPA service work and the unconditional kindness and support of my group, I have a renewed sense of dignity and purpose as I follow through on tasks, and I earn trust and respect from my fellows as I model the CPA way of doing service. "Slow and steady" is my CPA service motto.

Shortly after I began my Twelve Step journey in CPA, I became interested in service, which I know is part of working the program. I asked my sponsor about the CPA service structure flow so I could understand how information was transmitted, how requests were made, how decisions were made, and how the equality was practiced in CPA. It was a structure of clear communication and a fellowship of equals, and it left room for flexibility of service, when people had to bow out when necessary.

This made me realize that because I was living with chronic pain and chronic illness, the service chart had to change in my own house. Although there were areas where I couldn't contribute, there were others where I could. I didn't have to do it all. That is a beautiful reminder I learned in CPA. No one person is running the show. We work in concert with one another.

I have hesitancy to commit to something when I don't know how I will feel, hour by hour. I have concerns about signing up for things I may not be able to complete. But in Tradition Nine I understand that is okay. CPA is not rigidly organized. When one of us can't fulfill our service commitments, we ask for help from others and they step in. And there is forgiveness and compassion. It is not harsh, as I experienced it to be in the work world. I stepped down from a position in CPA, and it wasn't a big deal, and no one judged me negatively.

I was taken by surprise when I realized my Higher Power was asking me to volunteer for a position that I didn't believe I was qualified for, but the desire to do it was strong. I am so grateful for the apprentice approach to service in CPA. It allows me to gently ease into new responsibilities, slowly and with support.

    This gives me confidence to try new things I never thought I would be capable of—especially with chronic pain and chronic illness—in CPA, as well as out in the world. It is wonderful to be able to set aside my fear and be mentored to grow through new experiences.

Today I was attending a CPA committee meeting where I was the minority voice. I knew my solution would work for the best benefit of CPA, and I found my passion to explain and persuade was causing my voice and my tone to rise. In my mind, I heard the slogan

"Do I want to be happy or be right?" I took a breath, slowly said the Serenity Prayer, and dropped not only my shoulders but my voice as well. I remembered that in these committees I am not only responsible to the CPA fellowship but also to my fellow committee members. I could see my passion was putting people on the defensive instead of clarifying my point. I was so busy trying to be understood that I could not hear what anyone else was saying.

This pause served me well. My mental and emotional balance was restored, and I was once again able to offer positive contributions instead of selfish, self-centered arguments. Others were able to hear me instead of just my passion and defensiveness, and we came to a decision everyone was pleased with. I am responsible not only to those I serve but also to those I serve with.

I am an organizational enthusiast. When I am feeling overwhelmed, I will organize a drawer, and it always makes me feel better. What a lovely way of saying I try to control and direct outcomes to feel safe; it is my great obsession. There is no harm in organizing a drawer, but when I try to organize other people or institutions, such as CPA, my life quickly becomes unmanageable. Surprisingly enough, people don't like being told what to do. And I have come to realize that my desire to control to feel safe only separates me from my Higher Power and creates resentments in those around me.

I respect others by trusting that they have a Higher Power and I'm not it. I maintain my humility by not being a know-it-all and by practicing gratitude for others' willingness to serve. Besides, life is easier when I let my husband do the dishes his way.

I was preparing for a massive yard sale and asked my wife to help. I asked her to do a specific task and then told her how to do it. She said, "Sweetheart, you can tell me what do, but not how to do it." My need for control, to have things done my way, was disrespectful. To think someone can't carry out a task is unkind. In CPA, I've learned that when I delegate, I do so to a trusted servant, and I don't have to micromanage. This has helped my relationship with my wife, especially when we are working on a project together.

I reached out to a friend for help with a project in my home. I asked her when she could come over. She asked if Monday was okay. It turned out I would be in my CPA meeting at the time she wanted to come. I told her the door would be left open and trusted she knew what to do.

I asked her to pick up a task where I had left off. No matter what she does, I will be happy with it. I trust her; even if the task is not done the way I would do it. I am grateful for her assistance. It doesn't have to be my way. Her help will help me get my life more organized.

I am grateful to CPA for helping me to let go and trust—to live life more freely and with ease.

After I had been in CPA for a while, I realized that I had been in delusion, and I realized I needed help.

I hadn't been honest with my doctor. I was just smiling and being the good patient—not clearly communicating. So I wrote him a letter, listing all the things I couldn't do, explaining that I was declining. He responded immediately.

He couldn't be a trusted servant until I informed him about what was happening. And I needed to be honest with myself before I could be honest with him.

WORKING TRADITION NINE

CPA, as such, ought never be organized, but we may create service boards or committees directly responsible to those they serve.

The following questions can help deepen your understanding and application of Tradition Nine in your recovery and in all your affairs. Use these questions with your sponsor or sponsee or your CPA group, or explore them on your own, selecting the ones that are relevant.

1. Is everyone in my group encouraged to participate in service work?
2. How does my group support CPA's service bodies?
3. How does my group connect with the worldwide fellowship?
4. How am I contributing my talents to CPA, either in my group or on a service body?
5. Have I served on a committee in CPA? Was that different than other kinds of service?
6. How does service work benefit my recovery?
7. How do I support the importance of rotation of service?
8. Can I leave a service role gracefully?
9. Do I practice patience, flexibility, and humility in any CPA service position I take?
10. Do I appreciate those who serve? Am I critical of their efforts?
11. Am I familiar with the CPA Twelve Concepts of Service?

12. How does communication flow in CPA? Am I familiar with the Service Structure Flow Chart?
13. How do I create structure in my personal life without being rigid?
14. Am I willing to give up control of those around me?
15. How do we decide who does what in our home?
16. How do I make decisions with my healthcare professionals? Am I clear about my responsibility?
17. What do I consider unacceptable behavior? How do I communicate this?
18. Can I be flexible and adapt to changes and the needs of others?
19. How am I a clear and honest communicator?
20. How do I take responsibility for my best interest and well-being in a difficult relationship?
21. What does applying Tradition Nine in all my affairs look like today?
22. In what areas of my life do I already practice and understand the need for:
    - Most participation, least control
    - Clear flow of information
    - Trusted servants
    - Fellowship of equals
    - Structured service bodies
23. How can I include these spiritual tools where they may be missing in my life today?

Tradition Ten

Chronic Pain Anonymous has no opinion on outside issues; hence the CPA name ought never be drawn into public controversy.

> **Chronic Pain Anonymous has no opinion on outside issues; hence the CPA name ought never be drawn into public controversy.**

CPA takes no sides on public issues. We do not respond to the public, positively or negatively. We guard the fellowship by not allowing anything that is going on outside the meetings to divide us, which in turn protects our unity. We concentrate on our common bond and not on differing opinions.

SPIRITUAL TOOLS FOR PRACTICING TRADITION TEN

- Our common bond
- Mutual respect
- Individual opinions, no collective view
- Personal anonymity
- Anonymity as a member or in our group
- Sharing with awareness
- Focus on recovery
- Recovery-focused public outreach
- Commitment to non-controversy

APPLYING TRADITION TEN

I. In Our Groups

OUR COMMON BOND
Members of CPA come from many different backgrounds and have many different viewpoints. We are a diverse group, and taking sides on any of the things that make us so would divide us when an open-minded and uncontentious atmosphere is needed

for recovery to flourish. We have a common bond and a primary spiritual aim that is our sole concern: recovery from the challenges of living with chronic pain and chronic illness. We don't take a stand against or even propose a point of view about any public or social issue or cause. In this way, we can welcome all who come to our fellowship, and each of us can find the recovery we need.

In our meetings and in our shares, we keep our primary purpose in mind and set aside differences. The health and strength of our program is maintained when we are committed to our common welfare and our unity. Because we focus on ourselves and those who want the recovery available in CPA, we don't engage in public or outside issues. One example of outside issues would be when a member who belongs to another fellowship shares on those issues, which are unrelated to chronic pain and chronic illness.

Practicing Tradition Ten also means we are mindful when things are going on in the world that truly affect our hearts and minds. Outside the meetings, we can support any cause and state our opinions as strongly as we need to. But we need CPA to be CPA, and we will lose our way and our singleness of purpose if we get involved in outside issues in the meeting rooms.

Commitment to Tradition Ten is a matter of survival for our fellowship. Our spiritual foundation upholds us, and our Higher Power will support us. We have found that when we remain true to our CPA message and focus on our common bond, we can make it through any challenges. This keeps us strong and ensures that an undiluted, unified program will be there for all who will come after us.

By practicing this Tradition, we are participating in anonymity, unity, and our primary purpose, both as individuals and as a group.

MUTUAL RESPECT

The fellowship is essential for our recovery, and we guard it by allowing no controversy on outside issues in our meetings. Members may have different politics, religions, or languages, but this Tradition allows us to come together and share our experience of living with chronic pain and chronic illness in an atmosphere of mutual respect. We concentrate on our common bond, not on our differing views. Meetings are not the place for personal opinions on worldly topics or current affairs. No matter what may or may not be going on in the world outside our meetings, when we join together for recovery in CPA, we have come to a safe haven.

We want and need comfort and understanding. However, if there is controversy, our meetings will not be a safe place for our recovery. We need to be free from dissension and avoid angry confrontation, and this applies both to outside issues and to conflicts that may arise within our meetings. No matter how strongly we feel about a particular issue, we are mindful to speak to one another with mutual respect. In this way, we create a safe environment for all our members. We risk alienating newcomers and longtimers alike if we share our opinions on outside issues or if we confront one another aggressively.

We consider the effects of our speech and deeds on the fellowship, and we don't give each other advice in CPA. When we refrain from voicing a position on non-CPA issues, we are practicing anonymity and humility. In our meetings, our only perspective is that CPA works, and that is the message we carry.

This Tradition protects the spiritual nature of our program. We use the Steps, Traditions, and literature approved and written by the CPA fellowship, which ensures group unity. Although groups are autonomous and can decide what to read, by using Conference Approved Literature we preserve a consistent message about the Steps, Traditions, and principles of our program. It is truly a relief to enter into the rooms knowing all we will find there is CPA recovery.

INDIVIDUAL OPINIONS, NO COLLECTIVE VIEW

We each have a private life. As individuals, we have the right to be involved in any cause or to engage in any controversy, but we keep CPA's name out of it. If we fail to observe this Tradition, the fellowship may be harmed.

We all have opinions, and we can share our opinions outside of our meetings. But we don't have opinions as a group. If we are speaking about CPA as a member, we don't speak on outside issues. For instance, we may find ourselves speaking to our friends, even our friends from program, about a specific politician or governmental policy. We make it clear that this is our personal opinion and that CPA has no point of view—on this or any other topic. CPA has no collective point of view on any outside issue.

PERSONAL ANONYMITY
We practice anonymity as the foundation of our life in CPA. Anonymity protects us and keeps us equal and humble. It doesn't matter who we are or what we do outside the meetings. What matters is that we work the Steps, follow the Traditions, and have a desire to recover. We stay anonymous when we are in our groups.

We may need to practice awareness of our social media involvement and use of digital communication platforms to keep the CPA message of recovery set apart from non-CPA messages we may want to share with others. We never use our CPA membership as a means to obtain power, money, or fame (see Tradition Six). Nor do we mix CPA with the myriad opinions we may express on social media.

How this looks will differ for everyone. We may choose, for example, to create separate social media or email accounts so that our online CPA identity is never mingled with who we are outside the rooms. Or we may choose to never mention our membership in CPA in any online format. We each practice this Tradition in our own way, and in our technologically interconnected world, we need to pay attention and make good choices that protect both ourselves and our program.

ANONYMITY AS A MEMBER OR IN OUR GROUP
We protect our anonymity by keeping what we do, who we are known as, and our personal opinions outside of the meeting. When we share and sponsor, we don't tell others what they should

do; instead, we share about what we have done and experienced. We talk about our feelings, hopes, and recovery, not our opinions. There is no conflict when we talk about our experiences and concentrate on what we have in common. And when we speak in our group, we speak as an individual, not for the group.

A CPA meeting exists specifically for all of our recovery. We don't engage members to share our individual social causes or political events. We don't solicit others to purchase or use a product or to participate in a non-CPA group. Having no opinion on outside issues means we don't promote businesses in the group. CPA is a program of attraction, and one of the things that makes it so attractive is its detachment from the rest of the world's focus on opinions and personal agendas. There are no hidden ulterior motives in CPA; we simply focus on our recovery.

By honoring the Traditions and specifically practicing Tradition Ten, we offer a clear and simple message. If we were to express opinions on matters outside our recovery, we might offend or drive away those who hold different opinions, which would interfere with our primary purpose. We need to be a safe place for anyone who wants CPA recovery—not only those who agree with our opinions on other matters.

It's important to remember that we also don't share opinions about other members' choices. Any opinions we hear shared in the meeting are those of the speaker. We take with us what works for us, and we leave the rest. Once we are outside the meeting, we don't share what we have heard. This maintains the safety and anonymity of every speaker. As we consciously apply this Tradition, we let go of needing to take a stand on institutions, religious beliefs, or medical treatments. Although a member may wear a political T-shirt, it is not our business. We don't have to agree with everyone, nor do we need to express our disagreement. We pray for open-mindedness and tolerance when others are different from us, and we stay out of situations that are none of our business.

When our service work is done from a stance of anonymity, we no longer seek recognition or to be seen as having all the right answers. We follow the spiritual principle of *Live and Let Live*. We may struggle with accepting the majority view when it is different from our own; if this is consistently difficult for us, we may need to look at our character traits. If we are often having a hard time letting go of controversy, we can turn to the Steps, our sponsor, and our Higher Power.

SHARING WITH AWARENESS
Sharing is a personal and courageous act. We each know this, and we respect one another's bravery and honesty. We don't regulate the shares of other members: sometimes there is an expression of raw emotion; sometimes shares are thoughtful; sometimes an opinion is implicit in what the speaker is saying. There is no perfect sharing, nor need we ever strive for such a thing. We may get lost in the details and struggle to get to the essence of what is on our minds. When it is challenging to find the message of hope and strength in our experience, we look inside for our motive in sharing. It doesn't have to be elegant or tidy; however, we want to ask if we are adding in any way to diversion or division.

Mindful awareness as we speak with a clear focus, doing our best to leave out opinions, makes our message compelling and easily received. We share, both when we speak and by example, through our actions. For example, if we become aware that we are reacting emotionally or that our shares are motivated by a desire to be right, we can reach out to a friend and reason things out, and then make new choices in alignment with our recovery. Practicing doing things differently is a great way to carry the message of hope.

Not taking a stand supports not only our anonymity but also our inclusiveness. Chronic pain and chronic illness affect us all differently. In CPA, there are no policies on medications or treatment programs. Those are outside issues—individual matters between a person and their healthcare providers.

When we share about our Higher Power, we do so without indicating a specific faith. This is a practice of anonymity as regards our religious affiliation (or none), and it keeps the meeting safe and welcoming for everyone. We share without singling out names, organizations, or treatment programs. We may find that we need to develop this as a skill and find our own ways of talking about things that are important to our shares without naming them. This happens over time and sometimes with help from our sponsor and program friends.

Our primary purpose is expressed in our groups. If there is a disruption, we consciously practice Tradition Ten, inviting harmony and unity so we can stay focused on our message of recovery. We learn how to communicate so we can say what we mean without causing harm to others and concentrate on our common bonds rather than on our differences.

FOCUS ON RECOVERY

In our meetings, we have only one message: that although we live with chronic pain and chronic illness, we can find a new, deeply satisfying way to live. We provide help to others and receive their support. We preserve our energy for our spiritual recovery and do not expend it on controversy or outside issues.

One of the most powerful ways we carry the message is by listening—both to our Higher Power and to one another. When we no longer are attached to our own opinions, we can respect the consensus of the group conscience. In this way, our Higher Power can guide all of us. We turn our attention solely onto our recovery. When we listen to others' experience, strength, and hope with an open mind, we are more receptive to new ideas, which may be greater than what we had originally envisioned when we first joined CPA.

Recovery is a process of constant change. Our perceptions, attitudes, and values may shift and alter over time. By sharing our experiences with each other and bringing new perspectives into our recovery journey, we discover that together, focused fully on our shared purpose, we can live peacefully, joyfully, and comfortably, no matter our physical condition or what is happening in the outside world.

II. In Our Service Bodies

RECOVERY-FOCUSED PUBLIC OUTREACH
We participate in communities outside our meetings so that other people with chronic pain and chronic illness have a chance to hear our message. When we speak to others, we are clear about our purpose and practice restraint regarding our actions and words by keeping the Traditions in mind. We differentiate our own opinions from those of CPA, remembering that no one speaks for CPA.

When our service to CPA is out in the public, we need to be familiar with the basic guidelines of interacting with those outside of the fellowship. We don't need to do it alone; we can use the support of our literature and other members. If we follow the principles of our Traditions, especially Tradition Ten, it will be easy to avoid controversy. We first identify our message and how we want to carry it. We then share our experience, strength, and hope and how CPA has helped us in our recovery. If we state an opinion on anything other than our message, we may alienate people who can benefit from our help. To avoid this, we *Keep It Simple*, focus on recovery, and stay clear of all the issues that are not our business.

When we share outside of meetings, we focus more on carrying the message and less on ourselves. We share about how CPA works for us and what CPA is (and is not). We don't accept or create invitations, whether explicit or not, to get caught up in arguments, and we don't discuss the merits of other approaches. Just as in our meetings, we don't discuss treatments, medications, healthcare organizations, or other outside issues. We trust that we are practicing *attraction rather than promotion* (Tradition Eleven) when we share about the tools of the program and how they change our lives in positive ways. Tradition Ten keeps us focused on recovery.

COMMITMENT TO NON-CONTROVERSY
Being in service positions beyond the group level, such as Intergroup Chair, Meeting Liaison, or Chair of the Literature Committee, means that our decisions can have a significant impact on CPA. We may discover that we become more bold about our opinions than we were when doing service at the group level; if this happens, we remember to honor the service contribution each person offers and don't seek recognition or victory.

There are times when there can be controversy between members in our service bodies, and we can get diverted from our primary purpose if we get caught up in disagreeing about issues. We remember to protect the program that has brought us our recovery. Keeping Tradition Ten in mind, we listen to each other and practice respect and mutual problem solving, in service to unity.

It is important to be teachable and to have an open mind. We are never alone in our service work; we work together to explore issues and find a solution that benefits the whole. As we meet in an open forum, in an atmosphere of kindness and compassion, and discuss the issues, each of us has a voice. In the process of coming to a group conscience, we are guided by a Higher Power.

III. In All Our Affairs

"We don't speak as one voice on outside issues. We leave that which is not ours to manage to those whose business it is to do so." This is one possible way to reword Tradition Ten for use in our personal lives and other affairs.

In our relationships, we find it best to not argue about things we can't control and avoid outside situations that are none of our business. There are times we can agree to disagree on some issues and leave it at that, practicing the slogan *Live and Let Live*.

How do we do this?

We don't offer advice unless it is requested and don't comment on outside issues that are not our business—unless our opinion is being requested. We don't criticize others, directly or indirectly.

(Others' behavior is, to us, an outside issue.) We find ways to say what we mean without being mean, as we speak from an intention for connection and understanding. We practice not taking others' opinions personally and not being defensive when the other person doesn't agree with our point of view. People can say hurtful things while thinking they are being helpful. Just as we develop skillful ways of sharing in meetings, we can develop new ways of responding respectfully, without being pulled into controversy.

We pay attention to our own behavior and become aware of ways that we may be contributing to controversy. When we have a different or even strong opinion, we don't have to voice it unless the matter involves us directly. We can have thoughts without voicing them and can choose to not respond to others when they comment on issues that are not our business. We follow the spiritual principle of detaching with love.

We notice our habits around sharing with those we encounter in our daily lives. Family members, caregivers, and healthcare professionals don't have to hear all our opinions. We don't judge how others may do tasks. When we mind our own business and keep focused on our primary purpose, for each relationship we are in, we do not waste energy on matters that don't directly affect us or are not really important. We may find that reciting CPA's Serenity Prayer is a great reminder of how to stay on our own side of the street. It can free us from a sense of urgency during difficult moments.

> *God, grant me the serenity*
> *to accept the things I cannot change,*
> *the courage to change the things I can,*
> *and the wisdom to know the difference.*
> *Thy will, not mine, be done.*

We learn how to work through disagreements toward a mutually satisfying solution rather than maintaining controversy. If there is no agreement, we pause. In this pause, we can pray, meditate, or talk to our sponsor; we can ask our Higher Power for guidance and for the ability to have an open mind to alternative solutions. We concentrate on changing ourselves only. If we have a strong emotional response, we find someone to talk to and help us reason things out. And we can always decide it is okay to have different opinions.

In our relationships with others, we stay out of issues that are not our concern. If we find it too difficult to do this, we can consider applying Step Four or Step Ten and look at how we are contributing to the controversy. What feelings or old patterns are in play? How important is the issue? Are we damaging our relationship? Have we talked with our sponsor? Have we turned to our Higher Power?

Part of applying Tradition Ten in all our affairs means remembering that we don't have to listen to everyone's opinions about our care or treatment plans. We can respond as we need to, without disrespect or inviting conflict. We can say, *"Thank you for caring. However, this is not information I need at this time."* All decisions about our care need to be made by us, even though there may be others who will be affected and who we need to include in our process. We do this with respect and an open mind, and being considerate of others' needs and feelings. We remember to focus on our common bond, possibly on the love we share, and not on our differing perspectives. We stay focused on unity and the greater good.

ASSOCIATED SPIRITUAL PRINCIPLE: *Recovery Focus*

In CPA, we stay focused on our own recovery and avoid controversy. We have a responsibility to CPA as a whole and do not bring issues or opinions about public life into our program. As a CPA member, we choose to operate and share within these limits.

TRADITION TEN IN ACTION
Chronic Pain Anonymous has no opinion on outside issues; hence the CPA name ought never be drawn into public controversy.

VOICES OF OUR MEMBERS

I attended a meeting where one member would wear attire with language that was sometimes offensive. I had such a hard time with it. I questioned why he was bringing controversy to meetings. I talked to my sponsor, and she reminded me that what he was wearing was none of my business. I finally got to a place where I could separate what he was wearing from the actual message of the meeting. I began to feel safe in the meeting again, knowing that it does not matter what someone wears when I am there to work on my recovery. I realize that the discussion, and my focus in our meetings, needs to stay on our own individual experience with CPA recovery. Now, what I see is our common bond rather than outside issues.

The way this Tradition has particularly impacted me is finding that there is no opinion in CPA on the use of narcotic medications prescribed for pain. I have been brought into great awareness about the consequences of addiction. I know that there is big controversy over these medications, and I wouldn't want CPA to be pulled into those controversies. I have seen the effects narcotics have on others, and I bite my tongue. It is not my place to say anything.

In CPA meetings, I keep my anonymity as a member of another Twelve Step fellowship to myself. When fellow members mention by name, practice, or phrases of another Twelve Step program, my focus is pulled away from the CPA program. In a CPA meeting, this practice is just a distraction.

I was in fellowship, after a meeting, and I found myself very uncomfortable because of the nature of the humor being shared. Following this Tradition, I took what I liked and left the rest, let go of it and moved on. It was offensive to me, but I didn't jump in and say anything, as there are no guidelines for sharing in our social time. I didn't really know how to handle that except to observe, turn it over, let it pass, and in the future to make a note that if things seemed like they were headed that way again, I would go somewhere else. I would simply leave the gathering and search for what I needed in fellowship, elsewhere.

I find it's best not to mention at a meeting what medications I'm using to treat chronic pain and chronic illness. When I share so specifically, people sometimes come to me because they want to get permission to also use what I use or take what I take, or they want a referral to the doctor I go to because they think that that doctor will then help them. I had an experience where one woman did do that. She actively pursued my physician, and he turned her down and said he would not take her as a patient. I prefer not to invite this kind of controversy, so I keep my specific healthcare protocols out of my shares.

I was in a videoconference meeting, and one of the members had their video off so their image was set to display a political message. It quickly became clear that I wasn't the only one who noticed it, and a chat message that was meant to be privately addressed to that person accidentally showed up for everyone to see. I started privately chatting with another member about it, who confirmed that the person had been asked to change their image. They also thought the image was political and associated with racism. But, while the image was upsetting to me as well, I remembered Tradition Ten. If another member is displaying their political beliefs in their personal image online, it is none of my business. The member with the political image refused to take it down, and although it went against my beliefs, they had the right to display the image.

If as a meeting, we wanted to discuss it and come to a group conscience about whether this kind of use of our non-video presence was bringing an outside issue into the meeting, I realized we could do that and that I could bring it up at a business meeting.

I have been in meetings, both in groups and service work, as well as outside CPA, and have experienced people, without realizing or meaning to, put down some aspect of my personal experience. It can feel hurtful, whether or not they know they've done it.

In one case, I mentioned it, and upon doing so, realized it was my issue. That even if someone doesn't *approve* of my experience, that is their right, based on their understanding—and it is valid. It doesn't invalidate who I am or what I'm doing. It's not even personal. And my feelings are also valid.

When I do service work, as well in all my affairs, I now practice *Live and Let Live*. Anyone can say anything, and I know in my heart of hearts, I am okay and in the care of my Higher Power. Nothing can harm me then. And I am able to carry the message of CPA without needing to comment on others' opinions or invite controversy.

In the course of doing community public outreach service, I was asked to include a visit to a local pain management and addiction treatment clinic that specialized in a new medication and treatment modality. While there, I was handed a large stack of their brochures and business cards to share with members of my CPA group. I explained that I was grateful for all their efforts to reach those suffering with chronic pain and chronic illness, but CPA does not endorse or affiliate with any facilities or treatments. Returning the items, I gently said that CPA was not a professional healthcare organization and that we did not have opinions on outside issues.

As I left, I wondered whether these professionals would share CPA information with their clients, as I was unable to share their information in CPA. Months later, I spoke with someone they had referred to our program. It was a wonderful reminder that Higher Power is in charge of outcomes, and all I have to do is kindly abide by the principles of the program.

Tradition Ten reminds me that the controversy I create *within myself* when struggling with what action to take (or not take) can snowball into overwhelm and paralysis. My opinions, fears, and obsessions are often in the form of catastrophizing and "futurizing." When I let this controversy unfurl, I am drawn further away from my Higher Power's caring guidance. Time and time again, hindsight demonstrates that solutions are present for me, often before the challenges even enter my mind, and I can choose to tap into these solutions by turning to my Higher Power through present-moment mindfulness. I set aside what I think I know (my opinions) and all the "shoulds," and I surrender my self-will and become available for my Higher Power to reveal supportive, loving guidance.

It has been my experience that when I talk about my medical conditions, people tend to think I'm helpless and that I need help and direction...and that they need to give me meditation tapes, and they need to give me doctors' suggestions, and they need to tell me that I need to get a medical marijuana card, when they really do not know what the specifics of my medical condition are.

Is it the way that I present myself that causes people to treat me as helpless? Am I presenting as helpless? What is behind their response? Am I pulling this out of people, or is that just the way that people do respond? A trusted friend said, "People are just trying to be kind. They're not trying to be hurtful," and suggested that I try to see how that's their motive, and then to look at my side of the street. Am I trying to manipulate? Does it *sound* like I'm trying to manipulate? Does it sound like I'm being a victim? I don't want to be treated like that because I know that I'm responsible for being my own advocate. It is hard sometimes to do that alone, and I do need help.

I have found two or three people in my community whom I trust to go with me to doctors' appointments, patiently sit in the waiting room, and make no judgments. I'm grateful to have these safe friends in my life.

I am learning that practicing the Traditions can help guide my actions and how much I share with others and choose wisely with whom I share about my condition.

One of my treasured friends has different religious views from me. And that is none of my business. We relate to one another on profound spiritual levels. If I were to allow my focus to be on her religious life, it would jeopardize the friendship. Her religious practices are "outside issues" to me. Only how she and I relate to one another as human beings is what's important. We are speaking the same language of the heart.

Sometimes it surprises my friends that I don't need to agree with them politically. What I do need is that we agree as human beings on our common humanity and our common human struggles. I have some very valuable friendships with people who have divergent views, and I love that because I have an opportunity to learn. I might discover something new if I stay open-minded and listen; I also might find a best friend or a really good sponsor. If I limit my world to what I already know, I'm only going to receive what I already know.

In CPA, I'm learning more and more how self-care differs from person to person. What works for me may not work for you. It's none of my business how you practice self-care—it's an "outside issue"—just like it's none of your business how I practice mine. What is self-care for me in one moment, or one day, may cause harm in the next. What CPA has taught me is that we are all different in our diagnoses, medications, and treatments...and in our self-care practices. We are all the same in that we all need self-care to support us on our journey with chronic pain and chronic illness.

I keep my judgment out of my relationships and trust my Higher Power to guide me and everyone else. It is our Higher Power's job to guide us toward what is self-care to meet our daily needs.

WORKING TRADITION TEN
Chronic Pain Anonymous has no opinion on outside issues; hence the CPA name ought never be drawn into public controversy.

The following questions can help deepen your understanding and application of Tradition Ten in your recovery and in all your affairs. Use these questions with your sponsor or sponsee or your CPA group, or explore them on your own, selecting the ones that are relevant.

1. How do I focus on common bonds rather than differences?
2. Do I refrain from expressing my opinions on outside issues in a meeting?
3. What can I do if someone tries to promote or bring up an outside issue in a meeting?
4. What might be an outside issue for my group? Has this ever come up? If so, what did I do?
5. Can I share my experience, strength, and hope, and not make it be a CPA opinion?
6. In what ways do I ensure I don't breach this Tradition?
7. Do I understand that I can't control the thinking and beliefs of other people?
8. How do I manifest the spirit of this Tradition in all my affairs?
9. Do I hang on to my opinions, or is it easy for me to move on when I disagree with others?
10. Am I being courteous and respectful to those I encounter in all my affairs?

11. Can I allow others their feelings and ideas and not become resentful, defensive, or hurt?
12. Do I hold grudges? How can I forgive others?
13. Do I have to be right? How do I practice being happy instead of wanting to be right?
14. Can I disagree and still respect the other person?
15. What are some behaviors I have noticed (or participated in) that invite controversy, both overtly and covertly?
16. Do I understand that what may be acceptable to me may be controversial to another?
17. What does applying Tradition Ten in all my affairs look like today?
18. In what areas of my life do I already practice and understand the need for:
    - Our common bond
    - Mutual respect
    - Individual opinions, no collective view
    - Personal anonymity
    - Anonymity as a member or in our group
    - Sharing with awareness
    - Focus on recovery
    - Recovery-focused public outreach
    - Commitment to non-controversy
19. How can I include these spiritual tools where they may be missing in my life today?

Tradition Eleven

Our public relations policy is based on attraction rather than promotion; we need always maintain personal anonymity at the level of press, radio, television, film, and the Internet.

Our public relations policy is based on attraction rather than promotion; we need always maintain personal anonymity at the level of press, radio, television, film, and the Internet.

Through public information efforts, we practice attraction to let people know about CPA. We have nothing to sell—we simply let people know our program exists and, when invited, share in a friendly, welcoming manner how the program can help. We trust that CPA's effectiveness and value to its members will be attractive to those who may benefit from it. We publicize our program, not our individual members; we do not seek recognition, and there is no place for personal ambition in CPA; we are each a guardian of the fellowship. We protect our anonymity and the anonymity of other members by using first names or pseudonyms only. Anonymity guards both us as individuals and the reputation of the fellowship.

SPIRITUAL TOOLS FOR PRACTICING TRADITION ELEVEN

- Attraction, not promotion
- Anonymity
- Anonymity and outside organizations
- Attraction in public relations and the media

APPLYING TRADITION ELEVEN

I. In Our Groups

ATTRACTION, NOT PROMOTION
It is one of the spiritual tenets of Twelve Step programs that people are attracted to them because they are effective and safe places for recovery to occur. This Tradition states that attraction is a principle we adhere to and uphold. Why do we rely on attraction rather than promoting something we know is helpful and of such deep value?

Promotion suggests that we are selling something—advertising it, perhaps with a goal of benefitting ourselves. It is easy for a promotional approach to become, or feel, like a "hard sell." It implies that we are making promises or guarantees. It can be hard to trust someone who is promoting something—what's in it for them? CPA's integrity and real value are too important to risk that response in someone who might truly benefit from our program. In CPA, we don't tell people they will be healed or will feel better in a month. We don't try to sell the program or convince anyone of the merits of our approach.

Rather than promoting, we pay attention to what is attractive about CPA. Recovery from the difficulties of living with chronic pain and chronic illness is attractive. A safe, secure meeting environment with an atmosphere of friendliness is attractive. Also attractive: We are hospitable and empathic and offer compassion and kindness to each other. We are welcoming to anyone curious about CPA and only share our experience, strength, and hope. We practice the principles of the program and let the example of our recovery speak for itself. Every member has this responsibility. We trust that newcomers can decide for themselves whether CPA will be helpful to them.

A CPA meeting can provide a powerful experience of recovery. The spirit of a renewed life, of hope, and of strength in our meetings is attractive. Our diversity of ages, health conditions, and cultures, all being welcome and at ease together in our meetings, is attractive. We treat each person with dignity and respect. Whether we are at our first meeting or have many years as a CPA member, we are warm and caring toward everyone, and this is attractive.

There is nothing we need to sell. We simply need to be examples of recovery ourselves and share, honestly and simply, how the program is working for us. We behave in a way that shows that each of us matters. When we share from the heart, it can be attractive to a newcomer who may have been unable to articulate or express their feelings. There are no sales pitches in CPA; we simply share our stories.

People are attracted when they see how the program works in our lives. Recovery is not freedom from our pain and illness—we don't have a perfect life, nor do we strive for one. Instead, we discover how to navigate in new ways that bring serenity and contentment, understanding that recovery is a journey, not a destination. We don't promote CPA with excessive zeal or present a set of guaranteed results, as if they were available for purchase. We each carry the message of CPA by being examples of how recovery looks in everyday life. We live our program and warmly invite others to join us, and our message of hope is real and powerful. This is attractive. We make no promises but tell others about our recovery experience and have faith they will find what they need.

Our inner qualities are what attract people to us. When we practice the principles of the program in all our affairs, we are an example of how recovery works, and we attract others.

Living a life that demonstrates how we are capable of living peacefully, joyfully, and comfortably with chronic pain and chronic illness attracts others. Sometimes others notice the changes in us and inquire how we did it. If it is reasonable, we share our experience, strength, and hope with them, and we tell them about CPA.

On the CPA website, we attract by providing literature and meeting information. At our meetings, we can attract by sharing our literature; thus we do our part and leave the results up to a Power greater than ourselves. When we are welcoming and keep our message clear, we are being attractive to all people who may benefit and are serving effectively.

ANONYMITY

The principle of anonymity aids our spiritual journey. If we are going to practice this Tradition, we need to carry the message, and doing so anonymously gives protection to our own recovery.

Tradition Eleven focuses on personal anonymity, and Tradition Twelve is about anonymity as the core principle of all the Traditions. None of us speaks for CPA as a whole or for its members. There is no spokesperson for CPA. We are a fellowship of equals with no hierarchy.

This Tradition discourages our tendency to promote ourselves. Our service is not about achieving recognition; there are times we may do service that no one sees or knows about. We find that our self-obsession, an element of our problem, lessens when we put aside our needs for the good of the whole. Anonymity is a deep practice that brings relief from the part of ourselves that puts pressure on us to attain status and prestige.

Anonymity also assures the newcomer's safety, which is an attractive feature to people who are suffering and have often felt misunderstood. We all need to know that our anonymity is protected. In our meetings, we can decide to use our own name or a pseudonym. Our choice to be in CPA is personal, and we want to be confident that our names will not be taken outside of our meetings. Each of us has a responsibility to respect our own anonymity and that of our fellow members, being careful to always keep confidential what we hear in meetings or share one-on-one with each other.

We use our own discretion about how to apply the Traditions and how to practice anonymity in our personal life. CPA does not have the power to enforce members to keep either their anonymity or that of others. Rather, we each opt to voluntarily safeguard the fellowship and be obedient to the unenforceable.

Our personal anonymity is our own decision, and we can share our involvement in CPA with family, friends, or others, but we don't reveal the involvement of any other members. When we reveal our membership in CPA to friends, family, and healthcare professionals, we want to be living examples of our CPA recovery, having faith that this will reflect positively on CPA's reputation and how others view the program.

Anonymity allows us to be open and honest in our meetings. Without this safety, we would not be able to receive the gifts of CPA. Our practice of sharing authentically and letting others know us as imperfect humans, with all our strengths and weaknesses, is a form of attraction. We learn in the program that we are enough just as we are, and having this spiritual awakening of self-acceptance is attractive to others.

When we are in a leadership or service role, we treat everyone equally, with respect, civility, care, and appreciation. There is no special class of members; we all share in service, in various roles. Anonymity supports us in being a fellowship of equals; it safeguards CPA and protects the fellowship from our shortcomings. Consciously practicing anonymity ensures that no one can seek notoriety or use CPA for their own purposes outside the program. In this way, our message reaches beyond the limits of our personalities.

In our online presence, we need to consider how to maintain anonymity. We don't identify ourselves as a member of CPA through social media; we can say we are in recovery, but we don't specifically mention CPA. However, if we are in a private, closed, online group, we can share our CPA membership.

ANONYMITY AND OUTSIDE ORGANIZATIONS
There are times in business matters, such as acquiring a meeting space or working with various outside organizations, when we need to disclose our full name and role in CPA. (For instance, if we are the treasurer of our group, we may need to sign contracts or checks.) However, in dealing with outside organizations, it is best if CPA is not associated with any one person.

We may choose to share our role in CPA so as to be a credible source when dealing with outside organizations. In this situation, we can request personal anonymity or ask that a pseudonym be used when interacting with outside organizations. We are responsible for informing them about the need for our anonymity. If there is any media involvement, our personal anonymity, as well as that of other members, needs to be protected.

Outside organizations include the facility where we meet or digital platform we use. Our interactions with them, and with any outside entity, are public relations and reflect on CPA as a whole. We want to build trust and be responsible so that others in the community are comfortable and attracted to CPA. Our practice of goodwill and integrity in getting along with others helps our fellowship grow. We are each an agent of public information.

II. In Our Service Bodies

ATTRACTION IN PUBLIC RELATIONS AND THE MEDIA
This Tradition gives us guidelines to make the public aware of what we have to offer while keeping the individuals in the program anonymous. A good level of attraction brings new members, and this is how we grow—if we are too anonymous, to the point of being secret, no one will be able to find us. We want to inform the public and healthcare professionals about our program and the recovery CPA has to offer, and Tradition Eleven guides us to maintain the CPA spiritual foundation of anonymity while attracting those who are suffering.

Although we protect the anonymity of individuals, it is important that the CPA program is known. We want to help those with chronic pain and chronic illness find us and to make CPA available and accessible to whoever needs and wants it. We want people to know that our meetings are safe and to have an understanding of what we offer, and so we provide straightforward information so others can find us, including notification of the time and place of our meetings. We don't advertise anything beyond information about our meetings, our literature, and our program of Twelve Step recovery.

In order to reach those who suffer, we have relationships with organizations and people outside of CPA. To inform people in our community about CPA, we can print announcements of our meetings and make literature available, and we can participate in public discussions and make presentations to professionals. We also cooperate with healthcare professionals and share information about CPA as appropriate.

We explain the Tradition of anonymity when we interact with organizations or the media, informing them of the importance of not showing our faces and requesting that they only use our first name or an alias. This protects members and lets newcomers know that CPA is a safe place where they can stay anonymous if they choose. Breaking anonymity at a public level undermines the spiritual foundation of CPA, and we don't disclose our membership or that of another member at a public level.

CPA is not associated with any one person in any form of media. In general, when we interact with media directly, we don't share our full name or our role in CPA. However, when we are making arrangements with someone from the media, we may choose to share our role in CPA so as to be a reliable source, making sure to inform the media representative about the need for our anonymity. We request their cooperation in safeguarding our personal anonymity.

If we are speaking in a public forum to let others know about CPA, whether appearing in person, on film or radio, in print or online, we keep who we are in other areas of life out of the message. Certain public forums may require the use of our last name; if this is the case, we check in with our sponsor and our Higher Power and decide for ourselves if we are willing to share our name in public. We let the people we are speaking with know that breaking our anonymity is a choice we are making and specify to what degree we are willing to do so in order to be of service and let the public know about CPA.

As a general practice, we don't use our full face or full name in the media, on the Internet, or social media (except in private groups) identifying ourselves as a member of CPA. We can use our name and face when talking about our chronic illness and chronic pain as long as we talk about ourselves—but not our membership in CPA. We can say we are in recovery as long as CPA is not named. Discussing our health conditions and how we cope with them is personal.

III. In All Our Affairs

Practicing Tradition Eleven in all our affairs means bringing the gifts we have received from the program's anonymity into our daily lives. One of these is our release from self-obsession. Letting go of the need to be special or receive recognition supports being healthy in mind and spirit, and we see this expressed in our relationships.

We practice attraction rather than promotion through being respectful and courteous toward others. The way we live is an example of our recovery and program tools, and bringing the principles of recovery into all we do is what makes us attractive. Our actions speak loudly. We are mindful of our own behavior and motivations and concentrate on living a happy and joyful life filled with peace and serenity.

Growth through humility is rooted in anonymity. Humility is being teachable, with the ability to learn from anyone, and in all kinds of situations, especially as we deal with loss, unexpected changes, and new diagnoses. We don't discount messages based on whether or not we like the messenger. Just as we do in meetings, we have an attitude and willingness to grow from every challenge and situation and continue to be open-minded.

When this happens, we discover that living and interacting with others in this way is attractive and can increase the harmony and strengthen the bond of all our relationships. We experience new levels of ease in circumstances that we may formerly have found daunting.

We respect others' confidences and privacy; we don't violate trust. Applying Tradition Eleven means we consciously remind ourselves to do this with everyone we encounter, giving others the dignity to run their own lives. In any relationship, we speak only for ourselves; when we talk about the relationship to others, we do not reveal their personal information. This is how we carry the message of respect and dignity. When we protect another's anonymity and their right to share the details of their lives on their own terms, we build a new skill, one that increases our sense of integrity and self-esteem.

We treat ourselves with this same respect and dignity. Our needs may change, and often do, when we are living with chronic health problems. We pay loving attention and recognize when what we have been doing is not working anymore. How do we decide what to do differently? This is a time to ask our Higher Power for another way to do things and remember *GOD: Good Orderly Direction*. With dignity, we communicate our needs clearly and simply to those involved.

We allow others the freedom to choose how they will adapt to changes and practice patience as everyone adjusts. Changes to our healthcare plan naturally affect others in our lives. We notice if we have resentments toward anyone. We turn to our Higher Power, our sponsor, and whichever program tools will help us through the changing circumstances. We express gratitude to others for the support given to us, small and large.

Guided by our Higher Power, we can make choices about the quality of our life. We pray to practice *HOW: Honest, Open, and Willing*—and communicate in a respectful way as we speak what is true for us. We are responsible for our feelings; others are responsible for theirs. Feelings are not facts, and we do not judge ourselves or others for having them. We are all human. This is one way we practice anonymity in our relationships. We do not try to change others or make them live differently, nor do we accept the role of victim. Rather, we speak our truth as an equal member of our relationship.

Another element of anonymity in a relationship is not complaining when situations are changing and not going our way. We grow and adapt at our own pace and allow the same for others. This may mean keeping silent when someone makes a mistake or adjusts slower than we do. We can choose to keep our opinions anonymous.

> **ASSOCIATED SPIRITUAL PRINCIPLES:** *Attraction and Anonymity*
> We protect our program of recovery for both the individual and the fellowship as a whole through anonymity. We practice attraction, not promotion. We stay focused on our program and are examples of recovery as we "walk the talk."

TRADITION ELEVEN IN ACTION

Our public relations policy is based on attraction rather than promotion; we need always maintain anonymity on the level of press, radio, television, film and the Internet.

VOICES OF OUR MEMBERS

It's so tempting to recommend CPA to every ailing person I meet. I feel an urgency for everyone to join and find relief. However, I've learned that urgency is a call for stillness. People in my life have noticed the changes in me. If I come across someone who is suffering with chronic pain and chronic illness, I can direct them to the website and literature without mentioning I'm part of the fellowship. My intention is to enjoy my life. As a by-product, I can be of service by example.

The principle of "attraction rather than promotion" is powerful. In the world of chronic pain and illness, there have been countless experiences of someone being told what they "should" do to treat their condition. I came into CPA having never learned to listen to myself and my body. Instead, I was dominated by obsessive fear and endless medical and alternative care appointments. I used to rely on others to fix me. I am so grateful I was attracted to CPA and now have an entirely new, more serene relationship with myself and my body.

What does attraction mean to me?

    I know that when people compliment me on my resilience or when my husband says, "I don't know how you do this every day," CPA should get the credit. Working the Steps, staying involved in meetings and doing service work help me to be the person I want to be, amidst my chronic pain and chronic illness. My goal is to like the person I was today when I lay my head on my pillow at night. My dreams for my life have been completely altered since getting sick. I've had to let go and change all the plans I had. But I have the ability to live at peace with myself and my family. That is the gift of CPA.

    I share this gift everywhere I go by living authentically with my chronic health conditions. I don't have to hide it, and I don't flaunt it, I'm just me. I have a lot of friends outside of CPA who are sick with the same illness. In support meetings or advocacy calls with these friends, I often have the opportunity to share my experience, strength, and hope. And when people ask me how I'm emotionally handling my situation so well, I get to tell them a little about CPA.

I identify myself as a woman in long-term recovery. When I talk with people, or they ask me questions, I don't identify myself as a member of a specific fellowship. I say I am in a woman in recovery, and this is what CPA has done for me. When I talk with outside entities, I share my experience in CPA, but I do not speak for CPA.

    When a member uses their full name promoting and advertising Chronic Pain Anonymous, it makes it unsafe for everyone.

To protect the fellowship, we avoid being part of advertising or promoting. When newcomers see and experience what members who work a program receive, there is no need for promotion.

I had been a professional who worked in the field of pain and addiction. In CPA, my former profession was not part of how I identified myself at my meeting; I kept this part of my life anonymous. I got to be an equal participant in how I deal with pain and medication. As I watched others figure out what they needed to do by working the program, I got excited, seeing the results of what happens when someone works this program thoroughly. It renewed me and gave me faith in the program and Steps.

To trust this community to deal with tough issues for me means not talking about outside issues and leaving my profession out of my meetings.

When CPA started out, we were working on updating the website. We thought it would be great to have videos of our co-founder, in his wheelchair, talking about the Twelve Steps and how he applied them in his life. We thought it would be wonderful to have this well-spoken, inspiring man as our spokesperson. Then we realized: we can't do that, as CPA has no spokesperson. It would be great promotion, but not attraction. So today we have a quote of his on the website and trust in the attraction that provides, while preserving his anonymity.

Although CPA is an anonymous fellowship, we are not a secret one. Public information and outreach is one of my passions. It is a way to work my Twelfth Step. When I talk to the public or professionals, I share how I found CPA and the improvements it has brought into my life. Meeting me may be the only CPA experience a person may have, so I practice humility, honesty, and kindness. Higher Power is responsible for motivating a new member to join CPA. It is my responsibility to provide information about CPA in an attractive way so people can find the fellowship.

I belong to other fellowships where I know others have chronic pain and chronic illness, and as much as I want to stand on a chair and shout, "Join CPA, it will change your life!" I don't. However, I do share about my journey in CPA to gain emotional and spiritual recovery. Because of this, a woman in another program told me she knew someone who deals with chronic pain and chronic illness and asked if she could give her my number. I spoke to this person and told her about how CPA had changed my life, and she began coming to CPA meetings. That is one way I have practiced attraction, not promotion. And it is also how I found CPA. I was asked to chair a meeting in another program but shared that I couldn't do it because all that was on my mind were my health issues. Someone reached out to me after the meeting and asked if I had heard of CPA. They shared about their experience, and we talked on the phone, and I started attending CPA meetings and have continued ever since.

On social media I don't share about CPA, but I do share about my health challenges. Because of that, I've had an opportunity to share my CPA experience individually with people who reach out to me. They ask how my spiritual outlook changed, and I share some of my story.

One of the first pieces of hope I got for recovery was in the preface of *Recipe for Recovery*: "Many of us with chronic pain and chronic illness have cognitive and energy deficits, and reading can be challenging and overwhelming. We have written this book to present the Twelve Steps in a way that is manageable for anyone, whatever their condition." I had been drowning in search engine websites and articles that were overwhelming and increased my anxiety and hopelessness. I was grateful the CPA website was clear and easy to read. The book came, and I read those two sentences, and my heart sang with joy. That was the first thing that made CPA attractive to me. I knew CPA was for people just like me. CPA honors the realities of living with chronic pain and chronic illness, and although our circumstances and conditions differ, we have similar challenges.

In a conversation with someone or during a share, I will refer to an idea that someone else has shared that was helpful to me or touched me, and I make sure not to say the person's name. I may say that I have heard the idea from another member, but usually I just say something like, "I have heard it said…" and then talk about the idea. Part of keeping other members' anonymity, for me, is not repeating anything that has been shared during a meeting.

Another aspect of anonymity that I try to be aware of occurs when I see someone from the program somewhere outside of the program. If this happens, I make eye contact but do not let on that I know the person, which for me includes not addressing or approaching them. I just let them come to me and do not mention the program unless they do, especially if they are with other people I do not know.

A natural extension of this aspect of anonymity for me is keeping the voice and identity of members confidential during online meetings, fellowship, conversations, and any social time we share. Some of the tools I use during a meeting are using headphones whenever someone else is present in my home (or the physical space I am in) and not showing faces of members by switching off the screen if someone in my house walks into the room during a meeting.

I have had a couple of experiences while attending videoconference meetings in which I can see or hear other people in the background, and it is obvious that these people can see and hear me while I am sharing, which makes it difficult to share intimate feelings and experiences. I feel uncomfortable and vulnerable because I have not consented to these people who are not in the meeting hearing what I am sharing. I think it is a kind of pact of confidentiality and mutual respect that we enter into when we decide to become members of CPA and attend a virtual meeting.

I definitely appreciate it when people do their best to keep everyone who comes to meetings and people involved in the fellowship, as anonymous as possible. This helps me to feel we are creating a safe space for everyone.

I have printed black-and-white brochures from the CPA website and also ordered the CPA color brochures, such as *What Is Chronic Pain Anonymous?*, *CPA and Meditation*, and *One Day at a Time Explained*, along with CPA bookmarks. I have asked some of my doctors if they are aware of CPA and that it is for people in chronic pain as well as people with a chronic illness. After a short conversation about CPA, I then ask for permission to leave CPA literature in their waiting room. Every doctor I have asked has given me permission to place brochures and bookmarks in their waiting room.

Talking, even in goodwill, about someone who shared in a meeting is breaking their anonymity. Even in the guise of, "How are you doing? I heard you were not doing well," that is breaking a person's anonymity. This happened to me in CPA and made me very uncomfortable. I shared about my health decline and expected that no one would share outside of the meeting what I'd said. Someone who was not at that meeting came up to me later and asked about what I had shared, which I had trusted would not be passed on to others. We do care about each other, but it is breaking confidentiality to share what someone says about their condition in a CPA meeting.

The anonymity of our specific diagnoses is important. I don't discuss the specifics of my conditions in meetings or in fellowship. However, I have developed friendships with people in CPA where we have talked privately, and I have disclosed things about my condition. One time, someone said, "So-and-so deals with that too." And I really didn't care for that. I don't like the idea of my conditions being revealed to other people.

I had a situation where I met a woman in CPA, and we became friends and talked about our diagnoses. She was recently diagnosed with a condition I knew a longtime member of CPA dealt with. I was careful to respect both of their anonymities. I asked this woman if she might want to talk to someone with the same condition. I went to the other person and said there was a newcomer dealing with her condition and asked if it was okay to give her their number. I respected their anonymity and got their permission before putting them into contact with one another.

It was in the six-month gap between doctors' appointments when I discovered CPA. At my next visit, my doctor asked, "What has changed, what has happened in the last six months?" I had a CPA brochure in my purse. I shared it, and his eyes lit up, and he said he'd never heard of it and thanked me for sharing it. He said he would share information about CPA with his patients and colleagues because he thought the difference in my attitude and sense of well-being was noticeable. Now I get phone calls from that office, asking for brochures.

I was on the phone with technical support for the CPA website and the person I was speaking to wanted to know more about CPA. When I described the program, he said he has a friend, a 19-year-old woman who got into an accident and has pain and is miserable. I told him about some meetings she might want to attend. We are always practicing attraction, even when we interact with businesses when we are taking care of the operations of CPA.

Each member attracts other people to Chronic Pain Anonymous by living the program. I do not tell people in my life or in waiting rooms that they must join CPA. Instead, I model my ability to live peacefully, joyfully, and comfortably with myself and others. It is one way I am of service and carry the message of CPA. I am compassionate, kind, empathetic, and a good listener. I greet people with a smile and friendly words and actually stop to listen to their responses. Even if I do not have a conversation with everyone I see, I smile at each person I make eye contact with when I have the pleasure of seeing another person. It is when people ask me something along the lines of how I can appear so joyful that I may ask them if they have heard of Chronic Pain Anonymous, which is for people with chronic pain and chronic illness.

I am a member among members in CPA. Regardless of the length of time I've been in the program, I'm just a member. I am a worker among workers in my CPA service, regardless of the position I hold. Yet, when I get home to my family, I begin to think I am entitled to certain accommodations because of my chronic pain and chronic illness. In fact, I am a family member among other family members. I have limitations, as do my other family members. And I can be caring and sensitive about their needs. They are also processing and grieving the change that has occurred. I have found that equanimity and compassion require practice and are a necessary ingredient as we all adjust to change.

Before joining CPA, when I went out with friends and I was having a bad day, I would let them know: "I am having a hard time, I don't know if my brain will work, I may have to leave early." I wasn't anonymous about what was going on with me. Because of CPA, I have learned to have humility. They have stuff going on too, but they are not announcing it. Why do I need to announce what is going on with me ahead of time?

I have learned to practice anonymity. Sometimes I need to share what is going on with me, and sometimes it's unnecessary. I do share when it is happening in the moment and is important to my safety and well-being. But generally speaking, people don't need to know what I am struggling with that day. I don't need to announce my dietary restrictions, for instance, when I'm out with others at a restaurant. When I am a guest, I may privately let the hostess know ahead of time.

The anonymity suggested in Tradition Eleven is a spiritual tool that when I use it makes me feel both more attractive and more at ease, wherever I go.

When I first came to CPA, one of the things that was happening was a symptom that affected my brain in ways that caused reactivity. I often became moody and overreactive at home. After a little time in CPA, I have developed compassion and a sense of humor about this. It occurred to me that when my husband is behaving badly, why not let him have a turn? I no longer get to be the only one acting badly. Neither of us is perfect. He gets to have a turn now.

In CPA, I am learning how to be a kind and gentle person, regardless of my resentments. It is not my place to step in and tell someone, "This is not how to do things." I am learning to be loving and gracious. My top resentment is with my mother. Because I practice this program, I can treat her as I would treat someone in a meeting. In a conversation the other day, she said she thought she was becoming depressed. She talked for 30 minutes about what was going on. I didn't change the subject—didn't make my problem front and center. I was happy to listen. She really opened up when I listened without judgment, without trying to fix her problems. As a result of my recovery, I now walk in the world with graciousness and loving-kindness. That is the humility of anonymity.

For some time, I allowed my diagnosis to become my identity. There is "always something wrong with the wife" was said in jest, by me. It was a brutal comment. In CPA, I get to be anonymous—not identified as my diagnosis, or as a wife. I get to just be me. I am not my roles in my family. I may be a daughter, a sister, a mother, or an employee. I'm also still me: a human being. I am not my diagnosis, not my illness, and not my condition of the day. The practice of anonymity is freedom.

WORKING TRADITION ELEVEN

Our public relations policy is based on attraction rather than promotion; we need always maintain personal anonymity at the level of press, radio, television, film, and the Internet.

The following questions can help deepen your understanding and application of Tradition Eleven in your recovery and in all your affairs. Use these questions with your sponsor or sponsee or your CPA group, or explore them on your own, selecting the ones that are relevant.

1. What does my group do to let those in our community know about our group? What do I do?
2. How do I share about CPA with others? When do I choose not to?
3. How do I share my experience, strength, and hope in meetings so it is attractive?
4. Are the qualities of my recovery attractive to others who live with chronic pain and chronic illness?
5. Do I share about CPA in all my affairs in such a way that it is attractive?
6. What role did attraction play in my finding CPA? How does that affect how I relate to newcomers?
7. How do I keep the confidences of fellow members?
8. Why is it important to practice anonymity in recovery?
9. How do I maintain anonymity at the level of press, radio, television, film, and the Internet?
10. Am I always careful to keep the confidences of people in my life?
11. Are there ways I seek attention and recognition?

12. How can I express feelings without blaming, shaming, or attacking others?
13. How do I communicate to the people who matter to me when I need to make changes in my care?
14. How do I accept others as equals?
15. What does applying Tradition Eleven in all my affairs look like today?
16. In what areas of my life do I already practice and understand the need for:
    - Attraction, not promotion
    - Anonymity
    - Anonymity and outside organizations
    - Attraction in public relations and the media
17. How can I include these spiritual tools where they may be missing in my life today?

Tradition Twelve

Anonymity is the spiritual foundation of all our traditions, ever reminding us to place principles before personalities.

> **Anonymity is the spiritual foundation of all our traditions, ever reminding us to place principles before personalities.**

This Tradition is the foundation of all the principles of our program. Anonymity means everyone in our program is equal; there are no hierarchies based on who we are or what we do. Maintaining anonymity safeguards all of us and is a protection for the fellowship and for each of us in our program of spiritual recovery. Humility is expressed through anonymity; we give up our natural desire for distinction, personal glory, and our own will. Focusing on the principles of our program, rather than individual members or points of view, creates a foundation of safety and inclusivity for all who may benefit from CPA.

SPIRITUAL TOOLS FOR PRACTICING TRADITION TWELVE

- Program of "we"
- Spirituality in action—principles before personalities
- The journey of recovery
- Humility
- Safety

APPLYING TRADITION TWELVE

I. In Our Groups

PROGRAM OF "WE"
As the foundational spiritual principle of all Twelve Step groups, anonymity is an applicable part of all of the Traditions. We are one among many, seeing how, within anonymity, we are no better or worse than our companions. We leave our professional role, social status, and affiliations outside of the meetings. We are all on

equal ground, no matter how much time we have in the program, no matter what service position we may hold, and all have an opportunity for recovery. With the protection of anonymity, we have spiritual safety and can witness a Power greater than ourselves working in our lives and the lives of our fellows. When we see the miracle of recovery occurring, we start to believe in that force as a presence for goodness.

Because of anonymity, people with many different health situations can come together and find recovery, no matter how diverse their issues may be. We identify with feelings and thoughts and with recovery experience. Every member's experience, strength, and hope—not their position, status, or diagnosis—are the key to our recovery. We don't focus on our illness or our pain but instead let go of our self-obsession and resist focusing our shares on how sick we are or how wonderful we are. We are one among many, and we feel that clearly, in an environment of anonymity. And as we witness our common humanity, we discover our love for each other.

This is a program of "we." Each of us is, first, a person in recovery, and second, a personality. In the atmosphere of anonymity and equality, those of us who struggle with feelings of self-worth can begin to develop self-respect as we experience mutual kindness, acceptance, and love. We are not defined by our successes or our failures when we are anonymous. We don't have to be perfect or polished. This makes it possible for us to know that no matter our situation, we all contribute to the common welfare that fosters improvement in our personal recovery, one day at a time.

Regarding names, members sometimes ask: Can we share last names with one another? This may be beneficial at times. When someone is hospitalized, it helps to know a last name to be able to reach out to that person.

When we leave our other affiliations outside the meeting, we acknowledge we are here for a common problem, in support of our primary purpose. There is no confusion or dilution of the message of recovery we came to CPA to hear. We find a place we belong and realize we are responsible for our own spiritual recovery by focusing on principles before personalities—our own and others'.

In other arenas of our life, we may be used to getting recognition for our contributions and efforts. However, in CPA, our spiritual growth is rooted in our humility—in being one among our fellows. Through the principle of anonymity, we are freed of the desire for status, and we can share our recovery easily, without expectations. The rooms of CPA may be the first place we have ever experienced this. For the common good, we surrender being unique, and we discover that our personal good is facilitated by promoting the good for everyone. Anonymity means that who we are "known as" does not matter. Instead, we are free to make changes that are good for us, without needing to explain or justify them based on an old idea of self. CPA remains strong, supported by this spiritual foundation.

It is in a meeting that most people first encounter CPA. So, the more our group embraces the gentle guidance found in the Traditions, the more capable we are of developing and maturing in recovery and carrying the message to newcomers. Anonymity as a spiritual foundation sets the attitude for this service work and makes our meetings a safe place for the priceless gift of recovery. We serve without expectation of reward and contribute to the spirit of kindness. It becomes evident, joyful, and easy to recognize that we are all on this journey, together.

SPIRITUALITY IN ACTION—PRINCIPLES BEFORE PERSONALITIES

Anonymity underlies all of the Traditions. Not just the practical aspects of anonymity—like no photos or last names. There is a deep spiritual significance that occurs when we sacrifice our personal aspirations for the general welfare of the fellowship. We find freedom from the grip of our personalities, and we discover the deeper truths of who we each are. This is only possible when there is no hierarchy—to protect ourselves from, to be chosen by, or that invites comparison of one another. There are no honors or awards in CPA, no distinctions made. This protects us from the temptations we all have for personal recognition and self-centeredness. And it allows us the opportunity to invite a Higher Power to be the only authority, so we may each truly recover.

We can't have unity without the spiritual practice of anonymity. When we focus on principles and not our unique personalities, our unity becomes clear. We are united for one purpose: recovery from the effects of living with chronic pain and chronic illness. The spiritual action of Tradition Twelve, for some of us, is sacrifice. We learn to give up our personal desires in service of our primary purpose—we find this is the only way for us to recover and that it supports CPA on all levels. We are truly being of service and perhaps understanding this feeling for the first time. This spiritual foundation of anonymity is the starting point of parity, creating a space where we each can recover in dignity.

One of the gifts of anonymity is that we see others with new eyes and find ourselves accepting each other. What is not important is who we are or where we come from, what we have done in the world, or our medical situation. If or how we move our body, the functionality of our five senses, the ways we attend a meeting—these don't matter. As we grow in the program, we realize we can learn and work with different kinds of people with varying capabilities. Until we come into the meetings of CPA, we may not realize that in the past, we were not seeing others in this way. In CPA, we underline the principles, which are trustworthy, rather than the personalities, which are imperfect.

Anonymity as a practice continually provides opportunities for spiritual growth. Sometimes this means doing something for somebody else and not letting the receiver know we were the giver. We become right-sized as we carry the message and let our ego's desires fall away. All we do is share how the Steps have worked in our life, how we have faith in them, and that they can work for others. We don't always know who needs this message, who is ready to hear it, or even if we are the best person to deliver it. We simply stick with our commitment to our recovery and let our Higher Power be in charge of outcomes.

Being of service is one way to actively practice putting principles before personalities. It takes us out of ourselves and focuses on the needs of others. It gives us concrete opportunities to shift away from self-obsession and do something different. Our spiritual growth benefits, and so does the fellowship. We receive immeasurable gifts from our CPA recovery, the generosity of our sponsor, and from the experience, strength, and hope we hear in our meetings. We serve from the motivation to give back and find we are freed from our self-centeredness.

The relationship between Tradition One and Tradition Twelve holds us together—both keep the focus on our common welfare. Each of us is a part of the fellowship and contributes to fostering hope and a new way of life for ourselves, our fellow members, and those who have yet to find CPA.

All the Traditions give us a foundation for learning how to love and live with others. Our recovery is defined as the ability to live peacefully, joyfully, and comfortably with ourselves and others, and the Steps and Traditions show us how to do this. In Tradition Twelve, we practice putting principles before personalities by upholding our foundation of anonymity.

THE JOURNEY OF RECOVERY

We are here to help each other and experience joy in seeing each other recover, one day at a time, and we celebrate each other's growth. Before coming to CPA, we may have felt isolated, fearful, and worthless. We were most often focused on ourselves, even when we did not know it. As we start supporting each other in recovery, we begin to feel a sense of belonging and connection. We begin to know a new satisfaction as we see ourselves as useful. Through sharing our recovery, we see how useful and worthy we are as we give to others.

We each can recover in grace because there is a Power greater than ourselves present in the process. Our will doesn't determine reality. We experience connection with our Higher Power when we are not attached to our personal preferences and the stories we tell about our life. The Steps show us we are powerless over most all the things we thought we were supposed to have power over. Once we recognize this, not only do we feel relieved, we can now hear the wisdom of our Higher Power and understand that our efficacy comes from our Higher Power, not just from our own abilities and virtue. We begin to feel truly engaged in life, in new and real ways. Most of us find this unfolds slowly; indeed, recovery is not a one-time event but a new way of life.

As sponsors, we don't tell our sponsees what to do but guide them to help themselves and stay in contact with the guidance of their Higher Power. Our role is to help them identify the program tools and principles that will support them. We trust that people will see what they need to see when they are ready. In this way, each of us, without exception, can grow in awareness and capacity for joy, compassion and love—for ourselves and for others.

We don't have to like everyone on this journey, nor will we. Some members will not like us. We all have challenges with members or encounter behaviors and personalities that we struggle to tolerate. When this happens, we remember why we are all here and focus on our own recovery rather than on how we wish others might behave. It helps to shift our focus to our reaction and away from the behaviors, people, or situations we are reacting to. When we are having a hard time, we can ask our sponsor and Higher Power for help. In this way, we receive guidance, relief, and personal growth.

When we no longer focus on what others think of us and stop judging them, there is space to try something new, stretch beyond our comfort zone, and open our minds to new ideas. Within the compassionate and loving environment of the fellowship, we can continue to find harmony in our lives. Our growth in program is nurtured in the safety of anonymity. As we witness inner and outer changes in our life, we want to keep coming back

We learn to trust the process. We take care of ourselves and reach out to serve others and the fellowship. We see how all of our ideas and contributions shape CPA, and we value the wide variety of perspectives and work together in a spirit of equality and graciousness. We offer our time, energy, and talents, with no expectation of receiving something in return—and find this is not hard to do. We care because we are united in working together. Our strength lies not in individual people but in the fellowship.

No matter where we are in our recovery journey, we are part of the group. We extend respect to others and to individual differences. We learn to trust and to be trustworthy, rather than to judge or be judged. When we pay attention to principles and not personalities, we can listen to the message and not the messenger. This is simple, anonymous service.

HUMILITY

Practicing humility in our group protects our recovery. It is appealing to be recognized by the group, whether for being an especially deserving victim or being the soul of recovery, but this desire for recognition can threaten our recovery. Consciously putting Tradition Twelve into our toolbox and committing to the spiritual foundation of anonymity means we are all special in our own way. No one is put above or below others. We all need each other, so it's vital that no one is put on a pedestal or belittled. Our meeting rooms are safe places of recovery for all, for we all have challenges and need support, whether we have spent a day, a month, or years in the fellowship. We serve and share, not for acknowledgment or validation but to help carry the message to the person who still suffers. In a spirit of anonymity, we acquire a new understanding of humility. We enjoy its freedom and remember the importance of unity.

Anonymity as humility means that where we live, what car we drive, how our body does or does not function, are not who we are. We know each other not by our external life but by our inner sharing of our heart and mind. We are helping others without pay or recognition. There is no room for—and no need for—self-glorification or pride. We bring our humility, a willingness to learn, and gratitude for the gifts of the program.

Guidance from our Higher Power is greater than any one of us. There are times when we are the one who gives and times when we are the one who receives. We help others and stay open to receiving and accepting help, even when this is challenging. The stability of our fellowship and our groups is assured when we choose principles over personalities.

No one is perfect. What would being "perfect" even mean? Being alive and in recovery gives us compassion for each other and a joy in letting go of perfection as a concept. We can have high standards for our recovery and even for ourselves, but we come to see that those standards are best set by our Higher Power, not by ourselves or others. We seek humility, not perfection, and humility is expressed through anonymity, which allows us to work together in unity, which in turn is where we find our spiritual strength and receive healing for our spirit.

We are each unique beings with far more in common than we ever suspected, and in CPA we are never alone. Our courage and clarity come from being part of a group conscience derived from a Power greater than our own. We turn over our will to that of our Higher Power and to the group conscience.

SAFETY

Anonymity supports our inclusiveness. As anonymous members of our fellowship, we are all equal and accepted. The particulars of our life are left outside the meeting, for there is safety when we find we are not judged by where we live, our financial circumstances, our politics, or medical diagnosis. These things are not relevant to our recovery and membership in CPA. We come into meetings where no one is better than any other member. Understanding that we are safe and equal to others in the group leads us out of isolation.

We feel safe to share honestly and openly, knowing what we are sharing is confidential. Our names, faces, and stories are held in the confidence of the group. Members can even use an alias if they prefer. We trust that what we share is kept private, and we don't engage in gossip or pry into people's private lives—we trust they will give us the details they want to share.

Confidentiality means that what we hear in the meeting does not leave the meeting. This gives us all the ability to share from the heart without concern about public disclosure. We each play a role in keeping our group a safe shelter so we feel protected and free to be ourselves.

Although we all understand and are responsible for the privacy that is important for everyone's safety, it is possible that not everyone in a meeting knows this right away. For example, some members may be in the middle of their journey working on not gossiping. If there is something so private that we could not bear it being mentioned in any way, we may want to share that kind of detail and information only with our sponsor. The sponsor-sponsee relationship is where we can share our most personal experiences.

Newcomers come to meetings and experience our openness and acceptance. They learn as we share how chronic illness and chronic pain have impacted us. We may talk about our struggles, fears, grief, and frustrations and how the program helped us regain our balance and sanity. This is how we all recover together. If the rooms are not safe, our shares might not be deep, authentic, and honest enough to support our emotional and spiritual recovery. We honor our anonymity by not sharing outside the rooms what we hear and whom we see in the rooms.

With Tradition Twelve, we can let go of drama and the need for attention. Our personality, which may have caused emotional pain, is not the focus. Within our anonymity we discover safety and ease. We are focused on one thing: our recovery from the disabling effects of chronic pain and chronic illness. We all share the same goal and have a shared primary purpose: to carry the message to all who still suffer.

II. In Our Service Bodies

All of our service work in CPA is grounded in the spiritual principle of anonymity. This is described specifically in each of the preceding chapters. We can trust CPA service and outreach to be based on principles, to be transparent, and to be aligned with the fellowship. We commit to doing service as one member among many. In applying the spiritual foundation of anonymity, we benefit, and in turn so does the fellowship and so do all those who need CPA to be there today and in days to come.

III. In All Our Affairs

In our relationships outside of CPA, we place principles before personalities by treating others with respect and equality. We avoid gossip and criticism and practice honesty, tolerance, and kindness in all our affairs.

When we choose to live a life of recovery, we turn to and accept the guidance of our Higher Power. We experience the spiritual principle of anonymity in our fellowship and find that it works wonders for our well-being and harmony in all our relationships. Our life becomes one of honor, honesty, and dignity in all areas. We choose to see the good in others—to not focus on their faults but to focus on what we have in common rather than our differences. We are committed to keeping an open mind and don't discount people in our relationships when we disagree with them. As we detach from personalities, actively applying the principles of unity and anonymity, we find peace of mind.

We practice these behaviors, first in the rooms and service in CPA, and then find we are able to apply them everywhere. As we practice, we become more skillful. Our communication becomes genuine, thoughtful, and respectful. We listen without judgment. We don't criticize or gossip, so there is safety and trust in our relationships. We use the tools of the program to help us learn to not be critical of others or their personalities. When there are conflicts, we trust our Higher Power will lead us to solutions we may not have considered on our own.

We remember not to place anyone, including ourselves, on a pedestal. We practice humility and feel free to be ourselves in situations where we used to feel pressure to meet expectations. We embrace our self-worth, no matter our physical condition. We value ourselves as a right-sized human being, in a real relationship with a Power greater than ourselves. We are good enough just as we are, and so are others. No one is invisible, and everyone is vital to the whole.

> **ASSOCIATED SPIRITUAL PRINCIPLE:** *Principles Before Personalities*
>
> The spiritual foundation of anonymity expresses itself in our humility, deepens our own spiritual growth, and is a safeguard for CPA as a whole. When interacting with others, we place principles before personalities, focusing on what we have in common rather than our differences. We seek to hear what is being expressed, not to measure the person expressing it. This is a "we" program, and we thrive when we support each other in our journey of recovery.

TRADITION TWELVE IN ACTION
Anonymity is the spiritual foundation of all our traditions, ever reminding us to place principles before personalities.

VOICES OF OUR MEMBERS

Placing principles before personalities has been a great part of my recovery, and I get lots of opportunities to practice it.

There are some people who say a lot about their medical history when they share in a meeting or are specific about the religion that they follow. While I am annoyed when this occurs, I can still feel compassion when these people express their vulnerability and what they are dealing with in their lives.

At times, I have felt hurt or rejected by a particular person. For example, there was one specific chairperson who I felt greeted other people with more warmth than they did me. I felt slighted and tearful to the point that I was considering not introducing myself when this person was the chair of a meeting. But I reminded myself about putting the principles of the program before personalities and that I had just as much right to participate in meetings as everyone else. Instead of withdrawing, I decided to make an effort to be warmer to that person when I spoke. Immediately that person responded with warmth to me. I felt closer to them and relieved of my hurt feelings.

I remember when I went to my first meeting, held in an affluent part of town. I am basically middle class, and my perception of the people at this meeting was that they were a few notches above me, and I was feeling intimidated and out of place. The people at the meeting did nothing to cause me to feel this way—it came from inside of me. Tradition Twelve addresses situations like this: when it comes to recovery, we are equals.

Things like financial status, where I live, politics, etc. do not make a difference in our fellowship. We are all working toward the common goal of recovery from the debilitating effects of chronic illness and pain; that is our common bond. Anonymity means that it does not matter how much money I make, what my job is, whether or not my child is an honor student, or how far I have progressed in my career. Anonymity keeps us together, supporting each other and encouraging each other in working our program.

When I am interacting with others in Chronic Pain Anonymous, I focus on a person's recovery—experience, strength, and hope—not on any of the outside elements of a person's life. In this program, we are transparent, supporting, welcoming, and caring to everyone we meet. I have found safety and welcome in CPA and want to share my recovery with others. Tradition Twelve gives me the freedom to do that and relieves me of the burden of feeling separate.

I am so grateful that when I enter a CPA meeting, it doesn't matter who I am, it doesn't matter where I live, it doesn't matter what car I drive or what kind of cat or dog I have. I get to drop all of that, as well as all of my professional credentials. It's such a relief. As a professional, I'm expected to maintain a certain level of authority. In CPA, I've got no authority. I am not the person at the front of the classroom, and I'm not the person in the back. I'm the person in the middle. That's a relief to me.

Our sponsors don't tell us what to do, and when we sponsor someone, we don't tell them what to do. That's a relief. I know I don't take well to being told what to do. I have turned my will and my life over in such a way that I honor and respect what my current CPA sponsor says to me. I trust that the guidance comes from a place of love, kindness, and safety. I'm grateful that I don't expect that someone is going to tell me how to handle any particular situation.

About safety: there are times I can only share certain things with my sponsor, but two or three years later, when they don't have an emotional charge anymore, I can share them with anyone. I never thought I'd come to a place in my life where I could openly say I'm a childhood incest survivor. If that's what needs to be said at a meeting, or with a person I'm talking to one-on-one, I'm totally open about it now. There were many years where I didn't share it at all.

I shared something with my sponsor yesterday that I'm not comfortable sharing with a whole group of people. But maybe, a few years from now, I will be willing to share it and I'll be able to help someone else through that process.

Early in my recovery, my sponsor told me to tell the story of my truth because someone else out there might have had that experience. Healing happens over time, slowly, and it's not necessary to put it out there while it's still raw. Many of us experience deep grief related to our pain and our illness. Sometimes we can share about it right away, but we don't always want to share publicly the deep grief part while we are going through it. Once we've gotten through it, then we can talk about how we got through it and offer some experience, strength, and hope.

When I was exploring my behavior around gossip, I thought that I wasn't a gossip. But then I realized I had a tricky way of doing it. I'd be in a group, and I would know something was going on with someone and would just bring their name up, innocuously, knowing it would start gossip, and I would stand there feeling smug because everyone else was gossiping.

Another issue I explored in myself was "one-upmanship" around my suffering. I deserve to have the same kind of care and loving generosity toward myself that I crave from others. Until I believe this, I will continue trying to convince you how bad it is through telling you how tough my life is.

Because CPA is a safe place to recover, I can explore parts of myself I'd never otherwise be willing or ready to look at.

I've told people that my doctor says I've got the worst case, that I'm the rare person, that they've "never seen a case like this before." I do this to bring attention to myself. And in my meetings, I don't have to do that. Even if no one has ever seen what I've got, so what? What difference does it make? It's no big deal. It just is what it is. In CPA, I am one among many others, recovering from the effects of chronic pain and chronic illness. That is so freeing. I need not pursue status here to belong.

I understand the need for anonymity in our meetings, but this got me thinking. How could I send flowers or cards to a CPA friend who was in the hospital? How could I send a care package to a member to brighten their day? Now, I ask my CPA friends if I can have their last names and mailing addresses. Some have been hesitant to share their personal information; others ask why I want it, perhaps thinking I am prying or being nosey. I honor their concerns by explaining my intent and promise to keep their information confidential. Clear and kind communication always improves my relationships and assists me in connecting in multiple ways.

Some members have their last names listed on their profile pictures when attending a videoconference meeting. I have seen members tell such folks, "We do not use last names." I believe it is each member's choice—to share their last name, or not.

Personally, I find it helpful to know someone's last name, especially in the case of common first names like John and Mary, but it is up to each person how they want to be identified. Some people use an initial of their last name if there is someone else with the same name.

I have an incredibly unique name, and I had to come to terms with lack of personal anonymity from the very beginning of my Twelve Step journey. I thought of changing my identifiable name, but part of my healing is practicing being my authentic self and turning my fears and "shoulds" over to my Higher Power. I protect others' anonymity, and I am free to make choices around my own within CPA.

I love the words "handi-capable" and "flawesome." Before my illness and disability, I felt sorry for handicapped people, as I could not bear the thought of something like that happening to me. I prided myself on my strong body and multitasking mind. If my body was ever less than perfect, I believed I was of little worth. Because of this erroneous belief, when I developed chronic pain and chronic illness I quickly slipped into depression and suicidal ideation. Then I found CPA.

My journey of recovery began when I saw members attached to medical equipment or confined to wheelchairs or beds laughing and talking about renewed purpose through the CPA service they were doing. Because I could finally see beyond their bodies, I could come to believe that I too could have a purpose-filled life. It would simply look different with my chronic condition.

Thanks to CPA's "come as you are" environment of unconditional kindness, honor, and respect, I am able see the principles of the program, not the differences in our bodies. No one is discounted based on their abilities or lack thereof, and I attribute this to CPA's spiritual principle of anonymity. We keep the focus on all the spiritual principles in each of the Twelve Steps, Traditions, and Concepts as we journey together—not on individual personalities or conditions.

Today, I call myself "flawesome," which acts as a reminder that I am just like everyone else, regardless of pain and illness, circumstances, and appearances. I am perfectly imperfect, and so is my body, and I still have a lot to contribute. I am human, and thanks to CPA and anonymity, that's finally okay with me.

I remember when I first began attending Twelve Step meetings, I was always kind of in awe of whoever led the meetings. I thought that this person must be special in some way or have some power or seniority. I looked up to them as a leader and believed they had some kind of status. As time went on, I discovered, much to my surprise, that this was not true.

In CPA, anyone of us can lead meetings, even someone who is fairly new. No one is more "special" than anyone else. We do not do service work because we are set apart or special, and we are not set apart or special because we do service work. In Tradition Twelve, anonymity can mean that we are all valuable and are all able to perform service work, whether it is leading a meeting or being treasurer or GR or sponsoring someone. The principles of anonymity and giving back are foundations; personalities are less significant. We are a fellowship where every member has value and worth. Things such as prestige, money, and power are not of any use to us. We all can find ways to give back by doing service work. It helps others, but it also strengthens our own recovery.

When I decided to launch a new CPA meeting, I received support from a fellow CPA member. I was very grateful for this, especially as I was new to CPA and Twelve Step programs. I was also rather overwhelmed by the idea of starting a new meeting, but I felt guided, and ready to step up and do service.

My fellow member showed a great degree of enthusiasm and support, helping to develop the format and letting others know about the meeting. We had what I considered to be a constructive conversation to discuss the essential aspects of the meeting (day of the week, time, etc.) and they offered to fill a service position. It became apparent shortly afterward that there had been a misunderstanding, and the person took umbrage with certain things I'd said. They declined my offer to have a "clear the air" discussion to try to resolve the misunderstanding, and shortly afterward they decided to withdraw their support for the meeting.

My initial reaction was disbelief, disappointment, and anger. I was new to the program and felt rejected and alone. I immediately reached out to my sponsor and another longtime CPA member. They both reminded me of the Twelfth Tradition: "principles before personalities"—that we focus on our own recovery rather than trying to direct how others behave. They both emphasized the importance of keeping my "side of the street clean" and of asking my Higher Power for guidance.

I went ahead with creating the meeting. During its early weeks, at times there were only a few members attending. I was discouraged after one meeting in which only I and one other person were there. I thought of canceling the meeting but instead asked my Higher Power for assistance in making the right decision. In a short period of time, the meeting attracted new members, and it soon had over 10 regular members, with new people showing up each month.

I am grateful that I had the spiritual principles and other members to guide me as I learned how to practice and apply Tradition Twelve to what was initially a very difficult episode in program for me. I learned that no one person makes a meeting happen, and that even when feelings are aroused by clashing personalities—my own and others'—recovery is our primary purpose.

I was just thinking about the concept of anonymity as freedom from my *own* personality...some state of consciousness where I'm standing back, looking at myself. So I can say, when some aspect of my personality arises in meetings, "Oh, there you are, Judger," and just sort of label it. I used to feel upset and berate myself or jump into some tool to fix that about myself, and now, by just labeling it and saying, "Oh, there you are. Wink. Wink. You can sit right here beside me, and maybe you want to relax a little bit." That makes it a lot easier to separate the "I from the Me," to separate "the Special One, among others who are less or more than I consider myself to be," from the me who is simply a recovering person among other recovering people.

We don't brag about what we do in service work. We don't take credit for what we do. I love that. I love that we do it because we do it freely. In any given day, I can choose how much I have to offer. I don't have to be held to yesterday's standard today. If today is not a good day, if I'm tired or hurting, I can let you see all of it, and that's okay.

I have been contributing service on a project, which I shared about to my mother. She said, "They better be paying you." And I said (laughing), "It's a volunteer gig. We're all volunteers. Everybody participating in this project are volunteers who want to help other people living with chronic pain and chronic illness to find some emotional and spiritual support, and love and kindness." The whole point of the CPA service work is to get the message out. If I was in my position at my job, it would be considered service to be voluntarily contributing to a project together. I don't need the credit. I am happy to contribute something I enjoy doing that doesn't hurt my body.

I attended a group conscience open forum for the CPA fellowship. The person who led our discussion was kind and compassionate. She said that all shares are welcome and encouraged at CPA meetings. This message helped me open my mind and change my opinion about, and especially my attitude toward, another member whom I didn't like.

The way the group conscience event was handled helped me look at myself and how I had put personalities before principles regarding the member I didn't respect. I discovered a resentment I wouldn't have seen as such, and followed that with Step work, talking with my sponsor about the source of the resentment, and so on. I began to see fear in the person I disliked rather than arrogance. I sincerely care about her now and am going to call and ask how she is today.

What a spiritual gift I was given. Learning about listening to others without condemnation helped me change. My Higher Power spoke kindly through the member who led this CPA event, and for that I am grateful.

When I began service work in CPA, I discovered all the principles at work. I felt responsible to those who might come after me. My purpose was to ensure the projects were implemented with consideration for, the Twelve Steps, Twelve Traditions, and Twelve Concepts. I saw how important it was for service bodies to be open to all who wished to serve and be heard. Even when difficult decisions were to be made, the debate was not about who was right or wrong—it was about what aligned best with the spiritual principles of CPA. It was not important that others knew I served, but I did share in meetings how service expanded my program, my sense of purpose, my appreciation for all those who do serve, and, without question, my respect for how CPA works together to ensure the strength of the fellowship as it expands. I am not only honored to be able to serve, I am grateful to how such service has strengthened and broadened my understanding of how these spiritual principles work.

Serving on task forces in CPA has shown me Tradition Twelve in action. The members with more years in CPA treated one another the same as they treated me. Everyone's ideas were considered—even this "newbie's." We focused on the tasks required for the benefit of CPA's continued growth. Laughter and a light atmosphere were a part of it all, too. It turns out that anonymity was what we were practicing. All of us were considered equal members. Just because others had more experience or a position on the CPA Board, their ideas did not count more than my own. It did mean they knew more about how CPA operated, so they enhanced our efforts accordingly. We did not discuss accomplishments in our professional, personal, civic, political, or any other arenas. This would have made some seem more important than others.

Tradition Twelve also guided us to place "principles before personalities." In other words, we discussed ideas and how they supported what was best for CPA. We focused on our goals serving CPA's primary purpose. I ended up looking forward to working on the task force each week because there was no stressing about whose opinion mattered more, arguing, members taking offense, or others needing to prove themselves. We treated one another with kindness and respect. Even if we did not agree with an idea, we stated our viewpoint calmly and matter-of-factly. I learned to put my ego aside and practice being yet another member of the team. It wasn't easy at first. Yet we got so much done for CPA because we did not spend time resolving personality conflicts. This was a payoff much more valuable than a pat on the back for a personal contribution. CPA had been saving my life, and all that mattered was giving back to keep it going. Today I am so grateful for Tradition Twelve and the principle of anonymity and "principles before personalities." I even do my best to apply it to all areas of my life now.

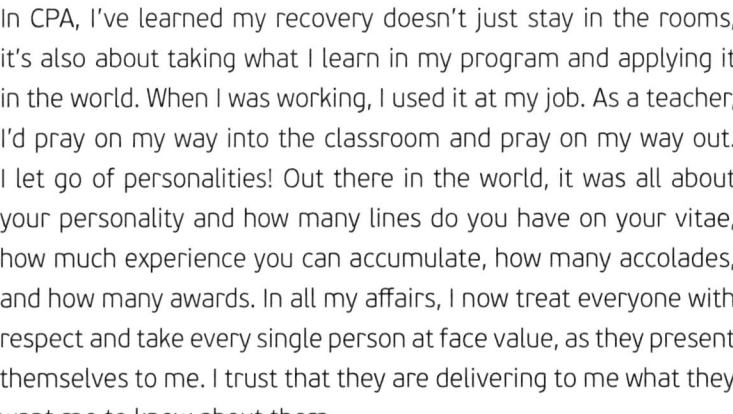

In CPA, I've learned my recovery doesn't just stay in the rooms, it's also about taking what I learn in my program and applying it in the world. When I was working, I used it at my job. As a teacher, I'd pray on my way into the classroom and pray on my way out. I let go of personalities! Out there in the world, it was all about your personality and how many lines do you have on your vitae, how much experience you can accumulate, how many accolades, and how many awards. In all my affairs, I now treat everyone with respect and take every single person at face value, as they present themselves to me. I trust that they are delivering to me what they want me to know about them.

We are all equals, inside the rooms and outside the rooms. Even if the person I'm talking to doesn't know that or even believe that, I am thinking about that. One more person thinking about that is having a positive effect out there. It's those little ripples. I can be kind and generous to a scheduler who calls about my surgery. I can say, "I hope you're doing well." I can wait and listen while she responds to me with a couple of lines about how she is doing. That is me taking my recovery into "all our affairs." Whether it's the grocery clerk or the overworked administrator at my doctor's office, I treat them with the same love and kindness I would give to my CPA friends.

I can be miserable, or I can be happy. It's often my choice. I've been practicing recognizing moments of joy, and they can be very simple moments. I hear the birds singing—that brings joy to me. I've found that one of the practices that feeds joy for me is seeing the good in others. It's true. People can irritate me. I can get so lost in that…and I don't have to gossip out loud; I'm just gossiping in my mind and making myself miserable, ranting about someone who is irritating me or something they did. I can choose to see the good or the bad in anyone. If I can take a moment to see the good, that means I'm going to practice "principles, not personalities," and the principle is: I see the good in this person. It helps me change my mind, and then I get to have peace of mind.

It's not always easy. There's a certain person that I'm struggling with. It stretches me...Where's the good? I like practicing that. That's a principle I bring to all my affairs: Where's the good in this person?

For years, I have had a number of chronic illnesses. As my illnesses progressed, I gradually became more dependent on other people to help me with the basic activities of living. This situation brought a bucket of tumultuous emotions. I was just figuring out how to grow up and be self-sufficient with the help of a Higher Power, when, by necessity, I became more dependent. One of the hardest areas for me to navigate was caregivers and the agencies for whom they worked.

A series of caregivers entered my life. It was hard having to deal with their differing personalities. Some did not seem to care about their job at all, some did only a small amount of work, some cared and got work done but insisted on being in charge of my apartment and life. Actually, many of them insisted on being in charge. Many of them were sure they knew what was best for my life. I spent a great deal of the little energy I had standing up for myself, trying to explain my philosophy that a disabled person could require help and still have say over their own situation, arguing with the agencies, and getting upset about my situation. I dreaded each day, not knowing if someone was going to show up or what mood they would be in if they did.

One day, I confided to a friend in CPA that I was so very tired of the power struggle. She quietly said, "Well then, let go of the power struggle." After a few minutes of thought about what this meant I said, "AHA!" I promptly went through Steps One, Two, and Three, focusing on how they applied to my relationship with caregivers. I asked for my Higher Power's help and guidance with the seemingly impossible situation. I also reminded myself that I could not change who they were or what they thought. I asked for HP's help in accepting this. In a way, I had been trying to control them even as they tried to control me. A sense of peace came over me.

After that, when they did or said something I considered inappropriate, I quietly said a prayer. When they got angry at a boundary I set or a reply to their mean comments, I remained calm and thought to myself, I will let them have their feelings. I do not need to react. I do not need to change them. I only need to take care of myself to the best of my ability.

They didn't change. They quit. A few at a time. Then several wonderful people came. I still had some difficult people on weekends, but I was able to calmly talk to the agency and request they not come back. I know things will not be perfect from now on, but I have my Higher Power and the Steps and Traditions of CPA to turn to for help.

It's actually enjoyable now for me to discover how the CPA Traditions support the Steps and how I can practice them in all my affairs. In this case, Tradition Twelve—"placing principles before personalities"—led me to confide in a CPA friend (two principles of the program: sharing honestly and asking for help), which led me to Steps One through Three (the Steps are the foundational principles of the program), and what I got was release from the grip of my desire for things to be different than they were. When I practice recovery in CPA, I get serenity, ease, and agency.

WORKING TRADITION TWELVE
Anonymity is the spiritual foundation of all our traditions, ever reminding us to place principles before personalities.

The following questions can help deepen your understanding and application of Tradition Twelve in your recovery and in all your affairs. Use these questions with your sponsor or sponsee, or your CPA group, or explore them on your own, selecting the ones that are relevant.

1. How has practicing anonymity in CPA affected me?
2. What is my part in helping CPA fulfill its primary purpose?
3. Do I actively participate in keeping my meetings safe for all by practicing the Traditions?
4. Have I let my personality, pride, selfishness, or arrogance disrupt a meeting or the unity of CPA?
5. Am I able to share and perform service without seeking recognition?
6. Do I refrain from complaining about other members?
7. How do I protect my anonymity? That of my fellow members?
8. How does my understanding of the Traditions benefit my recovery? Benefit my group? Benefit CPA as a whole?
9. Which spiritual principles are most challenging for me to practice?
10. How do I practice anonymity in all my affairs?
11. What does humility feel like? Where do I see it in myself, in others?

12. How does serving with humility benefit my spiritual growth, both in CPA and in all my affairs?
13. Am I able to see the good in others, even those whom I don't like?
14. How do I practice placing principles before personalities? When is this hard for me to do?
15. How do I practice tolerance, respect, and unconditional kindness?
16. What does applying Tradition Twelve in all my affairs look like today?
17. In what areas of my life do I already practice and understand the need for:
    - Program of "we"
    - Spirituality in action—principles before personalities
    - The journey of recovery
    - Humility
    - Safety
18. How can I include these spiritual tools where they may be missing in my life today?

Conclusion

The Traditions are the glue that keeps our fellowship together and functioning smoothly. It is important that we are familiar with these principles and how they can be applied in our groups, in our service bodies, and in all our affairs. They create the foundation for the unity that sustains and supports the survival of CPA. The Traditions ensure the continuance of CPA by providing guidelines that complement and support our personal recovery using the Twelve Steps. They show us how our program of action looks in our relationships with others as a member of CPA, as a trusted servant, and as a human being.

The Twelve Steps offer a solution, a way out of the misery, confusion, and disruption of life with a chronic health condition. Someone shows us how to work this simple program, and we turn around and help others who are struggling, just as we were helped. It is through our example, in word and action, that we show others how the program works.

The Traditions serve the same purpose, but unlike the Steps, which are about our individual recovery, they are focused on how groups interact and stay on track without falling apart. They are universal principles, and they work. They offer clear guidelines for interacting with unity, humility, love, and selflessness. The Traditions may have similar attributes, but each one focuses on a specific aspect of group interaction. To maintain the strength of our fellowship, we need to practice all of them. However, no one is forcing us. The Traditions are not rules or bylaws; no one is thrown out for not following them. We just recognize that upholding them is how we can ensure CPA stays together, intact, and on purpose, today and in the future. We trust in our goodwill and our desire to support our unity. Each of us can choose to be a member of CPA and to follow the guidance of the Twelve Traditions.

Becoming familiar with and applying the Traditions helps us create an atmosphere of recovery, safety, and caring in which we can experience identification, empathy, hope, and compassion. They help us stay on course and work together in the spirit of harmony. The Traditions suggest clear ways of interacting with others and the world so that we are kind, productive, and respectful, seeking not glory but recovery. We learn how to be a member of a fellowship and how to grow together in our recovery, regardless of our differences.

We apply these principles to the best of our ability, one day at a time. We will all make mistakes. We need to remember we are in the care of a loving Higher Power, and we trust in this ultimate authority. The spiritual principles of the Traditions and the love of our Higher Power keep us steady and give us tools for working together, as equals. They ensure that our personal recovery and our fellowship remain strong and can withstand challenges that will arise. If we head in the wrong direction, we can correct our course. There is room for us to learn and grow. In CPA, we practice forgiveness and experience renewal.

Guided by the Traditions, we stay focused on our primary purpose and are able to help those who still suffer. We do this together, not alone. We all know the despair and tear in the fabric of our lives as the result of chronic pain and chronic illness. We come together in CPA and share the responsibility of maintaining our fellowship, which has saved our life and which we believe can save others.

We serve with humility, carrying the message simply and honestly, and we grow together. In unity, love, and safety, we find serenity within a caring community that supports us in our spiritual journey.

How will you integrate the Traditions into your life in CPA and in all your affairs? The tools, materials, and questions in this book are here to help you on your journey.

Glossary

The Traditions provide guidelines for group governance. This glossary provides a shared understanding of the terms used in our Traditions.

affiliation—To bring into close association or official connection.

anonymous—Not named or identified. Lacking individuality, unique character, or distinction.

attraction—Providing something of value without promoting a particular benefit or outcome.

autonomy—Freedom to determine one's own actions and behavior.

common welfare—What is beneficial for and agreed upon by all or most members of a given community.

cooperation—Working or acting together for a common purpose or benefit.

debilitation—Impairing strength, causing weakness or lack of vitality.

govern—To control, direct, or strongly influence the actions and conduct of others.

group—When two or more members of CPA gather for the purpose of recovery.

HP—An abbreviated term people use for Higher Power.

primary purpose—Primary is defined as what is most important. CPA's primary purpose is to carry the message of hope and recovery.

principles—An accepted or professed rule of action; guide for conduct.

promotion—Trying to persuade someone of the worth or value of a product or institution.

service body—A group formed to provide specific services to the fellowship.

spiritual—Relating to inner values and meanings, as distinguished from material things or anything of a physical nature. A subjective experience of a sacred dimension.

unity—The state of being joined together in agreement with oneness of mind bound into a whole in accord and harmony. Singleness and continuity of purposeful action.

Appendix A

The Twelve Steps of CPA

1. We admitted we were powerless over pain and illness—that our lives had become unmanageable.
2. Came to believe that a Power greater than ourselves could restore us to sanity.
3. Made a decision to turn our will and our lives over to the care of God *as we understood Him*.
4. Made a searching and fearless moral inventory of ourselves.
5. Admitted to God, to ourselves, and to another human being the exact nature of our wrongs.
6. Were entirely ready to have God remove all these defects of character.
7. Humbly asked Him to remove our shortcomings.
8. Made a list of all persons we had harmed, and became willing to make amends to them all.
9. Made direct amends to such people wherever possible, except when to do so would injure them or others.
10. Continued to take personal inventory and when we were wrong promptly admitted it.
11. Sought through prayer and meditation to improve our conscious contact with God *as we understood Him*, praying only for knowledge of His will for us and the power to carry that out.
12. Having had a spiritual awakening as the result of these steps, we tried to carry this message to others with chronic pain and chronic illness, and to practice these principles in all our affairs.

Adapted by permission of Alcoholics Anonymous.

Appendix B

The Twelve Traditions of CPA

1. Our common welfare should come first; personal recovery depends upon CPA Unity.
2. For our group purpose there is but one ultimate authority—a loving God as He may express Himself in our group conscience. Our leaders are but trusted servants; they do not govern.
3. The only requirement for CPA membership is a desire to recover from the emotional and spiritual debilitation of chronic pain or chronic illness.
4. Each group should be autonomous except in matters affecting other groups or CPA as a whole.
5. Each group has but one primary purpose—to carry its message to people living with chronic pain and chronic illness.
6. A CPA group ought never endorse, finance, or lend the CPA name to any outside enterprise, lest problems of money, property, and prestige divert us from our primary purpose.
7. Every CPA group ought to be fully self-supporting, declining outside contributions.
8. Chronic Pain Anonymous should remain forever nonprofessional, but our service centers may employ special workers.
9. CPA, as such, ought never be organized; but we may create service boards or committees directly responsible to those they serve.

10. Chronic Pain Anonymous has no opinion on outside issues; hence the CPA name ought never be drawn into public controversy.
11. Our public relations policy is based on attraction rather than promotion; we need always maintain personal anonymity at the level of press, radio, television, film, and the Internet.
12. Anonymity is the spiritual foundation of all our traditions, ever reminding us to place principles before personalities.

Adapted by permission of Alcoholics Anonymous.

Appendix C

Twelve Concepts of Service

1. The final responsibility and the ultimate authority for the CPA World Services should always reside in the collective conscience of our whole Fellowship.
2. The CPA groups delegate complete administrative and operational authority to their World Service Conference and its service arms.
3. As a traditional means of creating and maintaining a clearly defined working relationship among the groups, the World Service Conference, the Service Board of Trustees and its service corporation, staffs, and committees, and of thus ensuring their effective leadership, it is hereby suggested we endow each of these elements of World Service with a traditional "Right of Decision."
4. The "Right of Participation" ensures equality of opportunity for all in the decision-making process. Participation is the key to harmony.
5. Throughout our structure, a traditional "Right of Appeal" ought to prevail, so that minority opinion will be heard and personal grievances will receive careful consideration.
6. The World Service Conference recognizes the chief initiative and active responsibility in most world service matters can be exercised by the trustee members of the Conference acting as the Trustee Board.
7. The Trustees have legal rights while the rights of the Conference are traditional.

8. The Trustees are the principal planners and administrators of overall policy and finance. The Service Board of Trustees delegates full authority for routine management to its executive committees.
9. Good personal leadership at all service levels is a necessity. In the field of world service, the Service Board of Trustees assumes the primary leadership.
10. Every service responsibility should be matched by an equal service authority, with the scope of such authority well defined.
11. The General Service Virtual Office is composed of the Executive Director, selected committees, and staff members.
12. The Conference shall observe the spirit of CPA tradition, taking care that it never becomes the seat of perilous wealth or power; that sufficient operating funds and reserves be its prudent financial principle; that it place none of its members in a position of unqualified authority over others; that it reach all important decisions by discussion, vote, and whenever possible, substantial unanimity; that its actions never be personally punitive nor an incitement to public controversy; that it never perform authoritative acts of government; that, like the Fellowship it serves, it will always remain democratic in thought and action.

General Warranties of the Conferences

- Warranty One: "that it never becomes the seat of perilous wealth or power"
- Warranty Two: "that sufficient operating funds and reserves be its prudent financial principle"
- Warranty Three: "that it place none of its members in a position of unqualified authority over others"
- Warranty Four: "that it reach all important decisions by discussion, vote, and whenever possible, substantial unanimity"

- Warranty Five: "that its actions never be personally punitive nor an incitement to public controversy"
- Warranty Six: "that it never perform authoritative acts of government; that, like the Fellowship it serves, it will always remain democratic in thought and action"

Appendix D

Additional Literature Resources

Chronic Pain Anonymous offers other literature that will offer guidance and support to groups as they apply the Twelve Traditions. These include information on group inventory, group conscience, business meetings, and much more. There are also many other pieces of literature on other topics provided to our members. Please be sure to visit the CPA website to find all that is available.

CPA literature can be purchased or downloaded at http://www.chronicpainanonymous.org.

Want to learn more?

To contact CPA, visit the website at http://www.chronicpainanonymous.org, or write to:

Chronic Pain Anonymous Service Board
8924 East Pinnacle Peak Road, Suite G5-628
Scottsdale, AZ 85255

Index

acceptance
    in all our affairs, 52
    and anonymity, 233, 237
    and attraction, 47
    of help, 142, 145, 237
    and leaving professional roles outside, 158
    of newcomers, 4, 56, 63, 238
    of others as equals, 63, 228
    of others as they are, 23, 52
    of physical pain and illness, 58
    self-acceptance, 62, 79, 81, 212
    and trust, 14
    unconditional, 48–49, 64
accessibility, 50–51, 59, 106, 149, 213. *See also* carrying the message
accountability
    and finances, 128–29, 134, 153
    and integrity, 156
    and open communication, 154
    in personal relationships, 176–77
    practice of, 164
    in service, 8, 90, 152, 153–55, 166, 169, 174
affiliations
    and anonymity, 212–13

affiliations *continued*
    and assessments of others, 163
    and boundaries, 108
    and consistent messages, 6
    and focus on primary purpose, 106–7, 110
    and individual choice, 48
    and non-affiliation, 112
    and outside literature, 3, 6, 75–76
    and program of "we," 230–32
    religious, 193–94
    and self-support, 123
    and sharing, 119
    and singleness of purpose, 109
    and unconditional acceptance, 48–49
anonymity
    and acceptance, 233, 237
    and attraction rather than promotion, 217, 219
    in common bonds, 189, 241
    and equality, 212
    as freedom, 226, 247–48
    and humility, 190, 215, 225–26, 236, 37
    and inclusiveness, 193–94
    and leaving professional roles outside, 219

anonymity *continued*
    as a member, 191–93, 206, 221–22
    and mutual respect, 190
    in our online presence, 212
    and outside organizations, 199, 212–13, 228
    personal, 191, 206, 210–12, 244–45
    practice of, xiv, 206, 210–12, 228, 254
    and principles before personalities, 232–34, 236, 240, 250
    and program of "we," 230–32
    and public relations, 213–14
    and reciprocal support, 151
    in relationships, 215–16
    safety of, 153, 192, 194, 211–12, 214, 230, 231–32, 235, 237–38
    and service, 152, 173, 192–93, 239, 246
    and sharing, 151, 193–94
    of specific diagnoses, 223
    spiritual practice of, 232–33, 236–37, 239, 245
apprentice/apprenticeship, 7–8, 19, 160, 181
asking for help
    and accountability, 8
    in all our affairs, 131–33
    and boundaries, 141–42
    and compassionate participation, 130

asking for help *continued*
    Higher Power, 92
    and humility, 127
    and listening, 14
    and perfection, 18
    and principles before personalities, 253
    of professionals, 164
    and self-support, 129, 138, 140
    in service, 168
    and special workers, 162–63
    as trusted servants, 152
    and unity, 16
attraction
    and acceptance, 47
    and anonymity, 217
    and autonomy, 67
    and carrying the message, 87, 88, 218, 224
    and detachment from opinions and personal agendas, 192
    in public relations and the media, 213–14, 227–28
    rather than promotion, 195, 208–10, 215, 217–18, 219, 228
    and sharing, 212
autonomy
    and balance, 69, 75–76, 79
    and boundaries, 67–68
    definition of, 66
    and interdependence, 71, 75
    and mobility aids, 140
    and personal relationships, 72–74

autonomy *continued*
   practice of, xiv, 67, 81–82, 167
   responsibility for unity, 69–71
   in service, 72

awareness
   and autonomy, 66
   of common welfare, 10
   and controversy, 197
   and group conscience, 27, 70
   and listening, 38
   and personal relationships, 73
   self-awareness, 71
   sharing with, 193–94, 206
   of social media involvement, 191
   that everyone has a voice, 31
   and well-being, 132

balance
   and acceptance, 238
   and autonomy, 68–69
   and common welfare, 9
   and complaining, 100
   of independence and responsibility, 81, 163, 168
   and our primary purpose, 130
   in personal relationships, 72–74
   practice of, 82
   and self-support, 124, 129
   in service, 98, 182
   and the Traditions, xiv

belonging
   and acceptance, 48
   and accountability, 8
   and connection, 49–50, 52
   and inclusion, 46–47, 51
   and the journey of recovery, 234–35
   and newcomers, 5
   and our primary purpose, 232
   practice of, 64
   and self-worth, 61
   and service, 32, 91
   and status, 244

Board of Trustees, xii, 115, 116, 134, 153, 155, 160–61, 175

boundaries, 9, 67–68, 82, 108, 111, 116, 119, 120, 141, 152

business meetings, 7, 12–13, 27, 37–38, 40, 69–70, 76, 144, 167–68, 178, 201

caregivers, 82, 103, 111, 140, 177, 197, 252

carrying the message
   and autonomy, 67
   and balance, 100–101
   and communication, 88
   consistency, 6
   and differences, 64
   to newcomers, 96, 232
   and our primary purpose, 84–87, 91, 97
   and outreach, 195
   practice of, 103
   and responsibility, 71, 88, 149, 151

carrying the message *continued*
  and self-support, 122
  and service, 72, 174
  and sharing, 11, 89, 93–94
  and singleness of purpose, 109
  and unity, xiv
Chronic Pain Anonymous Service Board (CPASB), xii, 50–51, 124–25, 153–54, 160–61, 170, 175
clear flow of information, 169–70, 185
collective view, *190–91, 206*
common bonds, 188–90, 198, 199, 206, 241
common welfare
  in all our affairs, 8–10, 12, 21
  and autonomy, 81
  and equality, 6, 172
  and group conscience, 167
  and our primary purpose, 189
  and principles before personalities, 234
  program of "we," 231
  safeguarding, 5, 16
  and surrender, 7
  and the Traditions, xiv, xvii
  See also unity
communication
  in all our affairs, 9, 73, 111, 177, 216, 228, 239, 244
  and being critical, 103
  and carrying the message, 88
  and clear flow of information, 169–70, 185

communication *continued*
  digital, 191
  and inclusion, 61
  and our primary purpose, 194
  practice of, 23
  and self-support, 140, 141–42
  in service, 33–34, 72, 91, 180
  and supporting the whole, 124–25
  and trusted servants, 183
  and unity, 5–6
  when making decisions, 81
  See also listening
compassion
  in all our affairs, 92, 111, 176
  and attraction rather than promotion, 209
  and carrying the message, 99
  communicating with, 9, 88
  and contributions, 128
  and non-controversy, 196
  in our meetings, 13–14, 18, 151, 241, 248
  and our primary purpose, 85, 124
  participation, 129–30, 146
  and perfection, 237
  on recovery journey, 235
  self-compassion, 89
  and service, 90, 139, 181
  and sharing, 158
  towards others, 23, 57, 103, 225–26

Conference Approved Literature (CAL), 6, 68, 119, 190
confidentiality, 211, 222, 223, 237–38, 244. *See also* anonymity
connection, 3, 10, 16, 42, 49–50, 51, 52, 64, 84–85, 197, 234–35
consistent message, 6, 23, 68, 89, 170, 190
controversy, 36–37, 109, 189–91, 193, 194, 195, 196–98, 199–202, 206
cooperation
   in all our affairs, xv, 34–35, 111, 131
   in group conscience, 30
   and inclusivity, 51
   and interdependence, 71
   with other organizations while maintaining boundaries, 108, 116
   with others, 9, 44, 137
   practice of, 120
   and public relations, 213–14
   in service, 33
   and the Traditions, xiv
   as trusted servants, 171
   crosstalk, 16

debilitation, 47, 53–55, 58, 59, 85, 106, 109, 139, 172, 241
diversity, xiii, 5, 31, 188, 209

enterprises. *See* affiliations

equality
   and acceptance, 228
   in all our affairs, 9, 34–35, 131–32, 155, 176–77, 239, 251
   and anonymity, 191, 212, 219, 230
   and contributions, 60, 128
   and decision making, 41
   fellowship of, 172–73, 177, 185, 211–12
   and integrity, 156
   in the journey of recovery, 113–14, 236
   in leadership, 212
   and learning on the job, 152
   and leaving professional roles outside, 158
   practice of, 23, 185
   and program of "we," 231
   and recovering together, 150–51, 241
   safety of, 153, 237,
   and scorekeeping, 20
   in service, 124, 160, 250
   structure of, 30, 180
   and trusted servants, 171
   and unity, 6, 31
everyone has a voice, 31, 44, 167

faith, 28, 36, 44, 54, 68, 126, 27, 137, 160, 100, 210, 219. *See also* Higher Power
fellowship
   and anonymity, 200, 208, 211–12, 217, 223, 230, 237, 239

fellowship *continued*
   and attraction rather than
      promotion, 219–20
   and autonomy, 66, 75
   and balance, 68–69
   and boundaries, 15, 67–68,
      108
   and clear flow of
      information, 169–70
   and common bonds, 189
   of equals, 172–73, 177, 185,
      211–12
   everyone has a voice, 31
   and finances, 128
   focus of, 84
   and focus on primary
      purpose, 107
   freely sharing in, 148
   and group responsibility, 89
   and group participation, 168
   and humility, 236–37
   and inclusion, 47, 50, 53, 61
   and integrity, 156
   and interdependent
      autonomy, 71, 75
   larger, xvii–xviii
   leaving credentials outside
      the, 153
   and mutual respect, 189–90
   and newcomers, 5, 94–95
   and obedience to the
      unenforceable, xvi–xvii
   and other organizations, 108
   and principles before
      personalities, 232, 246
   and the recovery journey,
      235–36

fellowship *continued*
   representing the, 81
   and responsibility for unity,
      69–70
   safeguarding the, 3, 188
   and self-support, 122, 129
   and service, 7–8, 33, 51, 59,
      72, 90, 151–52, 166,
      195, 234, 239
   and the Service Board, 175
   and singleness of purpose,
      109–10
   as solution-focused, 16
   and special workers, 153–55
   and spiritual strength, 127
   and structure of service, 29–
      30, 124–25, 173–75
   support, 78, 133
   and the Traditions, xiii–xvi,
      13
   and trusted servants, 171–72
   and unity, 2–3, 6
   and willingness to serve,
      32–33
   worldwide, 33, 122, 124–25,
      168, 175, 184

finances
   and accountability, 128–29,
      134, 153
   honesty about, 128–29, 146
   and inclusiveness, 237, 241
   integrity, 175
   and our primary purpose,
      130
   and paying it forward,
      161–62
   responsibilities, 160

finances *continued*
- and self-support, 123–24, 128–29, 139–40, 142–43, 156
- singleness of purpose, 109–10
- support, 133
- transparency, 115–16, 132–33
- and willingness to give, 127–28, 137

flexibility, xiii–xiv, 3, 9, 23, 28, 37, 44, 170, 176, 178, 180, 184–85

focus
- and attraction rather than promotion, 217
- and awareness, 193
- and common bonds, 189, 198, 205, 239, 240
- on common welfare, 21
- and compassionate participation, 130
- and Higher Power, 131
- and listening, 38
- on not harming others, 82
- and outside issues, 199, 203, 241–42
- on personal recovery, 109–10, 113, 192, 198
- and personal relationships, 74
- on prestige, 109–10
- on principles before personalities, 50, 51, 230, 232–34, 238, 245, 247
- program of "we," 231

focus *continued*
- and public outreach, 195
- on recovery, 194, 206
- and recovery journey, 234–35
- self-centered, 12
- of service, 110, 120
- shifting of, 52, 61
- singleness of purpose, 109–10
- on solutions, 4, 15, 16
- and unconditional acceptance, 48–49
- on unity, 2, 7
- *See also* primary purpose

General Advisory Council (GAC), 30, 33, 78, 125

General Service Virtual Office (GSVO), 50–51, 59–60, 128, 175

generosity, 14–15, 17, 19, 57, 126, 142, 144–45, 161, 170, 234, 243, 251

giving it away, 85–86, 103, 150

goodwill, 169, 213, 222

gossip, 4, 10, 91, 238, 239, 243, 251–52

governance, xiv, 26, 66, 171, 175

gratitude, 51, 87, 126, 132, 135, 137, 139, 144, 151, 176–77, 182, 216, 237

group conscience
- in all our affairs, 34–35
- and autonomy, 67
- and clear flow of information, 169

group conscience *continued*
   and controversy, 201
   and equality, 173
   everyone has a voice, 36–37, 136–37
   and group archives, 178
   and group autonomy, 167
   and group inventory, 70
   Higher Power expressed through, 6, 26–27, 30, 34, 36–39, 44, 126–27, 172, 196, 237
   and humility, 237
   and listening, 27, 28–29, 169
   and opinions, 27, 76, 167, 194
   participation in, 42–44, 64
   and patience, 27–28
   and principles before personalities, 248–49
   and responsibility for unity, 70
   scheduling of, 76
   and the Serenity Prayer, 17
   and service, 30, 32, 174
   and surrender, 7, 170
   and the Traditions, xix, xv
   and trust and faith, 28
   and unity, 3, 12, 28
   and the World Service Conference, 125
group inventory, 29, 44, 69–70
Group Representative (GR), 69, 72, 123, 125, 135–36, 144, 151, 169, 179–80
group responsibility, 89–90, 103

harmony
   in all our affairs, 73, 91, 131, 215, 239
   and autonomy, 69, 76
   and communication, 169
   and our primary purpose, 194
   practice of, 22, 43
   in service, 91
   and shared responsibility, 3
   through fellowship, 235
   and the Traditions, xiv–xvi, xvii–xviii
   and unity, 2, 70
Higher Power
   in all our affairs, 10, 34–35, 52–53, 73–74, 92, 118, 131, 156, 176–77, 197–98, 216, 239–40
   and anonymity, 193–94, 214, 233–34, 245
   and apprenticeship, 160
   and attraction, 220
   and autonomy, 79–80
   and caregivers, 252–53
   and choice, 48, 50
   and common bonds, 189
   and communication, 5–6, 169–70
   and controversy, 193, 202
   decision making, 13–14, 35
   expressed through group conscience, 6, 26–27, 30, 34, 36, 44, 126–27, 172, 196, 237
   and the gifts of recovery, 149
   and group conscience, 38

Higher Power *continued*
   and humility, 182, 237
   and the journey of recovery, 234–35
   and listening, 28–29, 34–35, 194, 249
   Live and Let Live, 201
   and the newcomer, 56
   and patience, 27–28
   and positions of responsibility, 168
   practice of, 37, 43–44, 62, 82, 103, 145
   recovering together, 150
   and self-support, 124, 126–27, 131
   and service, 7, 18–19, 39–40, 97, 142–43, 181
   and special workers, 163
   support of, 134–36, 139–40, 204, 247
   and the Traditions, xv, xvii
   and trust and faith, 28, 36
   and unity, 17
   and willingness, 58
home group, 27, 37, 40, 78, 96
honesty
   about finances, 128–29, 146
   in all our affairs, 131–32, 177, 239
   and anonymity, 211–12
   as basic value, xix
   and boundaries, 108
   and communication, 5, 141
   and humility, 127
   practice of, 140, 142–43, 183, 185, 220

honesty *continued*
   and safety, 237–38
   and sharing, 5, 55, 87, 89, 90, 159, 193, 209, 253
   and special workers, 155
   as spiritual principle, 160
HP. *See* Higher Power
humility
   in all our affairs, 10, 35, 215, 240
   and anonymity, 225, 226, 230, 232, 236–37
   and mutual respect, 190
   practice of, 159, 182, 184, 220, 254–55
   and recovering together, 150
   in service, 31–32, 152
   and spiritual strength, 126–27
inclusion
   in all our affairs, 52
   and anonymity, 230, 237–38
   foundation of, 46–47
   and not taking a stand, 193
   and participation, 15
   practice of, 50, 64, 114
   in service, 51
   as spiritual principle, 53
   and the Traditions, xiii–xiv
   and unity, 3
   and videoconferences, 12
independence, 72, 81, 122, 129, 139, 140, 146, 156
individual choice, 47–48, 64
individual opinions, 190–91

integrity
in all our affairs, 162, 216
and attraction rather than promotion, 209, 213
and boundaries, 67, 108
financial, 175
and non-endorsement, 117
and participation, 28
and special workers, 155
as spiritual principle, 156, 160
and the Traditions, xvi, xvii
and trusted servants, 161
as value, xix

interactions, 69, 71, 108, 140, 155, 170, 176, 212–13

interdependence, 71, 82, 124–25
interdependent autonomy, 71, 75

Intergroups, 33, 59, 124, 130, 168
Intergroup Chair, 196
Intergroup Representatives, 169

journey of recovery, xv, 85–86, 150–51, 194, 210, 234–36, 245, 255

kindness
in all our affairs, 52, 63, 176, 239
and attraction rather than promotion, 209
as basic value, xix
in communication, 9, 88, 103

kindness *continued*
and controversy, 196
experience of, 15, 18, 118, 158, 180, 220, 226, 242, 245, 250, 251
and group conscience, 29
practice of, 255
and program of "we," 231
in service, 33, 151
and the Traditions, xiv
and a willingness to give, 127

leadership, 17, 18, 29–31, 32, 44, 152, 171, 212. *See also* trusted servants

learning on the job, 152

limitations, 20, 39, 59, 61, 100–101, 133, 160, 225

listening
in all our affairs, 9, 21, 34–35, 91, 155, 239, 251
and attraction, 217
and carrying the message, 87, 194, 224
and controversy, 196
as equals, 151
and focus, 38
and giving it away, 85
and group conscience, 27, 28–29, 38, 169, 249
and Higher Power, 28–29, 34–35, 194
to opinions, 29, 198, 204
and our personal recovery, 40, 64, 103
and our primary purpose, 85, 169

listening *continued*
    and our willingness to give, 127–28
    practice of, 44
    and principles before personalities, 239
    and self-support, 122–23
    in service, 171–72, 174
    and sponsors, 14
    and the Traditions, xvii
    and unity, 5, 7
    See also communication

literature
    and attraction, 210, 213, 222
    and the Chronic Pain Anonymous Service Board (CPASB), 153, 170, 175
    and Conference Approved Literature (CAL), 68, 190
    and finances, 128–29, 144
    and group responsibility, 89
    and newcomers, 60, 94
    options of, 75–76
    outreach, 50–51, 133
    outside, 107, 119
    and service, 72, 174, 195
    and supporting the whole, 124–25
    and unity, 6
    and the World Service Conference (WSC), 175

love
    in all our affairs, 52, 91–92, 112, 197–98, 251
    and attraction, 47

love *continued*
    and Higher Power, 10
    and the journey of recovery, 235
    and principles before personalities, 234
    and program of "we," 231
    and sponsors, 242
    and trusted servants, 172
    and unconditional acceptance, 48

media, 212, 213–14, 228. *See also* social media

mentorship, 19, 32, 160, 171, 181

message of hope
    and attraction, 210
    and carrying the message, 11, 87, 88–89
    and giving it away, 85
    and the newcomer, 56
    and our primary purpose, 85
    practice of, 103
    and responsibility for unity, 70
    and service, 51, 60, 174
    and sharing, 93, 193
    and the Traditions, xviii

mutual respect, 169, 177, 189–90, 206, 222

newcomers
    and acceptance, 48
    and anonymity, 211, 214
    and attraction, 209, 219, 227

newcomers *continued*
  and carrying the message, 87,
    88–89, 232
  connecting with, 94
  and equality, 6
  experience of being a, 15–16,
    55–56, 113–14
  and the group conscience, 27
  and group meetings, 90
  and inclusivity, 47
  and interdependence, 71
  and practice, 81
  and our primary purpose, 84,
    85, 91
  and outreach, 51
  and recovering together, 151,
    159
  risk of alienating, 190
  and safety, 238
  and service, 31–32, 123, 167
  and shared responsibility, 3–5
  and singleness of purpose, 109
  in the structure of service,
    4–5, 30, 36
  and unity, 3, 12
  welcoming the, 49, 58,
    63–64, 102
non-affiliation, 112
non-controversy, commitment to, 196, 206
non-professionals, 151–53

obedience to the unenforceable,
  xvi–xvii, 3, 31, 69, 81
opinions
  in all our affairs, 9–10, 34,
    73, 196–98

opinions *continued*
  and anonymity, 191–92, 216
  and common bonds, 189–90
  and communication, 5
  differing, 82
  and group conscience, 27,
    76, 167, 194
  individual, 190–91, 206
  listening to, 29, 198
  minority, 44
  and non-controversy, 196
  and our primary purpose,
    112, 192
  and public outreach, 195
  and reactions, 14
  and recovery focus, 194
  and selflessness, 32
  and sharing with awareness,
    193
  on social media, 191
outside organizations. *See*
  affiliations

participation
  in all our affairs, 156
  in business meetings, 38, 40
  and clear flow of
    information, 169
  compassionate, 129–30, 146
  in fellowship, 2, 94
  and flexibility, 28, 37
  and giving it away, 85, 150
  and group structure, 166–68
  and interdependence, 71
  and newcomers, 15–16
  in non-CPA groups, 192,
    195, 213

participation *continued*
   and our primary purpose, 85
   and personal parameters, 132
   practice of, 22, 42–44, 144, 184–85, 254
   and principles before personalities, 241
   in service, 39, 59–60, 72, 82, 98, 124, 136
   shared responsibility, 3–5
   and surrender, 7
   and trusted servants, 39, 170–72
   See also group conscience

patience
   in all our affairs, 35, 216
   and clear flow of information, 170
   and compassionate participation, 130
   and listening, 29
   and making decisions, 27–28
   and newcomers, 56
   and our primary purpose, 85
   practice of, 23, 44, 57, 103, 184
   and service, 171, 174, 179
   as spiritual principle, 36

peacefully, joyfully, and comfortably, xix, 50, 84, 158, 194, 210, 224, 234

perfection, 18–19, 152, 163, 172–73, 177, 180, 193, 210, 211–12, 226, 231, 237, 244–45, 253

personal anonymity, 191, 206, 210–12, 214

personalities. *See* principles before personalities

personal relationships, xix, 22, 43–44, 72–73, 82, 91–92, 103, 111–12, 176

primary purpose
   and accountability, 154
   in all our affairs, 91–92
   and caregivers, 111
   and carrying the message, 87–89
   and common bonds, 189
   and controversy, 196
   focus on, 106–7, 120
   foundation of, 84–85
   giving it away, 85–86
   and group inventory, 70
   and group responsibility, 89–90
   and listening, 85, 169
   and opinions, 192
   and personal relationships, 91–92, 111–12
   practice of, 103, 120
   and sacrifice, 233
   and self-compassion, 89
   and self-support, 124
   and service, 90–91, 110, 130, 151–52, 174
   and sharing, 194
   and supporting the whole, 125

principles before personalities, xiv, 13, 29, 50, 51, 232–34, 236, 237, 239–40, 247, 249, 250–53, 254–55

professional roles, 153, 154, 158, 163–64, 230, 242
program of "we," 230–32, 255
promotion, 195, 208–9, 215, 217, 219–20
public information and outreach, 50–51, 195, 206, 208, 213, 219–20
public relations, 108, 212–14, 217, 228

reciprocal support, 148–56
religious affiliations, 193–94, 203
resentments, 132, 141, 182, 216, 226, 249
resources, 86, 106–7, 123, 125, 128–29, 130, 168, 170, 172
respect
    and acceptance, 245
    in all our affairs, 52, 91–92, 132, 177, 197–98, 215–16, 239
    and anonymity, 211–12, 223
    and attraction, 209
    and autonomy, 73
    and carrying the message, 88
    and communication, 5
    and controversy, 196
    and cooperation, 108
    and group conscience, 29, 38, 194
    and group organization, 168
    and humility, 182
    and inclusivity, 51
    and the journey of recovery, 236

respect *continued*
    listening with, 34, 40
    mutual, 169, 189–90, 206, 222
    and our primary purpose, 124
    and participation, 28
    practice of, 23, 42, 63, 144, 205–6, 255
    and principles before personalities, 250
    and service, 34, 39, 90–91, 180, 249
    and sharing, 16, 193
    of special workers, 155
    and sponsors, 242
    and the Traditions, xiv, xix
    of trusted servants, 152
    responsibility
    in all our affairs, 35, 64, 72–74, 81, 111, 131–33
    and autonomy, 66, 75–79
    balancing, 69
    and boundaries, 67–68, 116–17
    for carrying the message, 88
    in communication, 5
    and compassionate participation, 130
    of the group, 89–90
    and group conscience, 137
    and group organization, 177–78
    and inclusivity, 15
    and independence, 129
    and interdependence, 81
    to newcomers, 49, 58, 87

respect *continued*
   and our primary purpose, 107
   in personal relationships, 73–74
   in service, 30, 32–34, 72, 90, 123, 125
   shared, 3–5, 23, 33, 44, 128, 171
   and spiritual strength, 126
   for unity, 69–71, 82, 136
   and willingness to give, 127–28
   See also self-support
rotation of service, 32, 40, 167, 171, 173, 184

safety
   in all our affairs, 35, 176–77, 239
   and anonymity, 153, 192, 194, 211–12, 214, 222, 225, 230, 231–32, 235, 237–38
   and apprenticeship, 19, 160
   and attraction, 208, 209, 213
   and carrying the message, 88
   and communication, 5
   and connection and belonging, 49
   and control, 182
   and fellowship, 31
   and group responsibility, 89
   and Higher Power, 41, 131
   and humility, 236
   and inclusivity, 53
   and individual choice, 48

safety *continued*
   and mutual respect, 190
   and newcomers, 16
   and obedience to the unenforceable, 31
   and our primary purpose, 85, 107, 113
   practice of, 63, 254–55
   and service, 91
   and shared responsibility, 3–4
   and singleness of purpose, 110
   and sponsors, 242
   and the Traditions, xiv, 97
   and unity, 2
   and virtual meetings, 36–37
self-acceptance, 62, 79, 81, 212
self-awareness, 71, 73
self-compassion, 89, 90, 99, 103, 158
selflessness, 21, 31–32
self-obsession, 2, 7, 87, 211, 215, 231, 234
self-support
   in all our affairs, 131–33
   and asking for help, 138
   and communication, 140–41
   and finances, 123–24, 128–29, 139–40, 142–43, 156
   foundation of, 122–24
   healing journey, 139–40
   and independence and unity, 129
   and our willingness to give, 127–28
   practice of, 136, 143, 144–45
   in service, 123–24

self-support *continued*
   and spiritual strength, 126–27
   and supporting the whole, 124–25
self-worth, 33, 61, 118, 126, 128, 130, 139, 155–56, 162, 231, 240
serenity, 31, 43, 49, 56, 69, 86, 88, 111, 118, 126, 150, 177, 210, 215, 253
Serenity Prayer, 17, 27–28, 32, 42, 96, 140–41, 167, 182, 197
service
   and accountability, 153–55, 169
   in all our affairs, 176–77
   and anonymity, 192–93, 211–12, 213–14, 232, 239
   and communication, 169–70
   and compassionate participation, 129–30
   and equality, 172–73
   experience of, 15–20, 39–40, 59, 96–98, 134–39, 142–43, 160–61, 179–81, 201, 217–18, 224–25, 246–49
   focus of, 110, 120
   and gratitude, 126
   and group organization, 167–68, 173–74
   and humility, 31–32
   and inclusivity, 51

service *continued*
   as larger than ourselves, 31–32, 44
   and non-controversy, 196
   non-professionals doing, 151–53, 164
   and our primary purpose, 90–91, 130, 233
   participation in, 72, 82, 167–68
   practice of, 22, 43–44, 102, 119–20, 144, 163–64, 184–85, 254
   and principles before personalities, 233–34
   and professional roles, 153
   and public information and outreach, 50–51, 195, 213–14
   and reciprocal support, 148
   rotation of, 32, 40, 167, 171, 173, 184
   and self-support, 122–24, 133
   and shared responsibility, 33–34
   and special workers, 154–55, 174
   as spiritual principle, 178
   structure of, 4–5, 29–31, 69, 124–25, 166, 173–75
   and supporting the whole, 124–25
   and the Traditions, xiv–xvi, xviii
   and trusted servants, 170–72
   and unity, 7–8, 70, 196

service *continued*
    as volunteers, 171
    and willingness, 32–33, 44, 127–28
    See also Chronic Pain Anonymous Service Board (CPASB); World Service Conference (WSC)
Service Manual, 175
shared responsibility, 3–5, 23, 33, 44, 128, 171
sharing
    and affiliations, 119
    in all our affairs, 155–56, 197
    and anonymity, 200, 211, 222–23, 236–38
    and apprenticeship, 19, 160
    and attraction, 210
    with awareness, 193–94, 206
    and balanced autonomy, 76
    and carrying the message, 11, 87, 88, 89, 109
    versus explaining, 159
    the gifts of recovery, 148–49, 164
    and giving it away, 85
    and group inventory, 70–71
    and honesty, 5, 55, 87, 90, 159
    and integrity, 156
    the journey of recovery, 234
    in our meetings, 57, 157
    and the newcomer, 49, 63
    and our primary purpose, 96, 107

sharing *continued*
    and participation, 28, 136, 142
    practice of, 22, 63, 102, 119
    and recovering together, 150–51
    and safety, 243
    and self-support, 122–23
    and service, 15, 51, 78
    solution-focused, 16
    and unity, 16
    and a willingness to serve, 32
singleness of purpose, 46–47, 84, 85, 95, 109–10, 120, 189
social media, 50, 107, 115, 191, 212, 214, 220
special workers, 60, 154–55, 156, 160–61, 163, 174
spiritual condition, 7
spiritual debilitation, 47, 53–55, 58, 85, 109, 139
spiritual growth, 29, 33, 87, 99, 131, 148, 176, 232, 233–34, 240, 255
spiritual practice of anonymity, 232–33, 236–37, 239
spiritual principles, xiv–xv, xix, xvii, 33–34, 53, 192, 197, 230, 239, 245
spiritual strength, 126–27, 146, 237
sponsors
    and anonymity, 191–94
    and carrying the message, 87
    and change, 216
    and communication, 97, 177

sponsors *continued*
  and controversy, 197–98
  and decisions, 31
  and giving it away, 85–86
  and group organization, 168
  guidance of, 26, 60–61, 90, 113, 180, 199, 235
  and the media, 214
  and our primary purpose, 92, 130
  and "our side of the street," 53
  and our willingness to give, 127
  and principles before personalities, 234, 247, 249
  and reciprocal support, 148
  and self-support, 123
  and service, 19, 96, 180
  and sharing, 4, 11, 14, 54, 57, 159, 242–43
  and sponsee relationship, 152, 238
  and unity, 10
structured service bodies, 29–31, 124–25, 173–76, 178, 185
supporting the whole, 124–25, 145
surrender, xv, 7, 11, 23, 29, 74, 96, 139, 157–58, 170, 174, 202, 232
sustainability. *See* self-support

"Thy will, not mine, be done", vii, 18, 41, 50
  See also Serenity Prayer
Tools of the Program, 82, 87, 123, 137
  about, xiii, 18, 38, 58, 61, 102, 107, 113, 115, 136
  use of, 10, 15, 28, 46, 51, 59, 78, 97, 106,
Tradition One, 1–23
  communication, 5–6
  consistent message, 6
  equality, 6
  shared responsibility, 3–5
  surrender, 7
  unity, 2–3
Tradition Two, 25–44
  equality, 31
  group inventory, 29
  Higher Power expressed through group conscience, 26–27
  listening, 28–29
  participation and flexibility, 28
  patience, 27–28
  structure of service, 29–31
  trust and faith, 28
Tradition Three, 45–64
  connection and belonging, 49–50
  inclusion, 46–47
  individual choice, 47–48
  unconditional acceptance, 48–49
  welcoming the newcomer, 49

Tradition Four, 65–82
  autonomy, 67
  balance, 68–69
  boundaries, 67–68
  interdependence, 71
  participation in service, 72
  responsibility for unity, 68–71

Tradition Five, 83–103
  carrying the message, 87
  giving it away, 85–86
  group responsibility, 89–90
  hope and recovery, 88–89
  primary purpose, 84–85
  self-compassion, 89

Tradition Six, 105–20
  cooperation with other organizations, 108
  focus of service, 110
  focus on primary purpose, 106–7
  singleness of purpose, 109–10

Tradition Seven, 121–46
  compassionate participation, 129–30
  honesty about finances, 128–29
  independence and unity, 129
  self-support, 122–24
  spiritual strength, 126–27
  supporting the whole, 124–25
  willingness to give, 127–28

Tradition Eight, 147–64
  freely sharing the gifts of recovery, 148–50

Tradition Eight *continued*
  leaving professional roles outside, 153
  non-professionals doing service, 151–53
  reciprocal support, 148–50
  recovering together, 150–51

Tradition Nine, 165–85
  clear flow of information, 169–70
  fellowship of equals, 172–73
  most participation, least control, 166–68
  structured service bodies, 173–75
  trusted servants, 170–72

Tradition Ten, 187–206
  anonymity as member or in group, 191–93
  commitment to non-controversy, 196
  common bonds, 188–89
  focus on recovery, 194
  individual opinions, no collective view, 190–91
  mutual respect, 189–90
  personal anonymity, 191
  recovery-focused public outreach, 195
  sharing with awareness, 193–94

Tradition Eleven, 207–28
  anonymity, 210–12
  anonymity and outside organizations, 212–13
  attraction in public relations and the media, 213–14

Index   287

Tradition Eleven *continued*
   attraction rather than promotion, 208–10
Tradition Twelve, 229–55
   humility, 236–37
   journey of recovery, 234–36
   principles before personalities, 232–34
   program of "we," 230–32
   safety, 237–38
trust
   in all our affairs, 52, 131, 156, 176–78, 215, 239–40
   and attraction, 209, 213
   and boundaries, 68
   and confidentiality, 238
   and faith, 28, 36
   in Higher Power, 13–14, 26, 36, 37, 97, 131, 134–35, 156, 204
   and the journey of recovery, 235–36
   and leaving professional roles outside, 219
   and participation, 168
   practice of, 43–44, 183, 203
   and self-support, 124
   and spiritual strength, 126–27
   and structure of service, 30, 31
trusted servants
   in all our affairs, 176
   and apprenticeships, 8
   and the Chronic Pain Anonymous Service Board (CPASB), 175
   and clear flow of information, 169

trusted servants *continued*
   and equality, 173
   and flexible structure of service, 178
   and group organization, 170–72
   and honesty, 183
   and leadership, 30
   and participation, 179
   practice of, 42, 43, 183, 185
   and service, 39, 51, 60, 90, 152–53, 161, 174
   World Service Conference (WSC), 78
Twelve Steps
   and accountability, 154–55
   in all our affairs, 74, 80, 253
   and anonymity, 191, 193, 230, 233–34, 244
   application of, 96–99, 139
   and attraction, 208, 213, 218
   and balance, 69
   and controversy, 198
   and equality, 6, 30
   as example for CPA, 106, 109
   and focus, 15, 245
   giving it away, 85–86
   and group organization, 168
   and Higher Power, 10
   and inventory, 29, 70
   and the journey of recovery, 235
   and mutual respect, 190
   and the newcomer, 49, 55–56
   other fellowships, 23, 199
   and reciprocal support, 148–49

Twelve Steps *continued*
  and self-support, 140
  and service, 39, 137, 151, 180, 246, 249
  and sharing, 5, 11, 93, 114, 150
  and singleness of purpose, 95
  and sponsor/sponsee relationship, 19, 152
  and surrender, 7, 170
  and the Traditions, xiii–xvi, 31
  and willingness, 58

unconditional acceptance, 48–49, 63–64

unity
  in all our affairs, 8–10, 35, 52, 132, 198, 239
  and anonymity, 233
  in business meetings, 12
  and common bonds, 189
  and communication, 5–6, 72, 169
  and Conference Approved Literature (CAL), 68
  and controversy, 106, 109
  and equality, 6, 31
  foundation of, 2–3
  and group conscience, 28
  and humility, 236–37
  and inclusivity, 51
  and independence, 129, 146
  and individual choice, 48
  and interdependence, 71, 125
  and mutual respect, 190, 196

unity *continued*
  and our primary purpose, 86, 91, 194
  and our willingness to give, 128
  and personal recovery, 254
  practice of, 22–23
  and recovering together, 150, 158
  as requirement, 11
  responsibility for, 69–71, 82, 136
  and self-support, 123
  and the Serenity Prayer, 17
  in service, 7–8, 152, 174–75, 178
  and shared responsibility, 3–5
  and sharing, 16
  and singleness of purpose, 110
  surrender, 7
  and the Traditions, xiii–xiv, xvii
  See also autonomy; common welfare

videoconference meetings, 17, 59, 68, 94, 95–96, 125, 158, 167, 200–201, 244

virtual meetings, 19, 36, 57, 90, 109, 115, 125, 138, 222

well-being
  and accepting help, 142
  in all our affairs, 9–10, 35, 52, 111–12, 131–32, 177, 239

well-being *continued*
    and anonymity, 225
    and attraction, 224
    and autonomy, 73
    and balance, 69
    commitment to, 70
    contribution to, 145
    and gratitude, 126
    of the group, 129
    and group inventory, 29
    and honesty, 40
    and inclusivity, 46–47
    responsibility to, 185
    and self-care, 99
    and service, 90, 130
    and trust, 134

willingness
    and balance, 111
    to be teachable, 14
    and communication, 9
    and flexibility, 28
    to give, 127–28, 144, 146
    and group conscience, 29
    and humility, 215, 237
    to practice principles, 50, 58
    to serve, 32–33, 44, 123, 167, 182
    and spiritual strength, 126

World Service Conference (WSC), 6, 125, 135, 155, 161, 168, 174, 175

Notes

Notes

Notes

www.ingramcontent.com/pod-product-compliance
Lightning Source LLC
LaVergne TN
LVHW051543070426
835507LV00021B/2379